Inside the Campaign

COMMUNICATION
STRATEGY
AND POLITICS

COMMUNICATION, STRATEGY, AND POLITICS
THIERRY GIASSON AND ALEX MARLAND, SERIES EDITORS

Communication, Strategy, and Politics is a groundbreaking series from UBC Press that examines elite decision making and political communication in today's hyper-mediated and highly competitive environment. Publications in this series look at the intricate relations among marketing strategy, the media, and political actors and explain how they affect Canadian democracy. They also investigate interconnected themes such as strategic communication, mediatization, opinion research, electioneering, political management, public policy, and e-politics in a Canadian context and in comparison to other countries. Designed as a coherent and consolidated space for diffusion of research about Canadian political communication, the series promotes an interdisciplinary, multi-method, and theoretically pluralistic approach.

Other volumes in the series are

Political Marketing in Canada, edited by Alex Marland, Thierry Giasson, and Jennifer Lees-Marshment

Political Communication in Canada: Meet the Press and Tweet the Rest, edited by Alex Marland, Thierry Giasson, and Tamara A. Small

Framed: Media and the Coverage of Race in Canadian Politics, by Erin Tolley

Brand Command: Canadian Politics and Democracy in the Age of Message Control, by Alex Marland

Permanent Campaigning in Canada, edited by Alex Marland, Thierry Giasson, and Anna Lennox Esselment

Breaking News? Politics, Journalism, and Infotainment on Quebec Television, by Frédérick Bastien

Political Elites in Canada: Power and Influence in Instantaneous Times, edited by Alex Marland, Thierry Giasson, and Andrea Lawlor

Opening the Government of Canada: The Federal Bureaucracy in the Digital Age, by Amanda Clarke

The New NDP: Moderation, Modernization, and Political Marketing, by David McGrane

Gendered Mediation: Identity and Image Making in Canadian Politics, edited by Angela Wagner and Joanna Everitt

What's Trending in Canadian Politics? Understanding Transformations in Power, Media, and the Public Sphere, edited by Mireille Lalancette, Vincent Raynauld, and Erin Crandall

See also

Canadian Election Analysis 2015: Communication, Strategy, and Democracy, edited by Alex Marland and Thierry Giasson. Open access compilation available at http://www.ubcpress.ca/canadianelectionanalysis2015.

Inside the Campaign

Managing Elections in Canada

Edited by
ALEX MARLAND
and
THIERRY GIASSON

UBCPress · Vancouver · Toronto

29 28 27 26 25 24 23 22 21 20   5 4 3 2 1

Printed in Canada on FSC-certified ancient-forest-free paper (100% post-consumer recycled) that is processed chlorine- and acid-free.

Library and Archives Canada Cataloguing in Publication

Title: Inside the campaign : managing elections in Canada / edited by
   Alex Marland and Thierry Giasson.
Names: Marland, Alex, editor. | Giasson, Thierry, editor.
Series: Communication, strategy, and politics.
Description: Series statement: Communication, strategy, politics,
   ISSN (print) 2368-1047, ISSN (ebook) 2368-1055
Identifiers: Canadiana (print) 2020018413X | Canadiana (ebook) 20200184148 |
   ISBN 9780774864671 (softcover) | ISBN 9780774864688 (PDF) |
   ISBN 9780774864695 (EPUB) | ISBN 9780774864701 (Kindle)
Subjects: LCSH: Political campaigns – Canada. | LCSH: Campaign management –
   Canada. | LCSH: Canada. Parliament – Elections, 2019.
Classification: LCC JL193 .I57 2020 | DDC 324.70971 – dc23

Canadä

UBC Press gratefully acknowledges the financial support for our publishing program of the Government of Canada (through the Canada Book Fund), the Canada Council for the Arts, and the British Columbia Arts Council.

Publication of this book was also made possible with the help of funding provided by Université Laval and Memorial University of Newfoundland.

Printed and bound in Canada by Friesens
Set in Bodoni, Baskerville, and Myriad by Artegraphica Design Co. Ltd.
Copy editor: Dallas Harrison
Proofreader: Alison Strobel
Indexer: Hannah Loder
Cover designer: Kimberley Devlin

UBC Press
The University of British Columbia
2029 West Mall
Vancouver, BC V6T 1Z2
www.ubcpress.ca

Contents

Part 2: Campaign Offices and the Campaign Trail

Acknowledgments

ALL OF THE CONTRIBUTORS in this book followed imposing editorial guidelines and collaborated in speedy fashion. The editors wish to thank all of them for their investment in this project.

Inside the Campaign: Managing Elections in Canada exists because of a major commitment from UBC Press. Previously, it produced the digital publication *Canadian Election Analysis 2015: Communication, Strategy, and Democracy* featuring fifty-seven short contributions from sixty-six academics, students, and journalists. The publication was publicly available just three weeks after election day. Building on the success of that venture, UBC Press committed to produce a book that combines traditional academic formats with public engagement. In addition to rethinking its normal production process in order to fast-track publication – such as commissioning a book cover before the chapters were drafted – the Press boldly agreed to publish both a conventional peer-reviewed printed book and an open access publication. Aside from the obvious financial implications, this involved new ways of thinking about chapters to ensure that the content travels as stand-alone documents and identifying new ways to publicize them. The editors, participants, and ultimately readers are indebted to the willingness of UBC Press to support this venture, in particular Megan Brand, Laraine Coates, Kerry Kilmartin, Nadine Pedersen, Melissa Pitts, and Randy Schmidt. Thank you to Kimberley Devlin for designing the book cover, Alison Strobel for proofreading, Dallas Harrison for copyediting,

Hannah Loder for indexing, and Yann Minier for translating the chapter abstracts.

We are thankful to the three anonymous peer reviewers who read and commented on the manuscript in record time. The reviewers' feedback meaningfully improved the final product.

In addition to UBC Press commitments, the publication of this book has been made possible by a financial award from Memorial University of Newfoundland via its Publications Subvention Program, administered by the Office of Research Grant and Contract Services, and from a financial contribution of the Groupe de recherche en communication politique, based at Université Laval.

Abbreviations

CBC	Canadian Broadcasting Corporation
CDPP	Canadian Debate Production Partnership
CEO	chief electoral officer
CSE	Communications Security Establishment
CSIS	Canadian Security Intelligence Service
CTV	Canadian Television Network
EI	Employment Insurance
GDP	gross domestic product
ID	identification
MP	Member of Parliament
NDP	New Democratic Party
PBO	Parliamentary Budget Office
PCO	Privy Council Office
PM	prime minister
PMO	Prime Minister's Office
PPC	People's Party of Canada
PSAC	Public Service Alliance of Canada

Editors' Note

CANADIAN UNIVERSITIES, academic presses, and funding agencies are keen for scientific research to engage with the public. This book represents one such effort. As with its 2015 counterpart, and a handful of democracy-themed initiatives in Canada, the venture constitutes a social experiment.[1] Documenting our experiences with recruiting practitioners can help readers to interpret the final product and inform the efforts of academics who embark on future public engagement projects.

The chapters of *Inside the Campaign: Managing Elections in Canada* reveal the considerable strategic thinking and teamwork that go into the campaigning that climaxes on election day. Substantial planning and collaboration were likewise necessary to produce the book. From the outset, academic participants were aware that a condition of participation was to write with someone who could provide an inside perspective on what happens during a Canadian federal election campaign. The forty-third general election, scheduled for 21 October 2019, would be the anchor. The proposition of working with a practitioner was relatively seamless when a scholar could leverage an existing relationship. Others looked to us to put them in touch with someone. We collectively identified potential collaborators through our networks. In June 2018, we started contacting potential practitioner authors in order to introduce ourselves, the project, and proposed coauthors. Practitioners received a draft table of contents, academic bios, and a Q&A sheet about the project.

A coordination meeting with UBC Press followed a year later, in June 2019, at the annual conference of the Canadian Political Science Association, held in Vancouver. Soon afterward, the academic authors were required to submit initial drafts of their literature reviews as well as attend to administrative matters (e.g., author bios and backup contact information for practitioners) designed to elicit the commitment of their coauthors before election campaign duties took priority. In order to communicate a commitment to trustworthiness, each practitioner received a confidentiality agreement signed by the academic author and countersigned by an editor. The agreements affirmed that the practitioners' participation would not be publicly disclosed until after election day, including on social media. We even withheld the practitioners' names from UBC Press.

Some academics went through the project in a recurring state of uncertainty about the involvement of their coauthors. Some practitioners were always at the ready, others less so. Invariably, some campaign professionals were inaccessible at times. Yet all of those who ultimately coauthored chapters became available when called on. Adapting to different work styles was a reminder that public sector practitioners operate in a deadline-oriented environment and that for most of them publishing is an extracurricular activity. In a few cases, collaboration with someone involved in the previous campaign was necessary to generate inside information, supplemented by an interview with a 2019 counterpart after election day. Although two chapters were abandoned because of an inability to collaborate with a practitioner, as with *Canadian Election Analysis 2015* we witnessed that the post-campaign environment lends itself to focused writing and responsiveness to firm deadlines in a compressed production schedule. UBC Press received the draft manuscript for peer review within seven days of the polls closing on election day and received the revised post-review manuscript on the day that the new government was sworn in.

Consequently, some collaborations were smooth affairs, whereas others involved overcoming obstacles. As mentioned in the Introduction, many practitioners experienced difficulty engaging in critical perspectives on their work during the campaign period in contrast to the normal expectations of academic writing. An ingrained tendency to promote their own organization's accomplishments and to take no notice of its shortcomings put the academic coauthor in a delicate situation. Diplomatic exchanges sometimes resulted. The independent assessments of anonymous academic reviewers recruited by UBC Press served as invaluable tipping points to inject additional objectivity.

The main goal of this book, and probably its most useful contribution, is to describe how Canadian election campaigns are run from the inside, behind closed doors, in offices and war rooms, out on the campaign trail, and from planes, trains, and tour buses. It offers an interesting inventory of campaign work. We hope that readers find it useful.

Note

[1] See Marland and Giasson, *Canadian Election Analysis 2015;* Bratt et al., *Orange Chinook;* Koop et al., *Understanding the Manitoba Election 2019;* and Marland and Moore, "Democratic Reform on the Menu in Newfoundland and Labrador."

Bibliography

Bratt, Duane, Keith Brownsey, Richard Sutherland, and David Taras. *Orange Chinook: Politics in the New Alberta.* Calgary: University of Calgary Press, 2019.

Koop, Royce, Barry Ferguson, Karine Levasseur, Andrea Rounce, and Kiera L. Ladner. *Understanding the Manitoba Election 2019: Campaigns, Participation, and Issues.* Winnipeg: University of Manitoba Press, 2019.

Marland, Alex, and Thierry Giasson, eds. *Canadian Election Analysis 2015: Communication, Strategy, and Democracy.* Vancouver: UBC Press, 2015. http://www.ubcpress.ca/canadianelectionanalysis2015.

Marland, Alex, and Lisa Moore. "Democratic Reform on the Menu in Newfoundland and Labrador." *Canadian Parliamentary Review* 41, 1 (2018): 5–7.

Inside the Campaign

Introduction
Constantly Shopping for Votes
Alex Marland with Susan Delacourt

T his chapter begins by observing that Canadian political parties engage in a continuous quest to win public support between elections, known as the permanent campaign. We summarize the layers of election campaigning with a particular focus on communications. A brief synopsis of the 2019 Canadian federal election provides some context for the chapters authored by academics and their practitioner coauthors who share real-world experiences from inside the campaign. Each chapter's profile of work carried out behind the scenes of a Canadian election will be of particular interest to readers drawn to political management.

C e chapitre débute en notant que les partis politiques s'engagent dans une quête incessante visant à s'assurer de l'appui du public entre les élections, c'est-à-dire qu'ils mènent une campagne permanente. Les différents aspects d'une campagne électorale y sont également présentés sommairement; une attention particulière est portée à la communication. Une brève présentation du déroulement de l'élection fédérale canadienne de 2019 permet de définir le contexte dans lequel s'inscrivent les chapitres corédigés par des universitaires et des praticiens faisant part d'expériences électorales concrètes. Au sein de chaque chapitre, les descriptions de différentes tâches et fonctions menées en coulisse d'une élection canadienne sauront capter l'attention des lecteurs s'intéressant à l'organisation politique.

DESPITE CONSIDERABLE scrutiny of Canadian election campaigns and their importance in determining the formation of the next government, we know relatively little about the work that goes into them. Sometimes the journalists who criss-cross the country on leaders' tours expose their backstage moments. Occasionally, party strategists tell stories about their experiences many years later. After election day, academics write summaries of campaign dynamics and analyze voter behaviour data as they try to make sense of the election results. Deep descriptions of what happens on the ground are confined to a geographic area or one political party.[1] Rarely do we get an enduring sense of the labour carried out by the wide variety of people involved.

You are about to learn about the roles and responsibilities of some of the political actors who make Canadian democracy work. For the first time, academics and public sector practitioners have come together to provide an authentic look at what happens behind the scenes in Canadian elections. The objective of *Inside the Campaign: Managing Elections in Canada* is to describe, in plain language, the activities of people with varied responsibilities in an election campaign. Yet it is difficult to capture the profound emotional journey and intense stress that these personnel experience; as one veteran campaigner put it: "A lot of pressure goes with the responsibility."[2] Before we take a tour of the fourteen vocations examined in this book, let us consider some of the elements of the permanent campaign that lay the groundwork for the official campaign.

The Permanent Campaign

Politicians are always campaigning for public support. In *Fights of Our Lives: Elections, Leadership, and the Making of Canada,* political strategist John Duffy describes the pre-campaign and official campaign machinations of various Canadian prime ministers. Throughout history, they have concocted policies that cater to supporters and drive wedges between opponents. Their governments have changed election rules to benefit their own party. They have curried favour from financial backers, and they have turned to the latest communication technologies for a competitive edge. Duffy describes an extended period of campaigning that at times is indistinguishable from governing:

> Most of us think of election campaigns as the period from the call to Election Day. Politicos, however – a century ago as today – define the whole affair more broadly, with a pre-writ campaign leading up to the issuance, or "dropping," of a writ of election, and then a writ-period campaign until voting day. In our day the pre-writ and writ-period campaigns are equally important. A century ago the writ period was little more than a brute organizational effort that came at the end of an elaborate and more critical pre-writ battle.[3]

Today the activities undertaken during pre-writ campaigning are so similar to what happens during official campaigning that political scientists refer to the permanent campaign.[4] Permanent campaigning concerns political parties leveraging all available resources as they infuse campaign-style behaviours into the executive and legislative branches of the government. It reflects a competitive mentality to win all public battles – the news cycle, Question Period debates, public opinion polls, fundraising, and so forth. As in an official campaign, political staff rapidly respond to allegations and misinformation and strive to control the public agenda by implementing strategic communication plans. Politicians and their aides have a relentless motivation to shore up votes, especially as the next election approaches.

The rise of advertising and consumer culture has transformed political parties into marketing machines.[5] In Canada, political parties are relatively small operations that come to life as elections approach, and their marketing sophistication is limited compared to that of large corporate actors. But political actors do possess certain marketing advantages over those in the private sector – they have access to the list of electors to construct databases, donations qualify for generous tax reductions, and their leaders are regularly in the news. No sales event on the commercial calendar remotely compares with the scope of society coming together to vote.

Political parties are in constant pursuit of voters' attention, personal information, and dollars. Politicians push their brands and parties shop for votes with many of the same tools used in the consumer marketplace. Between elections, political parties make sustained pushes to add information about Canadians to relationship-management databases, just like the big stores that gather data on their customers. The parties solicit donations from supporters by asking them to "chip in," especially at the end of each quarter, when a party is judged by its standing in political fundraising horse-race data.[6] The quarterly fundraising reports are essentially political sales data.

A party that prioritizes political marketing infuses discipline into all aspects of its communication, especially what happens in the legislature. Members of Parliament (MPs) are expected to vote as partisan blocs; the leader's office coordinates MPs' activities in the House of Commons and on committees, including voting, and key messages are distributed so that everyone affiliated with the party brand will repeat the same corporate messaging.[7] The competitive drive to win every communication battle increases relative to the proximity of the next campaign. Periods of minority government are therefore especially prone to the characteristics of permanent campaigning. In all circumstances, election readiness builds as the parties recruit candidates, conduct public opinion research, plan their advertising strategies, and coordinate candidate training schools. The media report, to some extent, on this choreography but rarely on how the steps are plotted.

Permanent campaigning is especially pertinent to the governing party. A prime minister and cabinet have much more power than backbench MPs do. Political staff in the Prime Minister's Office (PMO) and senior public servants in the Privy Council Office (PCO) negotiate policies with ministers, their political staff, and their deputy ministers.[8] A political pollster can be embedded within the government to oversee public opinion research and to share polling insights with partisans sprinkled throughout government offices.[9] Senior political personnel strive to align all government communications, as one political scientist has observed:

> Every action, decision, and communication by government has been strategized, tested, and deliberately conveyed according to an overall theme or message designed to win public approval. The permanent campaign has implications for political communication, since it is essentially the conflation of campaigning and communications into permanent election communications. Governments must be able to consistently and effectively express what they are doing and why in a format that is both easily digestible by voters and appealing to core supporters.[10]

Elections are fundamentally different from permanent campaigning if only because during an official campaign period all politicians must interact with electors directly. Between elections, the executive branch of government is supposed to consider the views of elected representatives who, in theory, speak on constituents' behalf. Outreach to engage citizens in the policy-decision process can be perfunctory.[11] Limited consultation causes frustration when political actors challenge traditional power structures and believe that the public has a right to pass judgment on the social acceptability of government actions.[12] However, from the perspective of the governing party, Canadians collectively commented at the ballot box. The government believes that it has a mandate to follow through on implementing the promises outlined in the party's campaign platform, especially if it controls a majority of seats.[13] It matters little to the governing party that election campaigns are stage-managed events or that most voters base their decisions on partisanship and political values rather than on specific policy proposals.[14] Nevertheless, elections constitute the core of a democracy. This is when interactions between politicians, political parties, the media, interest groups, and citizens are their liveliest.

Behind the Scenes of Election Campaigning

Election campaigns provide people with knowledge that can only be learned by doing. At some point, everyone holding a role in a campaign – from the party leader standing on stage during a leaders' debate to the election scrutineer at a polling booth – has learned on the job. It is a high-wire act. Errors can be public and costly. Some of these on-the-job trainees will never again hold an official role in a campaign. The vast majority will return and build on their experiences.

Peruse a book written by someone who has been in the thick of a Canadian election campaign, and you will soon spot divergence among communication (the air war), national-level strategy (the war room), and the grassroots level (the ground war). *Inside the NDP War Room,* by former journalist James McLean, exposes the strategies and tactics of party operatives in the nerve centre of a campaign headquarters. Political personnel manage the message by disclosing controversial information about opponents and by coordinating rapid responses to repudiate criticisms of their own campaign. War-room personnel circulate talking points and key messages to support the leader's message of the day. They busily monitor all media interventions to isolate any instances of spokes-people going off-message and off-brand.[15] The need for communication control comes through in *Harper's Team: Behind the Scenes in the Conservative Rise to Power,* in which former Conservative strategist Tom Flanagan reveals the inner workings of a campaign operation.[16] Flanagan describes a seemingly endless inventory of details requiring attention in an intense environment in which a slip-up can be magnified into a public controversy that costs votes. How do we go about renting an airplane? What should be on the bus-wrap livery? What is the campaign slogan? Have we secured the rights to play a campaign song? Who is in charge of costing the promises in our platform? How do we ensure that the people travelling with the leader are synchronized with the people in the war room? What do we do when the leader's political instincts seem to be distorted by the bubble of the leader's tour? Who is responsible for dealing with the maverick candidate distracting from the party's messaging? Who is writing the leader's speeches? How many people need to sign off on a press release? Who is heading up our public opinion research? How does our polling inform our advertising? How are we going to pay for all this? *Harper's Team* is exceptional in its detail. No other academic work has divulged such a trove of inside information about the back rooms of a Canadian political party's election campaigns.

A national election campaign is an enormous operation that requires complete dedication from a tightly connected group willing to work long hours in a fast-paced, high-stakes atmosphere. Consider the work involved in putting on a political rally.[17] When a leader arrives in a community and enters a room full of cheering supporters waving campaign signs, all that most Canadians see is a brief media clip of something that the leader says, punctuated by visuals of the words on a podium sign and whoever or whatever is behind the leader. The goal is to create the look of a spontaneous show of adulation in an event the opposite of spontaneous. Campaign workers put a lot of effort into generating that brief media coverage. Tour advance personnel are tasked with scouting out a location and mapping an event scenario, with particular attention given to what cameras will catch. Sound systems, lighting, and teleprompters must be set up. In preparation for the rally, local candidates are engaged, and electronic invitations are issued to supporters in the party's database. On the day of the leader's visit, workers decorate the location with party colours and signs. An enormous Canadian flag is often draped on the wall so that the leader can stand squarely in the middle of the maple leaf, or perhaps workers wearing hard hats will stand on a tiered stage to form a topical backdrop. Supporters begin showing up hours before the leader arrives. Reporters might interview people waiting in line while protesters clamour outside vying for media attention. When attendees register, they can be given wristbands to authorize their entry. By registering, perhaps by showing an electronic ticket with a quick response (QR) code, they provide the party with additional information for its database. An invitation to a campaign event is considered a benefit for party supporters. As a former PMO director of communications puts it, "the daily rallies at the end of a campaign day are meant to reward the faithful for their hard work and contributions ... and to fire them up to keep pounding in lawn signs, knocking on doors, and adding new supporters into the party's database. They're also meant to bludgeon the ballot question into the travelling press pack's heads."[18]

The leader's arrival at a campaign rally is all about showmanship. Smiling supporters greet the leader before the entourage disappears into a hold room. Partisans with local profiles warm up the crowd in preparation for a grand introduction. As the party's campaign song begins to blare, the smiling leader takes the stage, with the crowd signalling its approval. The leader consults a teleprompter to deliver a variation of the script used at all of these packaged events. Talking points are emphasized, partisan jabs are thrown, and crowd reactions are elicited. When the speech is over – naturally to thunderous applause – supporters clamour for selfies with the leader. Staff begin the teardown process of removing chairs and signs, dismantling audiovisual equipment, and storing props. The whole thing is replicated elsewhere the next day as the leader's tour rolls through the country while, behind the scenes, the campaign wagon master worries about the logistics of transporting the large media entourage.[19] In some ways, the spectacle is relatively unchanged from the time when John A. Macdonald gave speeches from raised platforms decorated with bunting or when Wilfrid Laurier addressed crowds as he passed through their communities on a whistle-stop tour.

The media travelling with the tours willingly play along with this show – the journalists' presence and the bank of cameras reinforce the impression that something big is happening. Their reports on the events amplify the message, as politicians and journalists call the leaders' scripted utterances. This is a symbiotic relationship.

Of course, in some parts of Canada, it is not always easy to co-ordinate a rally, especially for an opposition party. Pseudo-events for opposition leaders are often little more than pop-ups. The leader stands at a podium outside a local campaign headquarters or a strategically selected location that fits the intended message. Candidates dutifully nod as the leader addresses the media. Staff huddle on the sidelines, busily checking their smartphones. The visuals give the impression of professional delivery, albeit without the aura of popularity, resources, or momentum. Walking through a restaurant and touring a local business are other practices. Whether the leader is available to speak with reporters has much to do with calculations of whether the message is controllable.

The experiences of local candidates in a campaign are diametrically opposed to those of national candidates. Imagine the excitement of being declared an official candidate and the rush of seeing your name on signs dotted throughout your community. It can be a thrill to talk policy on doorsteps and to network with public figures. Granting interviews to the media and watching your social media followers increase in number can make you feel like a VIP. Watching the tallying of votes on election day can be euphoric. Visions of being elected to Parliament and being able to fix Ottawa can be intoxicating.

In reality, being a candidate is as frustrating as it is exhilarating.[20] It is hard work, and you have to check your ego. People aspiring to run as candidates for a political party are required to fill out an invasive questionnaire and sign quasi-legal paperwork.[21] A vetting committee asks probing questions and scours the Internet for anything controversial. Much of this is done with journalism in mind, which has built up a new genre of political reporting in recent years, exposing flawed candidates with embarrassing details of their pasts. Punishment is usually severe for candidates outed this way in the media: swift ejection and public shaming. Prospective candidates who survive this intense screening process must then compete in a nomination contest to drum up local support.[22] The nomination is won by default if nobody else steps forward, which can signal that the party is weak in that electoral district. It is at this point that the nominated candidates are told that they must stick to the party message and never publicly contradict the leader. Candidates then begin to realize that the local media have limited interest in them and that it is difficult to get traction on local policy issues.[23] Those who have the privilege of being invited to stand with the leader at a campaign rally might be told just to smile and nod. By now, notions of being a political force have been tempered by the growing realization that candidates are cogs in the large party machine. Salvation is found in the camaraderie of a local team that works tirelessly to identify the vote, deliver brochures, and get supporters to the polls. Most of a candidate's local network consists of hardcore partisans, friends, and family members who must collectively interpret the instructions relayed from national campaign operatives. For many people, election campaigning can be considered a social event as much as a contest for power.

People experience the same campaign differently because they are exposed to different information and process that information in different ways. This has implications for how political parties deploy resources. As a Canadian political marketer once observed, the political views of a woman in downtown Toronto who likes organics and yoga are likely distinct from those of a young single guy working at Canadian Tire.[24] Likewise, how candidates campaign in densely populated, multicultural, urban areas home to many renters differs from how they campaign in vast rural areas with homogeneous and aging populations.[25] As well, political cultures, economies, and cleavages vary across the country.[26] Differences are pronounced in a fractured media market in which citizens choose to consume information that fits their political tastes – or perhaps to tune out of Canadian news altogether. Finding ways to get the right message to intended target audiences is a constant communication struggle, one made easier by advances in technologies.

As the communication landscape evolves, we develop a new sense of normal and forget what normal used to be.[27] Transformations in communication technologies indeed change campaign practices, even as basic principles such as voter identification persist. A generation ago campaigners were concerned with renting fax machines and land-line telephones, and election rules intended to level the playing field centred on limiting how much money candidates could spend.[28] Gradually, there were fewer community newspapers available to profile local candidates and issues, and campaign workers have acquired their own mobile phones. By the 2008 federal election, campaign news was criss-crossing the country in real time, and political parties busily uploaded to their websites raw video footage of campaign events. Social media were emerging in Canadian politics: the Facebook pages of party leaders were rarely updated and some leaders' Twitter accounts were created for that campaign.[29] Today social media are displacing mainstream news and advertising as the primary outlet for political campaigning. Political parties are using sophisticated computerized segmentation analysis to pinpoint potential supporters. They push micro-refined messages through database marketing and targeted advertising on social media.[30]

Digital strategists occasionally reveal the value that a national campaign attaches to digital data. "You don't win close campaigns trying to convince people something they don't believe," says the chief digital strategist of the Liberals' 2015 and 2019 campaigns. "It's totally inefficient and a waste of time. You win them by being efficient at finding and mobilizing people that already support you."[31] Digital platforms allow political operatives to test multiple versions of advertisements and word choices used in messaging. They improve the ability to monitor local outreach by tallying how frequently candidates and local workers are door knocking and placing phone calls. Across the country, they constantly upload data to a central database that becomes an arsenal of information to inform communication precision, from analytical modelling to get-out-the-vote operations. Literally thousands of variants of digital advertising are deployed to match targeted audiences.

The influence of digital media extends beyond party politics to empower activists who mobilize political protests and digital activism.[32] The visuals of conflict are attractive to news media. News organizations compete for audience attention and find it difficult to tell captivating stories about public policy. Similarly, social media outrage can be fodder for news content, causing every politician to be fearful of doing or saying something that goes viral and generates a pile-on. At the other extreme are the politicians who peddle soft messages on non-political programming, known as infotainment.[33] This too has evolved in a digital media ecosystem: during the 2019 campaign, Prime Minister Justin Trudeau engaged in a rare sit-down interview with the host of the Facebook Watch series *New Mom, Who Dis?* in which the studio audience was young schoolchildren.

The 2019 Canadian Federal Election

Most of the experiences described in this book are grounded in Canadian federal election campaigns. Many of the contributors know what it is like to work in campaign war rooms, to travel with the leader's tour, or otherwise to be involved in the cut-and-thrust of electioneering. They avoid discussing the minutiae of the 2019 Canadian federal election in order to explain how campaigns work in general. Here we provide a brief overview of that election as context for the chapters that follow.[34]

An element that courses through election campaigns is that they must often abide by new rules every election. The Liberal majority government led by Trudeau passed the Elections Modernization Act in time for the 2019 campaign. This act introduced spending rules for political parties and advocacy groups during the period leading up to the dissolution of Parliament. It expanded the scope of communication activities by Elections Canada and required online platforms to publish a registry of digital political advertising.

Through an Order-in-Council, the government created the Leaders' Debate Commission to organize two official national leaders' debates in English and French. Rules, of course, are subject to interpretation. One example of controversial decisions by non-partisan administrators included Elections Canada warning environmental groups that, in order to engage in political advertising about climate change, they would have to register formally as third parties; another was the commission's deliberations on whether to invite or exclude the leader, Maxime Bernier, of the recently formed People's Party of Canada.

As the forty-second Parliament ended, ministers fanned out across the country to make a plethora of spending announcements, and all parties busily recruited candidates. Justin Trudeau was still the country's most popular national party leader. However, the Liberals jockeyed with the Conservatives, led by Andrew Scheer, for top spot in public opinion polls. The New Democratic Party (NDP), led by Jagmeet Singh, had trouble with candidate recruitment because of a toxic combination of incumbents who did not seek re-election, money woes, and weak public support.

On 11 September, Prime Minister Trudeau asked the governor general to dissolve Parliament. A forty-day campaign would be held, culminating in a general election on 21 October, the date prescribed by law. At dissolution, the seat counts were 177 Liberal, 95 Conservative, 39 NDP, 10 Bloc Québécois, 2 Green, 1 People's Party, and 9 independents. Five seats were vacant.

Aggregates of public opinion polls forecast the Liberals picking up NDP seats in Quebec, which might compensate for seat losses elsewhere. The polls also predicted that the Conservatives would dominate the Prairies but that vote inefficiencies would make it difficult to win enough seats to form the government. They suggested that the NDP risked losing official party status (twelve seats) in the House of Commons.[35] The Greens, led by Elizabeth May, were poised for a breakthrough given a spate of recent electoral successes and global concerns about climate change. For the first time, the Green Party was competing with the New Democrats for third place in opinion polls. Many pundits thought that the Bloc Québécois, led by Yves-François Blanchet, would struggle to regain official party status or even survive the election. The People's Party – led by libertarian MP Bernier, a former Conservative – was a wild card. At the local level, two former prominent members of Trudeau's cabinet promised to be potential disrupters. Jody Wilson-Raybould and Jane Philpott, expelled from the Liberal caucus in April 2019 amid the SNC-Lavalin affair, were rare cases of independents with a chance of being elected.[36] As is so often the case, Ontario and Quebec would play formidable roles in determining which party would form a majority or minority government.

Normally, when an election is called, the media coverage is formulaic, focusing on the remarks of the prime minister outside Rideau Hall, the official residence of the governor general. That normalcy was disrupted during the 2019 election period by a *Globe and Mail* story that Prime Minister Trudeau's unwillingness to waive cabinet confidences was blocking the RCMP's investigation of the SNC-Lavalin affair.[37] The media then proceeded to report on controversial social media posts unearthed by the opponents of candidates, which led to some resignations. A week into the campaign, images rocketed around the world of Trudeau wearing brownface and blackface before he became an MP, throwing the Liberal campaign into disarray. Scheer was knocked off message multiple times, including on his personal position regarding abortion rights and by news that he holds dual American-Canadian citizenship. Singh found his stride by presenting a positive alternative to the main front-runners and through strong performances in the leaders' debates. Blanchet performed well in the French debates. Two instances of a "media tsunami" occurred, in which all news outlets converge on a single story and suggest a social crisis.[38] The first was the brownface and blackface photos and video; the second was climate change, peaking with protests during the Global Climate Strike day of action on 27 September.

As the campaign wore on, public opinion polls continued to place the Liberals and Conservatives in a statistical tie nationwide. The

Bloc Québécois and NDP rode the momentum of their leaders' debate performances while the two front-runners traded nasty barbs.[39] Among the more distinctive ways in which the Liberals sought advantage was coordinating a public expression of support from former US President Barack Obama, who tweeted his hope that Canadians would return Trudeau to office for another term.

Heading into election day, commentators observed that it was "a disgraceful election," reflecting on the fact that it was the first time in Canadian history that the two parties contending to form the government had garnered such low support in public opinion polls.[40] Pollsters largely predicted a tie between the Conservatives and Liberals in the popular vote but that seat counts would result in a Liberal minority government. They were right. The Conservatives marginally won the largest share of the popular vote, but the results in terms of MPs were 157 Liberal, 121 Conservative, 32 Bloc Québécois, 24 NDP, 3 Green, and 1 independent (Wilson-Raybould). The results exposed a divided country and were magnified by an electoral system that exposes regional concentrations. As Canadians began to process the implications of a return to minority governance, politicians and political staff turned their minds to the forty-third Parliament as the gears of permanent campaigning machinery restarted.

The Challenges of Political Management

Academic and media attention to campaign activities tends to focus on what is visible. Thus, we see the leaders' debates without being privy to the considerable planning required to pull off those high-stakes focusing events. We look at party platforms and advertising in the absence of the strategic considerations that contributed to their production. Some campaign tactics, such as digital fund-raising, are visible only to select people, and rarely do the media engage in public self-analysis of their role in reporting information. Some aspects of a campaign receive little attention, such as the work done by government employees while the campaign is under way or the electoral journey of an independent candidate. Furthermore, when these phenomena are explored, it is normally in the context of a specific election.

Inside the Campaign explores the inner workings of a Canadian election campaign. As indicated, books that combine both scholarly insights and voices of experience are rare. This book features chapters authored by academics collaborating with practitioner co-authors in their areas of expertise. The chapters encompass an array of partisan and non-partisan perspectives. Grounded in the 2019 federal election, the book attempts to present information relevant to understanding campaigns of the recent past and the near future.

The objective of this book is to profile campaign jobs and, by extension, to reveal the hidden work that occurs during a Canadian election campaign. It chronicles fourteen different types of actors as parts of the campaign infrastructure. The intended contribution to knowledge is to document professional practices that occur behind the scenes during elections. We anticipate that this book about the practical side of politics will appeal to anyone who studies Canadian politics or identifies as a political practitioner. It will be of particular value to those intrigued by applied politics, including those affiliated with Canada's first graduate program in political management at Carleton University. Political management is an emerging subfield that harnesses political science, political communication, and political marketing to provide a professional foundation for people who work in the political arena. The political management curriculum is skills-based and integrates interconnected subject areas that include "qualitative and quantitative analysis of survey research data, understanding of voter behaviour, campaigns and election law, information management, get-out-the-vote activities, microtargeting, grassroots organization, fundraising, strategic communications, strategic public relations, political branding, strategic thinking, the business of political consulting, issue advocacy, relationship marketing, civic engagement, political advertising, and more."[41] Many of these topics are addressed in this book and featured in other titles in the UBC Press Communication, Strategy, and Politics series in which it appears.

We might expect practitioners to be keen to profile their expertise in a volume that contributes to the development of political management as an academic subfield in Canada. However, Canadian practitioners are constrained in what they can say and how they can say it. People who work in ministerial or campaign offices, who are public servants, who are employed in the media or polling industries, or who are members of advocacy groups are subject to forms of reserve and discretion unfamiliar to those in academia. They must exercise caution about what they disclose. They might be averse to criticism because they are acutely aware of employer sensitivities and the risk of an opponent torquing a remark. Practitioners must be careful about casting doubt on their employers; after all, they are not shielded by academic freedom. Furthermore, being publicly self-critical can be anathema to their occupation and identity. Partisan politics is still at its core an ideological activity. For some practitioners, contributing to this book was an opportunity to provide a frank description of what goes on during campaigns, whereas for others pulling punches was a necessary condition of their participation. We hope that readers agree that the result is a valuable peek inside the countless hidden practices that occur in a Canadian election campaign.

Getting *Inside the Campaign*

This book is divided into two parts. Content in the "Caretakers and Participant Observers" section describes the work of people involved in caretaking and election-preparedness roles in the government and those who participate by commenting publicly on the campaign. The second section is titled "Campaign Offices and the Campaign Trail." It profiles the work of people who toil in campaign offices and out on the hustings. Each chapter is organized in a common manner, beginning with a summary of public knowledge about the profiled occupation that weaves together information from published sources. Next the authors demystify the profiled occupation by outlining hidden roles, difficulties, and time frames largely unknown to most Canadians. The chapters conclude with a vignette explaining the challenges in the federal campaign and how the obstacles were handled internally.

The first section begins with Chapter 1 and its look at the campaign from the perspective of Elections Canada. We learn how the non-partisan organization has responded to challenges to uphold the integrity of the democratic process. Andrea Lawlor builds on her work studying election administration. The chapter's profile of Elections Canada is punctuated with contributions from Marc Mayrand, a former chief electoral officer of Canada.

Chapter 2 discloses the work of political staff who remain in their departmental offices. They maintain connections with public servants as well as provide information and support to their ministers. In particular, the authors analyze the role of ministerial staff in the lead up to and during an election campaign. Paul Wilson, acting chief of staff to Prime Minister Stephen Harper during the 2011 campaign, writes about the role of political staff. He collaborates with Michael McNair, a former policy director for Prime Minister Justin Trudeau.

Next, we learn about the senior public servants during an election campaign working to support the transition to government. In Chapter 3, Lori Turnbull draws on her knowledge of public administration and her experience in the Privy Council Office when the Liberal government was formed in 2015. Donald Booth, a member of the Machinery of Government Secretariat at the Privy Council Office, joins her to reveal what happens as the public service awaits the formation of a new government.

Chapter 4 documents the deliberations held within the new federal Leaders' Debate Commission during the production of its first debates. That body sought to minimize uncertainty about debate formats and participation that climaxed when Stephen Harper was prime minister. Brooks DeCillia is a former CBC journalist turned academic. He collaborates with Michel Cormier, a former executive with Radio-Canada and the executive director of the commission in 2019.

Chapter 5 features a discussion about the evolving terrain of news production in a mediated environment fraught with the perils of fake news, cyberhacking, and evolving business models. News production has become highly metrics-driven, which has implications for campaign coverage and audience trust. Colette Brin harnesses her research examining changes in journalistic practice and is joined by Ryan MacDonald, a senior editor at the *Globe and Mail*.

Chapter 6 examines the interactions among media polling, party polling, and media reporting in the framing of an election campaign. The authors show that the role of opinion polling has come a long way from the neutral recording of citizens' views as once envisioned by acclaimed pollster George Gallup. André Turcotte has extensive experience in both studying and leading public opinion survey research for political parties. His coauthor, Éric Grenier, is familiar to Canadian political observers as the face of Poll Tracker on CBC News.

The second section of the book begins with an examination of the work of party fundraisers in Chapter 7. It considers how technological trends and the news cycle affect fundraising efforts. Erin Crandall leverages her expertise in studying election law to describe the parameters of fundraising by Canadian political parties. Michael Roy draws on his online fundraising experiences with the New Democratic Party in 2015. Their insights are punctuated by information obtained from conversations with some personnel involved with fundraising during the party's 2019 campaign.

Chapter 8 introduces the strategic objectives involved in building major party platforms in Canada. It examines the tactics involved in marketing the platform as party personnel attempt to set the media agenda. Jared Wesley researches public policy and electioneering. His coauthor, Renze Nauta, held a senior role in platform development with the Conservative Party in 2019.

Chapter 9 provides a job description of national campaign directors by examining what they do on a day-to-day basis. David

McGrane expands on his research on political marketing and electioneering. Anne McGrath, his coauthor, was the NDP's national campaign director in 2015. Their chapter includes insights provided by her 2019 counterpart. Collectively, they look at the chronological arc of a national campaign by exploring the various stages of preparation that a campaign director must oversee from appointment to election day.

Working closely with a national campaign director is the director of communications, a position profiled in Chapter 10. To assemble that summary, Stéphanie Yates leveraged her research on how communications and politics intersect. Coauthor John Chenery reflects on his experience as director of communications with the Green Party in 2019.

A related position is profiled in Chapter 11, in which we are introduced to political leads, also known as senior campaign advisers. This chapter provides an under-the-hood look at how senior advisers accompany and counsel political leaders about their public image on tour. In it, Mireille Lalancette evokes her past work examining how politicians and political strategists construct political images. Marie Della Mattia contributes her own insights gleaned from over three decades of experience working with NDP leaders.

This attention to image management transitions into a discussion about political advertising in Chapter 12, which looks at how advertisers leverage media platforms to share issue- and image-based political ads. It unpacks how advertising professionals reach out to specific target audiences in order to deliver messages appealing to narrow interests and objectives. Vincent Raynauld draws on his scholarship in political and digital communications. His coauthor, Dany Renauld, has extensive expertise in the advertising industry, helping to produce advertising for the Conservative Party in Quebec in 2019.

Building on this examination of political parties' communication strategies and tactics, Chapter 13 invites us into the complementary world of registered third parties, more commonly known as advocacy groups. The chapter focuses on the political orientations and strategies adopted by labour unions when registered with Elections Canada as third parties during federal elections. In it, Thomas Collombat builds on his research on the socio-political aspects of trade union activities, and Magali Picard shares her experiences as a senior executive with the Public Service Alliance of Canada during the 2019 campaign.

The final chapter will intrigue Canadians who have concerns about the gatekeeping role of political parties in the House of Commons. Chapter 14 profiles the opportunities and considerable challenges of being an independent candidate in a Canadian election campaign. Tamara Small, a leading expert in the study of digital politics in Canada, turns her attention to constituency campaigning. The focus is on the experiences of coauthor Jane Philpott, a high-profile former Liberal MP and cabinet minister who ran as an independent in 2019.

After this sobering tale, everything in the book is brought together in the Conclusion, written by Anna Lennox Esselment and Thierry Giasson. Drawing on their knowledge of political marketing practices, party politics, and electoral strategies in Canada, they summarize what we have learned about campaign workers in recent Canadian elections. The Conclusion includes a tour of recent findings about the nature of campaign work from past contributors to the UBC Press series.

We hope that you enjoy getting *Inside the Campaign*.

Notes

[1]   For example, see Sayers, *Parties, Candidates, and Constituency Campaigns in Canadian Elections;* Flanagan, *Harper's Team;* and McLean, *Inside the NDP War Room.*

[2]   Brook, *Getting Elected in Canada,* 68.

[3]   Duffy, *Fights of Our Lives,* 30.

[4]   For example, see Esselment, "The Governing Party and the Permanent Campaign."

[5]   Delacourt, *Shopping for Votes.*

[6]   Marland and Mathews, "'Friend, Can You Chip in $3?'"

7   For a good overview of a Canadian political party's use of political marketing, see McGrane, *The New NDP*.

8   Wilson, "The Inter-Executive Activity of Ministerial Policy Advisors in the Government of Canada."

9   Turcotte and Vodrey, "Permanent Polling and Governance."

10   Esselment, "The Governing Party and the Permanent Campaign," 24.

11   Turnbull and Aucoin, *Fostering Canadians' Role in Public Policy*.

12   Yates with Arbour, "The Notion of Social Acceptability."

13   For more, see Birch and Pétry, *Assessing Justin Trudeau's Liberal Government*.

14   Gidengil et al., *Dominance and Decline*.

15   McLean, *Inside the NDP War Room*, 67.

16   Flanagan, *Harper's Team*.

17   Some information in this section is drawn from Aiello, "Election 2019."

18   MacDougall, "Rallying the Faithful."

19   Rodier, "Confessions of a Campaign Wagon Master."

20   For an excellent account of life as a party candidate, see Richler, *The Candidate*.

21   See Chapter 2 in Marland, *Whipped*.

22   For more on candidate nomination processes, see Pruysers and Cross, "Candidate Selection in Canada."

23   Tolley, *Framed*, 145.

24   Delacourt, *Shopping for Votes*, 199–200; Flanagan, *Harper's Team*, 223–24.

25   For example, see Koop, *Grassroots Liberals*, Chapter 5.

26   See Wesley, *Big Worlds*.

27   Taras, *Digital Mosaic*, 2.

28   For example, see Brook, *Getting Elected in Canada*, 91; and Lawlor and Crandall, "Understanding Third-Party Advertising."

29   Small, "Still Waiting for an Internet Prime Minister."

30   Giasson and Small, "Online, All the Time."

31   Tom Pitfield, quoted in Raj, "How Justin Trudeau Didn't Lose the 2019 Election."

32   See many of the chapters in Lalancette, Raynauld, and Crandall, *What's Trending in Canadian Politics?*

33   Bastien, *Breaking News?*

34   For further communication-related information about the 2019 campaign, see Gillies, Raynauld, and Turcotte, *Political Marketing in the 2019 Canadian Federal Election*.

35   CBC, "Canada Votes 2019."

[36] For a summary of the SNC-Lavalin political controversy, see Chapter 11 in Marland, *Whipped.*

[37] Leblanc and Fife, "Ottawa Blocks RCMP on SNC Inquiry."

[38] Giasson, Sauvageau, and Brin, "From Media Wave to Media Tsunami."

[39] For example, see Rana, "Election Campaign One of the Dirtiest in Recent History."

[40] Coyne, "Can't They Both Lose?"

[41] Johnson, "Political Management," 1155.

Bibliography

Aiello, Rachel. "Election 2019: Anatomy of a Liberal Rally in a Key Bell-wether." CTV News, 26 September 2019. https://election.ctvnews.ca/election-2019-anatomy-of-a-liberal-rally-in-a-key-bellwether-1.4612846.

Bastien, Frédérick. *Breaking News? Politics, Journalism, and Infotainment on Quebec Television.* Vancouver: UBC Press, 2018.

Birch, Lisa, and François Pétry. *Assessing Justin Trudeau's Liberal Government: 353 Promises and a Mandate for Change.* Laval: Presses de l'Université Laval, 2019.

Brook, Tom. *Getting Elected in Canada: A Political Insider Demystifies the Canadian Election Process.* Stratford, ON: Mercury Press, 1991.

Canadian Broadcasting Corporation (CBC). "Canada Votes 2019: Poll Tracker." 2019. https://newsinteractives.cbc.ca/elections/poll-tracker/canada/.

Coyne, Andrew. "Can't They Both Lose?" *National Post,* 19 October 2019, A17.

Delacourt, Susan. *Shopping for Votes: How Politicians Choose Us and We Choose Them.* Madeira Park, BC: Douglas and McIntyre, 2013.

Duffy, John. *Fights of Our Lives: Elections, Leadership, and the Making of Canada.* Toronto: HarperCollins, 2002.

Esselment, Anna. "The Governing Party and the Permanent Campaign." In *Political Communication in Canada: Meet the Press and Tweet the Rest,* edited by Alex Marland, Thierry Giasson, and Tamara A. Small, 24–38. Vancouver: UBC Press, 2014.

Flanagan, Tom. *Harper's Team: Behind the Scenes in the Conservative Rise to Power.* Montreal and Kingston: McGill-Queen's University Press, 2009.

Giasson, Thierry, Marie-Michèle Sauvageau, and Colette Brin. "From Media Wave to Media Tsunami: The 'Charter of Values' Debate in Quebec, 2012–2014." In *From Media Hype to Twitter Storm: News Explosions and Their Impact on Issues, Crises, and Public Opinion,* edited by Peter Vasterman, 167–85. Amsterdam: Amsterdam University Press, 2018.

Giasson, Thierry, and Tamara A. Small. "Online, All the Time: The Permanent Campaign on Web Platforms." In *Permanent Campaigning in Canada,* edited by Alex Marland, Thierry Giasson, and Anna Lennox Esselment, 109–26. Vancouver: UBC Press, 2017.

Gidengil, Elisabeth, Neil Nevitte, André Blais, Joanna Everitt, and Patrick Fournier. *Dominance and Decline: Making Sense of Recent Canadian Elections.* Toronto: University of Toronto Press, 2012.

Gillies, Jamie, Vincent Raynauld, and André Turcotte, eds. *Political Marketing in the 2019 Canadian Federal Election.* New York: Palgrave Macmillan (forthcoming).

Johnson, Dennis W. "Political Management." In *The International Encyclopedia of Political Communication, Volume 3,* edited by Gianpietro Mazzoleni, 1153–57. Chichester, UK: Wiley Blackwell, 2016.

Koop, Royce. *Grassroots Liberals: Organizing for Local and National Politics.* Vancouver: UBC Press, 2011.

Lalancette, Mireille, Vincent Raynauld, and Erin Crandall, eds. *What's Trending in Canadian Politics? Understanding Transformations in Power, Media, and the Public Sphere.* Vancouver: UBC Press, 2019.

Lawlor, Andrea, and Erin Crandall. "Understanding Third-Party Advertising: An Analysis of the 2004, 2006 and 2008 Canadian Elections." *Canadian Public Administration* 54, 4 (2011): 509–29.

Leblanc, Daniel, and Robert Fife. "Ottawa Blocks RCMP on SNC Inquiry." *Globe and Mail,* 11 September 2019, A1.

MacDougall, Andrew. "Rallying the Faithful: The Secret to Conservative Success." CBC News, 3 August 2015. https://www.cbc.ca/news/politics/canada-election-2015-rallying-the-faithful-the-secret-to-conservative-success-1.3178046.

Marland, Alex. *Whipped: Party Discipline in Canada.* Vancouver: UBC Press, 2020.

Marland, Alex, and Maria Mathews. "'Friend, Can You Chip in $3?' Canadian Political Parties' Email Communication and Fundraising." In *Permanent Campaigning in Canada,* edited by Alex Marland, Thierry Giasson, and Anna Lennox Esselment, 87–108. Vancouver: UBC Press, 2017.

McGrane, David. *The New NDP: Moderation, Modernization, and Political Marketing.* Vancouver: UBC Press, 2019.

McLean, James S. *Inside the NDP War Room.* Montreal and Kingston: McGill-Queen's University Press, 2012.

Pruysers, Scott, and William Cross. "Candidate Selection in Canada: Local Autonomy, Centralization, and Competing Democratic Norms." *American Behavioral Scientist* 60, 7 (2016): 781–98.

Raj, Althia. "How Justin Trudeau Didn't Lose the 2019 Election: From Scandals, Spin and Slams to a Minority Government." *Huffington Post,* 5 November 2019, updated 17 November 2019. https://www.huffingtonpost. ca/entry/justin-trudeau-canada-election-how-did-they-win_ca_ 5dc0d8c1e4b0bedb2d519a3d.

Rana, Abbas. "Election Campaign One of the Dirtiest in Recent History, Say Political Insiders." *Hill Times* [Ottawa], 14 October 2019, 1.

Richler, Noah. *The Candidate: Fear and Loathing on the Campaign Trail.* Toronto: Doubleday Canada, 2016.

Rodier, David. "Confessions of a Campaign Wagon Master." *Policy Options,* 16 December 2019. https://policyoptions.irpp.org/magazines/december -2019/confessions-of-a-campaign-wagon-master/.

Sayers, Anthony. *Parties, Candidates, and Constituency Campaigns in Canadian Elections.* Vancouver: UBC Press, 1999.

Small, Tamara A. "Still Waiting for an Internet Prime Minister: Online Campaigning by Canadian Political Parties." In *Election,* edited by Heather MacIvor, 173–98. Toronto: Emond Montgomery, 2009.

Taras, David. *Digital Mosaic: Media, Power, and Identity in Canada.* Toronto: University of Toronto Press, 2015.

Tolley, Erin. *Framed: Media and the Coverage of Race in Canadian Politics.* Vancouver: UBC Press, 2015.

Turcotte, André, and Simon Vodrey. "Permanent Polling and Governance." In *Permanent Campaigning in Canada,* edited by Alex Marland, Thierry Giasson, and Anna Lennox Esselment, 127–44. Vancouver: UBC Press, 2017.

Turnbull, Lori, and Peter Aucoin. *Fostering Canadians' Role in Public Policy: A Strategy for Institutionalizing Public Involvement in Policy.* Ottawa: Canadian Policy Research Networks, March 2006.

Wesley, Jared, ed. *Big Worlds: Politics and Elections in the Canadian Provinces and Territories.* Toronto: University of Toronto Press, 2016.

Wilson, R. Paul. "The Inter-Executive Activity of Ministerial Policy Advisors in the Government of Canada." In *How Ottawa Spends 2016–2017: The Trudeau Liberals in Power,* edited by G. Bruce Doern and Christopher Stoney, 191–215. Ottawa: Carleton University, 2016.

Yates, Stéphanie, with Myriam Arbour. "The Notion of Social Acceptability: Lay Citizens as a New Political Force." In *What's Trending in Canadian Politics? Understanding Transformations in Power, Media, and the Public Sphere,* edited by Mireille Lalancette, Vincent Raynauld, and Erin Crandall, 257–75. Vancouver: UBC Press, 2019.

PART 1
Caretakers and Participant Observers

1

Election Administrators

Andrea Lawlor and Marc Mayrand

Whereas most Canadians tend to focus on parties and candidates during an election campaign, the work performed by an equally important set of actors – election administrators – is often overlooked. Election administrators are responsible for the procedural aspects of an election: implementing election laws, ensuring that campaign advertising and spending comply with the laws set out by Parliament, and most importantly facilitating the voting process for citizens. This chapter covers the work of Canada's election administrators – Elections Canada and the chief electoral officer.

Alors que la plupart des Canadiens se concentrent d'avantage sur les partis et les candidats pendant une campagne électorale, le travail effectué par un groupe tout aussi important d'acteurs – les administrateurs d'élection – est souvent négligé. Les administrateurs d'élection sont responsables des aspects procéduraux et logistiques d'une élection, c'est-à-dire de mettre en application les lois électorales, veiller à ce que la publicité et les dépenses électorales soient conformes aux lois établies par le Parlement et, surtout, faciliter le processus électoral pour les citoyens. Ce chapitre traite du travail des administrateurs d'élection du Canada, à savoir le Directeur général des élections et Élections Canada.

IN CANADA, THE task of administering federal elections is in the hands of Elections Canada. At the helm is the appointed chief electoral officer (CEO). The CEO is an officer of Parliament – politically independent and at arm's length from the government of the day. Broadly speaking, the job of Elections Canada and the CEO is to administer elections and referendums, implementing and ensuring compliance with election laws handed down by Parliament.

Elections Canada is an administrative agency entirely staffed by non-partisan bureaucrats. They normally include five hundred full-time members of the civil service: lawyers, policy analysts, auditors, and sundry administrative and technical staff. Their role includes facilitating the registration of parties, candidates, and third parties; conducting by-elections; and holding the rare referendum. They co-ordinate the monitoring and auditing of party/candidate spending and donations and, broadly speaking, ensure that campaign actors comply with the Canada Elections Act and other relevant election laws. There is also the considerable work of ensuring that the machinery of an election – everything from balloting to deploying the materials required so that millions of Canadians can vote – reaches each of Canada's 338 ridings without incident. During the campaign, this involves overseeing more than 235,000 temporary election workers, including polling clerks and returning officers.

At the helm is the chief electoral officer, appointed through a resolution of the House of Commons. The CEO advises Parliament, through its committees, to determine fair and enforceable rules for elections. The CEO has some discretion granted by Parliament to deal with emergencies that could affect the running of an election in any given constituency. Ultimately, though, the CEO defers to Parliament in the design of election legislation. Although not reporting directly to a single minister, the CEO is like a deputy minister – the most senior unelected official in the "department" – and as such it is the CEO's job to submit reports on matters related to elections to the Speaker of the House and to appear before committees that deal with electoral matters.[1] CEOs are typically pulled from the ranks of the civil service and have a history of public administration and management experience within the government. To preserve their neutrality and independence, they are not permitted to vote in federal elections, and as of 2014 they are limited to serving a ten-year, non-renewable term.[2]

The authority and limits of Elections Canada and the CEO are set out in the Canada Elections Act. The act was created in 2000, updating and consolidating pre-existing election laws as well as integrating some recommendations from the 1991 Lortie Commission. It is routinely updated by Parliament to address changes to the campaign environment and to reflect the government's preferences for how elections should be run.[3] Subsequent electoral legislation – such as the 2006 Federal Accountability Act and the 2014 Fair Elections Act, the 2014 Fair Elections Act, and the 2018 Elections Modernization Act – instituted changes to the election regime, some of which were lasting. These changes included alterations to campaign finance laws, voter identification rules, and responsibilities and permitted activities of the CEO. As a result, Elections Canada has seen its duties expand and contract depending on the legislative preferences of the government. The very act of governments legislating how elections should be run but "outsourcing" some implementation authority to Elections Canada is inherently political and positions the elections administrator as a powerful actor both within and outside the campaign period. Consequently, it could be argued that the emphasis on continually enhancing regulations has built an administrative apparatus that is its own centre of power in elections.

The job of the CEO and Elections Canada could be considered to fall into two distinct periods: the election campaign and the inter-election period. In practice, however, these periods are never truly distinct. Nonetheless, during the inter-election period, Elections Canada and the office of the CEO perform routine electoral administrative duties. They maintain the National Register of Electors; administer the Canada Elections Act and other relevant pieces of electoral legislation; promote the act of voting by ensuring that both polls and information about the vote are accessible;

and provide legal, technical, and administrative support to the commissions responsible for adjusting electoral boundaries. Elections Canada also has some limited duties regarding candidate nominations and leadership contests, such as registering the contests and monitoring compliance with election financial laws. At times, its office orchestrates educational outreach campaigns to improve public knowledge about elections.

Much of the agency's time during the inter-election period is spent monitoring and auditing financial contributions to parties to verify that they are being made in accordance with the Canada Elections Act. Elections Canada dedicates a considerable amount of time to conducting audits to ensure that campaign actors are compliant with election finance laws. Political parties and riding associations submit periodic financial reports, whereas candidates and third parties only submit a report following the election. Although election administrators do not pursue campaign finance violations – the commissioner of elections investigates any violations of the Canada Elections Act, and the RCMP investigate possible violations of the Criminal Code – they do follow up on concerns reported by citizens.

From time to time, Elections Canada might also issue public statements about the application of election laws to matters such as campaign or inter-election spending or advertising. Although such pronouncements might appear to be routine and administrative, at times their effects can be perceived to be controversial since any exercise of rules can have positive or negative implications for specific sets of campaign actors. In 2019, for example, the CEO had to issue a statement assuring environmental groups that they would not find themselves in violation of the Elections Act by publishing calls to fight climate change, despite that message being contrary to the position taken by the leader of the People's Party, Maxime Bernier.[4] Here it became essential for Elections Canada to clarify that advocacy groups were able to speak freely about issues that have political dimensions without being perceived to be campaigning.

In recent years, Elections Canada and the office of the CEO have shifted to meet the challenges of the new electoral environment. Their mandate has evolved to include enhancing physical accessibility to the polls, providing election data through their online portal, conducting research on voting and campaign innovations (e.g., online voting, digital advertising), and increasing general accessibility to populations such as youth, Indigenous communities, new Canadians, and individuals with disabilities who traditionally have voted in low numbers.[5] Furthermore, with the turn toward a digital style of electoral outreach, Elections Canada, under the guidance of the CEO, has worked with Parliament to monitor the digital transmission of information as it relates to the procedures for voting by electoral actors and to counter cyberthreats to our electoral system.

Duties in an Election Campaign

The careful stages of planning and laying the groundwork for a free and fair election get pushed into overdrive when the campaign writ is dropped. Although the regularity of election dates has been enshrined in Canadian law since the enactment of Bill C-16, An Act to Amend the Canada Elections Act, in 2007, the parliamentary system still gives the prime minister some ability to set the precise timing of an election. In a minority Parliament, a failed confidence vote can quickly send the country back to the polls. The independence of the CEO from Parliament means that individual does not have any advance knowledge of election timing. Thus, Elections Canada and the CEO have to be agile, responding to an election call at a moment's notice.

During this time, the CEO operates mostly behind the scenes. The constituency-level returning officers carry out most election day duties, and Elections Canada staff deal with legal questions as well as public and media inquiries.[6] Since a CEO's principal relationship is with Parliament, the role as adviser is engaged only when questions about applying election laws arise during the election.

Arguably, the measure of the agency's success is how little attention is paid to the CEO and team during the campaigns, for it signals few disruptions to the election. Yet challenges arise all the time. They can be minor (e.g., a misprint on a voter card) or major (e.g., misinformation about voting times and locations). Problems can arise from election laws themselves, such as how to implement a law coming into effect for the first time, or from an issue brought up by a member of the public or a political party. For example, just prior to the 2019 election campaign, Chief Electoral Officer Stéphane Perrault had to address requests and a Federal Court directive to review changing the election date because of a conflict with the Jewish holiday of Shemini Atzeret, which began the day before and ended the day after the election. This was a rare occasion of a CEO having to intervene publicly in some capacity during the campaign. No change was made to the original election date.

Part of the role of Elections Canada and the CEO is to lead critical planning exercises to handle any incident or disruption at the polls. This can include poor weather, challenges with infrastructure, security threats, or barriers to access. During the campaign, Elections Canada trains and deploys small teams to handle incidents or inefficiencies in the system. Back in Ottawa, members of these teams monitor risks and create contingency plans to ensure that the election proceeds without disruption. Although the number of incidents arising at the polls has been small historically, threats to personal security, such as concerns following the attacks on Parliament in 2015, are taken seriously; consequently, the CEO is in contact with relevant law enforcement bodies as needed.

Of course, most concerns that arise during the campaign are merely procedural. As election day approaches, Elections Canada must prepare all special ballots that permit individuals to vote remotely. The organization performs a risk assessment of each riding to determine where it might expect a higher than average number of administrative issues. They can include expectations of a high number of voters without identification, voters who are highly mobile (e.g., young people, students, those with no fixed address), or ineligible voters. To address these issues, the CEO's staff are in constant communication with the returning officers in the ridings, particularly on election day. At Elections Canada's head-quarters in Gatineau, rapid intervention teams are ready to be deployed to address situations such as staff absences or inadequate training, errors in poll locations, misdirected electors, or disputes between campaigns regarding the counting of ballots and the eligibility of voters.

Recently, Elections Canada has had to keep up with the changing landscape of campaign ads. It used to be the case that money was the metric to evaluate how much access a party has to the electorate. Parliament put laws in place to ensure that limits on spending would create the opportunity for an even playing field when it comes to election advertising.[7] Historically, the CEO's appointed broadcasting arbitrator was able to ensure that parties had equal access to purchase ad time. Today televised advertising is only a small part of the campaign backdrop. Partisan advertising has evolved from traditional means (e.g., billboards, radio and print ads) to modern approaches (e.g., social media, targeted online advertising). Modern-day campaign teams are adept at using digital media, automated calling, and other automated and resource-efficient means to tailor messages to specific populations.[8] Therefore, CEOs have had to work with Parliament to consider whether, how, and to what extent to regulate new technologies, many of which do not always rely on big-ticket spending and therefore cannot be easily evaluated according to the old "money as speech" criterion.

Similarly, CEOs and their office have acknowledged new challenges to their ability to orchestrate democratically fair and open elections. Since the mid-2010s, campaigns have increasingly become targets for actors who seek to disrupt the outcomes of elections either directly or indirectly. Election administrators must be aware of threats coming from anonymous sources insofar as they relate to misdirecting voters about dates, times, and locations of polls. They must cultivate the technical expertise to counter risks, including hacking, tampering with information, or misdirecting the public on the procedures of elections. However, to maintain its non-partisan nature, Elections Canada has a limited role to play in the mis/disinformation wars waged across Western democracies. The Canadian government and Elections Canada have signalled that they are alert to the possibility of undue campaign influence.[9] They are therefore putting in place measures to fight off attacks to Elections Canada's internal systems and databases. This preparation includes working with Canada's Communications Security Establishment (CSE), the organization responsible for monitoring the threat of cyberespionage and security and intelligence threats to elections. It incorporates the RCMP, Canadian Security Intelligence Service (CSIS), and Global Affairs Canada.[10]

Overcoming Obstacles

Recent challenges faced by Elections Canada have been unprecedented but not entirely unforeseen. The rise in threats to the integrity of democratic elections has been noted worldwide, stemming from the ongoing debate about the extent to which foreign entities meddled in the 2016 US presidential election. It is not part of Elections Canada's mandate to follow up on partisan or policy disinformation. However, the elections administrator can refer any detected threat to the integrity of the campaign to a new Critical Election Incident Public Protocol, composed of five senior-level, non-political government officials. Leading up to the 2019 election campaign, the CEO oversaw an increase in Elections Canada's resources dedicated to countering cyberattacks and commented that the organization was "pretty confident" that it was prepared for the threat of cyberattacks disrupting either the flow of legitimate information or even the election infrastructure itself.[11] Greater staffing resources were allocated to monitor social and digital media as well as its own systems to prevent the distribution of inaccurate information about dates and locations of polls and voter eligibility. The threat of attack to the integrity of the system is partly why the government and Elections Canada have taken such a cautious approach when considering the introduction of online voting.

Efforts to combat poor information were not made solely by the government. In 2018, it had called on large social media companies to take greater care in the dissemination of information. During the campaign, Twitter provided additional checks on the distribution of disinformation and monitoring of potentially volatile political discourse that could lead to misinformation or, worse, violence.[12] Twitter worked with Elections Canada's lists of third parties to verify that ads placed through Twitter conformed to the legislation that governs them.

Electoral finance posed some new but undoubtedly timeless challenges to the election regime. Third-party advertisers were scrutinized carefully by the media as concerns about anonymous funding grew. In the final weeks of the campaign, the media highlighted a possible loophole in third-party spending laws. A conservative think tank became the focus of media inquiry as routine financial disclosure brought to light donations of over $300,000 to various third-party groups.[13] Although the law requires that third parties disclose their sources of funding, there is no requirement that donors to third parties do the same. Thus, the think tank was compliant with the letter of the law, but it brought up concerns that legal drafters might not have anticipated. Elections Canada responded that the law does not prevent such activity and therefore did not act on it. These sorts of challenges often come up only once the policy is in place and electoral actors can test its limits. Elections Canada might be called on to advise Parliament on the unintended consequences of election laws as they played out in the 2019 campaign; however, it is not in its purview to initiate changes to the law.

Finally, we could consider the extent of regulation in Canadian elections to provide its own set of challenges. In contrast to some of our international counterparts, Canadian elections might appear to be heavily regulated, particularly in regard to issues of free speech. In the past, Parliament, civil society, and the Supreme Court of Canada have often been at odds on issues of campaign advertising, the transmission of election results, and third-party spending. These issues routinely engage both advocates and critics of the Charter of Rights and Freedoms, thereby posing challenges for Elections Canada, whose role it is to carry out regulations to remain out of the fray of explicitly political and partisan questions. A grey area exists with respect to advocacy groups' participation in public discourse. As the aforementioned ruling on public discourse about climate change illustrates, the exercise of fundamental freedoms can create friction with the regulatory activities that Elections Canada carries out.

As a further example, at the time of writing, there is considerable debate about changes made to section 91 of the Canada Elections Act, which states that publishing false statements about party leaders, candidates, and other individuals associated with political parties "with the intention of affecting the results of an election" is an offence.[14] Despite a previous amendment to section 91 that removed the notion that misinformation has to be transmitted "knowingly," the commissioner of Canada Elections noted that this section is essentially unenforceable. The combination of widely available digital technologies and platforms on which to express political views further introduces substantial complexity into what constitutes an offence under this section and which offences are to be prosecuted. Although monitoring such activities might not be directly part of the mandate of Elections Canada, inevitably it is alert to legislative changes that might contradict Charter rights or other laws and how that might affect its work in administering election laws. That said, the CEO cannot refuse to apply a provision of the act simply because it *might* be found to be unconstitutional. Until a court rules on the validity of the provision or Parliament changes the act, the CEO must apply the legislation as written. It is unlikely that Elections Canada will take a position on this matter, leaving it instead to the courts and Parliament to react to the issue. However, each decision made by Parliament to restrict or expand the authority of the elections administrator to limit speech will have inevitable implications for the freedom of parties, candidates, and perhaps even citizens to participate in elections.

The future of elections will inevitably engage serious questions for the public, the government, and the academic community about how the use of technology in campaigning and advertising affects voter deliberations and election outcomes, in addition to core matters of personal freedom. We suggest that these developments have put and will continue to put election administrators in an important but sometimes controversial spot. Election administrators are often placed in the background of conversations about elections. However, considering the changing campaign environment and the likelihood that political actors will use it in order to advocate for or against a stronger regulatory hand, we should continue to consider whether government policies pressure the administrator to take on greater capacity. In the absence of government directives on matters related to campaigns, the administrator might face challenges in upholding the election regime. For now, we can observe that Elections Canada is a long-standing institution with decades spent cultivating administrative expertise. Such institutions tend to be resilient even in the face of a change in government. Thus, despite governments' changing preferences, expect Elections Canada and the chief electoral officer to remain influential in the evolution of our electoral democracy.

Notes

[1] Massicotte, "The Chief Electoral Officer of Canada."
[2] Kingsley, "The Administration of Canada's Independent, Non-Partisan Approach."
[3] Elections Canada, *A History of the Vote in Canada.*
[4] Zimonjic, "Environmental Groups Can Still Talk Climate Change during Election."
[5] Ladner and McCrossan, "The Electoral Participation of Aboriginal People."
[6] Massicotte, "The Chief Electoral Officer of Canada."

7   See Crandall and Lawlor, "Third Party Election Spending in Canada and the United Kingdom."
8   See Pal, "Canadian Election Administration on Trial."
9   See Government of Canada, "New Initiatives to Safeguard the 2019 Federal Election."
10 Centre for International Governance Innovation, "Election Risk Monitor Canada," 12.
11 Bryden, "Chief Electoral Officer Worries Parties Are Weak Link in Cybersecurity Chain."
12 Paas-Lang, "Twitter Says Canadian Election So Far Free of Major Manipulation Attempts."
13 Keller and Cryderman, "Manning Centre Won't Disclose Source of Donations to Third Parties for Attack Ads on Liberals."
14 Canada Elections Act, section 91.

Bibliography

Canada Elections Act. https://laws.justice.gc.ca/eng/acts/e-2.01/index.html.

Centre for International Governance Innovation. "Election Risk Monitor Canada." Centre for International Governance Innovation, Waterloo, ON, 2019.

Crandall, Erin, and Andrea Lawlor. "Third Party Election Spending in Canada and the United Kingdom: A Comparative Analysis." *Election Law Journal* 13, 4 (2014): 476–92.

Elections Canada. *A History of the Vote in Canada.* 2nd ed. Ottawa: Office of the Chief Electoral Officer of Canada, 2007.

Government of Canada. "New Initiatives to Safeguard the 2019 Federal Election." 30 January 2019. https://www.elections.ca/content.aspx?section=med&dir=spe&document=jan3019&lang=e.

Keller, James, and Kelly Cryderman. "Manning Centre Won't Disclose Source of Donations to Third Parties for Attack Ads on Liberals." *Globe and Mail,* 15 October 2019. https://www.theglobeandmail.com/canada/article-manning-centre-wont-disclose-source-of-donations-to-third-parties-for/.

Kingsley, J.P. "The Administration of Canada's Independent, Non-Partisan Approach." *Election Law Journal* 3, 3 (2004): 406–11.

Ladner, Kiera, and Michael McCrossan. "The Electoral Participation of Aboriginal People." Working Paper Series on Electoral Participation and Outreach Practices, Chief Electoral Officer of Canada, Ottawa, 2007.

Massicotte, Louis. "The Chief Electoral Officer of Canada." *Canadian Parliamentary Review* 26, 3 (2003): 20–27.

Paas-Lang, Christian. "Twitter Says Canadian Election So Far Free of Major Manipulation Attempts." *National Post,* 24 September 2019. https://nationalpost.com/pmn/news-pmn/canada-news-pmn/twitter-says-canadian-election-so-far-free-of-major-manipulation-attempts.

Pal, Michael. "Canadian Election Administration on Trial: 'Robocalls,' Opitz and Disputed Elections in the Courts." *King's Law Journal* 28, 2 (2017): 324–42.

Zimonjic, Peter. "Environmental Groups Can Still Talk Climate Change during Election, Says Canada's Chief Electoral Officer." CBC News, 20 August 2019. https://www.cbc.ca/news/politics/climate-elections-canada-perrault-1.5253580.

2

Political Staff

Paul Wilson and Michael McNair

Many ministerial political staffers take unpaid leaves of absence to work on election campaigns. The opportunity to contribute to their political party in an election is a natural extension of their motivation to work in politics in the first place. However, since ministers remain ministers even during a writ period, some members of their political staff continue to be employed in their departmental offices to maintain connections with public servants and to provide information and support to their ministers. This chapter analyzes the role of ministerial staff during an election campaign.

De nombreux membres du personnel politique ministériel demandent des congés sans solde afin de participer aux campagnes électorales. La possibilité de contribuer aux activités de leur parti en période électorale est inhérente aux motivations qui les ont initialement poussés à faire de la politique. Toutefois, comme les ministres conservent leur poste en période électorale, certains membres de leur personnel politique continuent de travailler dans leurs bureaux ministériels afin de maintenir les communications avec les fonctionnaires, d'informer leurs ministres et de les soutenir. Ce chapitre analyse le rôle du personnel ministériel pendant une campagne électorale.

MANY PEOPLE GRAVITATE to political jobs because they love the adrenalin of campaigning and are committed to building support for their party. Predictably, when an election is called, most political staffers take unpaid leaves of absence to work on the campaign. However, some remain at their desks in ministers' offices, including in the Prime Minister's Office (PMO), in order to support the ministry that continues in power throughout the writ period. In essence, they act as democratic insurance so that even during an election period final government decisions and accountability rest with those who earned a democratic mandate in the previous election. These staff play an important role in maintaining information flow between departments and ministers as well as ongoing dialogue with the public service during the campaign.

Political staffers comprise a diverse part of the Canadian federal political community. Some, known as exempt staff, work for cabinet ministers, providing political support and advice. Some work for Members of Parliament (MPs), either supporting them in their House of Commons duties on Parliament Hill or dealing with constituents and local matters back in their home ridings. This "para-political bureaucracy" exists to serve politicians personally, and the jobs of political staffers depend on their bosses – and, for ministerial staffers, their party – winning re-election.[1]

Political staffers are paid out of public funds; hence, though their work is expressly political, it is not directly partisan. House of Commons resources, including employees, may be used "in the fulfillment of parliamentary functions only."[2] This explicitly excludes election campaigns. Similarly, ministerial exempt staff may only support ministers with "ministerial business, and not for party political activities."[3] Political staffers who themselves run as candidates in an election or participate full time in a campaign must either resign or take an unpaid leave of absence. Staffers who campaign only part time may stay in their day jobs but must campaign only on their own time outside office hours.

Except for Senate offices, all political staff jobs ultimately depend on the electoral results, so working or volunteering during elections is an important litmus test of commitment to the team. One survey found that 100 percent of ministerial policy staff respondents had volunteered at some point during an election campaign.[4] Some staffers work on the local campaign of their own minister or MP, some go to ridings that need more bodies or experience, and some work on the national campaign in the war room, on the leader's tour, or in a call centre.

Not all political staffers leave their usual jobs, however. MPs cease to be MPs as soon as the governor general dissolves Parliament, but their office budgets continue until the date of the general election.[5] They may continue to pay their employees, though MPs' offices are very quiet when Parliament is dissolved. Some political staff stay on their MP's payroll, sometimes volunteering on a local campaign after hours and sometimes not.

Ministers are usually MPs and need to run for re-election. Yet, during the campaign, ministers continue to be ministers. Government business continues, and they retain their legal authority from the Crown. However, it is not business as usual. The caretaker convention dictates that, when Parliament is dissolved and there is no confidence chamber to hold them accountable, ministers will exercise restraint.[6] Through such self-restraint, they show respect for democratic accountability. They also avoid any perception that the governing party receives electoral benefits from its executive privileges. This convention operates in Canada similarly as in other countries with a Westminster parliamentary system such as the United Kingdom, Australia, and New Zealand.[7] Usually, it attracts public notice only in times of controversy, such as the disagreement between Charles Tupper and Governor General Lord Aberdeen over appointments following the 1896 election, Kim Campbell's decision to approve a contract for the sale of Toronto Pearson International Airport in 1993, and the RCMP's announcement of a politically sensitive criminal investigation during the 2005–06 election.[8] Under the convention, routine administration continues, and ministers must still address urgent and unavoidable matters, such as natural disasters. However, generally they avoid making announcements, commitments, or decisions that an incoming government could not reverse.

Although most ministerial aides take leaves of absence to campaign, a coterie of exempt staffers remain at work in the PMO and in each department. They monitor government activity from the perspective of communication risk, act as liaisons between the minister and public servants, and provide the minister with information and advice in the exercise of their caretaker duties. The PMO political staff perform a particularly important role during the campaign period. They support the prime minister, who remains the head of government, and they interface with the Privy Council Office (PCO). The PCO is the prime minister's department and the public service central agency responsible for enforcing the caretaker convention across the public service. PMO staff have their own central role in coordinating all other ministerial offices.

Duties in an Election Campaign

As the date of the election approaches, ministers' offices must determine which staffers should remain at work during the writ period and who should take an unpaid leave to join a campaign. The assumption is that most staffers should contribute to the re-election effort. Typically, only a handful of ministerial staffers remain behind to assist ministers with their responsibilities during the caretaker period. Staffing decisions depend on several factors.

First, requirements vary according to the nature of the department since some departments are more likely to see significant issues emerge, such as Global Affairs or Public Safety, whereas others pose greater risk management challenges. Second, a minister's campaign needs can influence office staff disposition. A minister in a highly contested constituency might bring as many experienced staffers as possible to lead local volunteers, especially if the staffers have close personal connections to the minister and roots in the riding. In contrast, a minister running in a safer constituency can afford to leave more experienced staff in the department. Third, personal aptitude and circumstance make a difference. For example, it is easier for younger staffers without family obligations to uproot and couch-surf for several months while volunteering for a campaign on the other side of the country. Older staffers, especially those with young children at home, find this more personally disruptive, and some might find it impossible. Offices tend to take such factors into account when determining who will be on the campaign full time.

As in other ministers' offices, a handful of the normal staff complement remains at work in the PMO. They include representatives from many of its key departments, especially those related to its policy, media relations, and issues management teams. Typically, most of the senior PMO staff takes leave to work either in the party's national headquarters or on the leader's election tour. However, one of the senior staffers staying behind acts as the chief of staff to manage the office and to provide a senior point of contact with the prime minister, the campaign, ministers' offices, as well as the PCO.

Prior to the election, the Prime Minister's Office generally coordinates with ministers' chiefs of staff to ensure that satisfactory staffing arrangements are in place in order to cover a range of contingencies. Doing so ensures that the government is staffed and that experienced and motivated workers are available for the campaign. Offices must pay close attention to administrative details in order to ensure a strict separation between government business and election campaign activity. For example, a best practice is to change telephone voice-mail messages and email out-of-office responses to say that the individual is on leave, specifying a return date after the election. Before taking leave, staffers must hand in office property such as their government smartphones and other electronic equipment, their building access pass, and their key(s). Again, this is to ensure proper separation – and the appearance of proper separation – between the two worlds.

The daily rhythm of ministers' offices changes as soon as the writ drops and the caretaker convention comes into operation. The normally heavy volume of briefing notes from the deputy minister is reduced considerably. Oral briefings cease. Impromptu, face-to-face interactions with departmental officials become less frequent as the public service turns inward to focus on planning for post-election transition scenarios.[9] It is almost as if a curtain descends to separate the two worlds.

Nevertheless, since ministers continue to head their departments, they are entitled to be kept apprised of events within their portfolios since they might be asked questions at any time. They might even have to respond to urgent matters that cannot wait until after the election. Examples include international crises, ongoing Canadian military engagements, court rulings, domestic emergencies, and high-level negotiations such as for trade agreements. In these situations, ministers must be kept informed, make decisions, and give direction. Therefore, they require political staff who can be trusted to exercise sound judgment in deciding what information needs to be conveyed when to the campaigning minister. Political staff should have sufficient policy expertise so that they can engage with departmental officials and ensure that the minister is fully briefed, including by providing political context and advice.

Once the minister is engaged, political staff will often convey the minister's direction and facilitate the next steps if necessary. This might mean setting up a telephone call with the deputy minister or other ministers, depending on the scope of the issue. Political staff can carry out political legwork with other offices to ensure coordination. Sometimes specific documents need to be conveyed to the minister for signature. This is why one member of the minister's political staff is permitted to accompany the minister while campaigning yet remain as a government employee. This ensures a constant liaison between the department and the minister who can receive classified information if necessary. Just like colleagues remaining in the Ottawa office, this staffer does not take a full-time part in partisan campaign activities, though proximity to the minister is required.

Most departmental paperwork can wait until after the campaign. However, ministers are sometimes asked to take administrative decisions and these can be important and time sensitive. For example, if a government did not pass budgetary measures prior to the dissolution of Parliament, then ministers may request from the governor general special warrants granting urgent funding so that normal departmental operations can continue. Political staff would work with public servants to ensure that the minister was briefed, to send the proper documents to the minister on the campaign trail for signature, and to get them back to the department.

In normal times, ministers' offices devote significant effort to pushing out proactively the government's strategic messages.[10] During an election, however, the campaign team assumes almost all responsibility for public messaging. Ministers' offices, in contrast, adopt an entirely reactive and defensive approach to communication. Their goal is to manage and mitigate risk by identifying potential problems and neutralizing them before they become public controversies. This involves carefully monitoring news stories, including on social media, to identify negative stories relevant to the department, gathering background information from the department in order to understand the context, and recommending response lines. Ministers' offices maintain media relations capacity so that they can deal directly with journalists and answer questions about departmental business. To monitor potential issues across the government, the PMO creates a process so that early each day political media relations and issues management staffers from across the government can flag emerging issues and recommend responsive messages. These lines are then communicated to ministers so that they are prepared for government-related questions as they campaign at public events.

In a similar way, work in the Prime Minister's Office changes when the election is called. Political staffers in the PMO no longer work with the PCO on managing the cabinet policy agenda or coordinating long-term strategic communication efforts across the government. The clerk of the Privy Council significantly curtails the volume of daily briefing notes to the prime minister, though this reduction might reflect the prime minister's desire to focus on the campaign as much as a desire to defend the caretaker convention.

The PMO must always ensure that the prime minister is aware of key developments within the government. Of course, this includes information in priority areas such as the economy, national security, and international relations. However, details vary from day to day. Senior PMO staff may speak with the prime minister when required to answer questions and to pass on information that the prime minister needs to know, either to ensure smooth governance or to ensure that the prime minister is briefed on government business that might intrude into the campaign setting.

When appearing in public as a party leader, the prime minister simultaneously wears the hat of the head of government and is therefore always entitled to receive briefings on the status and impact of government programs across the country. The PMO may appropriately request these details from the relevant government department. However, the campaign and the PMO must respect caretaker convention limits. It would be improper to ask any ministerial staffers, as government employees, to use government time or resources to analyze opposition parties' election platform commitments, let alone to ask departments any long-term policy questions that would contribute to the incumbent's own platform. The PMO needs to exercise good judgment in these delicate matters.

Finally, though interactions between the PMO and the PCO are reduced during the campaign, there are opportunities for dialogue. PCO staff might wish to discuss "transition to government" questions with PMO staff. If the government is re-elected, might the prime minister consider machinery of government changes? Is the prime minister satisfied with the briefing processes in place, or could they be improved? Is the prime minister open to revising guidelines on conduct and accountability for ministers? Informal consultations on such matters might be helpful, though at this stage they would be only one-way conversations. For example, the PCO can solicit views from the PMO on such matters, but it should not offer any advice in return on matters of transition or on governing after the election.

Overcoming Obstacles

Sometimes obstacles emerge in the relationship between ministers and their offices and public servants in the lead up to and during the election campaign. Such obstacles are often rooted in a misunderstanding of the purpose and limits of the caretaker convention.

In 2015, Stephen Harper was the first prime minister to make the caretaker guidelines available publicly. Prime Minister Justin Trudeau also did so in 2019. This transparency helps the public to understand how the government works during an election and ought to provide more clarity across the federal government. In practice, there is still more work to do in understanding when the caretaker period begins, what is meant by the caretaker function, and where the limits of the convention can be found.

Election campaigns in both 2015 and 2019 occurred in the context of majority governments with a legislated fixed election date. This meant that everyone knew when the election would likely be held, though not when Parliament would be dissolved. In terms of political activity and public perception, this meant that the campaign seemed to extend back into the summer. To deal with this issue, the Trudeau government introduced changes for the pre-writ period to restrict government advertising and limit pre-campaign spending by political parties. These steps, combined with the fact that Parliament was adjourned but not dissolved, could lead public servants or even political staff to conclude that ministers were not permitted to operate as usual during the summer. Ministers' offices had to work to counter this perception by asserting, for example, their entitlement to information and briefings as usual. With the support of the PMO and PCO, the government operated as normal in the months leading up to the election call. However, additional clarity is needed to ensure that everyone recognizes that caretaker restraint only begins with the dissolution of Parliament and not in the period leading up to it.

Who is the caretaker? This concept has been a source of confusion. Are the deputy minister and senior officials now in charge of the department? Does the chief of staff now act as minister? The reality is far simpler and consistent with our democratic system of government. During the campaign, ministers sometimes choose to delegate more authority to their deputy ministers where appropriate and in coordination with their chiefs of staff. However, whether delegated or not, it is never public servants or political staff who act as caretakers or hold the authority or accountability of ministers. Rather, the government continues to be led by a political cabinet of democratically elected ministers who, in the absence of an elected House of Commons, act with self-restraint. The ministers are the caretakers.

Maintaining information flow to ministers through their offices as the caretaker period begins can be a challenge. Due to honest misunderstandings of the caretaker convention, some departments have initially reduced or even cut off services to their ministerial offices because they were wary of providing media monitoring and other sources of information to political offices for political purposes. The misunderstanding is that even though these offices are political, they are not engaged in partisan, political party activity. Rather they are supporting their politicians, the ministers, who remain in their legitimate roles. In these cases, a chief of staff would contact the PMO, which would work with the PCO, which would intervene to ensure that ministers and their staff continued to receive services that they required and to which they were entitled to do their job. These sorts of problems occur mostly near the start of the campaign period and are resolved through openness and collaboration between political staffers and officials. Good faith on all sides combined with clear public guidelines help to solve these issues quickly.

The public availability of the prime minister's caretaker guidelines is the key. It makes resolving matters much easier since everyone, including officials and staff inside the government and the public outside it, can refer to the same document. If ministers or their offices can justify their requests based on what the prime minister has approved, then the requests are legitimate. However, if any demands go beyond the guidelines, then the PCO will back up department officials and inform the PMO. Nevertheless, it is possible to overstate how much the caretaker convention constrains ministers. Again, clarity is in the guidelines themselves. A minister may act if any one of the following criteria for that action is met: the matter is routine, non-controversial, urgent and in the public interest, reversible, or agreed to by the opposition parties (in cases in which consultation is appropriate). Ministers are therefore far from incapacitated, though the point is not to take advantage of the fine print but to ensure continuing good government while respecting the democratic will. Ultimately, the caretaker convention is adjudicated politically. When to act – or not to act – according to these criteria is ultimately something that ministers must decide, and they are accountable to Canadians for their decisions.

In highlighting the role of ministerial exempt staff during an election campaign, this chapter augments the growing but relatively small body of research on political staffers in Canada. In particular, it emphasizes the significant role of political staffers as interlocutors between ministers and public servants during a campaign. It provides a better idea of the practicalities of how the government of Canada operates while under the caretaker convention.

Notes

[1] The term "para-political bureaucracy" comes from Williams, "The Para-Political Bureaucracy in Ottawa," 215.

[2] Canada, House of Commons Board of Internal Economy, *Members' Allowances and Services Manual,* Chapter 2, p. 4.

[3] Canada, Privy Council Office, *Open and Accountable Government,* 90.

4   Wilson, "A Profile of Ministerial Policy Staff in the Government of Canada," 464.
5   Feldman, *Transition to the 42nd Parliament,* 22.
6   Canada, Privy Council Office, *Guidelines on the Conduct of Ministers.*
7   United Kingdom, Cabinet Office, *The Cabinet Manual,* 17; Australia, Office of the Prime Minister and Cabinet, *Guidance on Caretaker Conventions;* New Zealand, Cabinet Office, Department of the Prime Minister and Cabinet, *Cabinet Manual,* 88–89.
8   Cappe, "The Caretaker Convention in Canada."
9   Zussman, *Off and Running,* 105–25.
10 Marland, *Brand Command.*

Bibliography

Australia. Office of the Prime Minister and Cabinet. *Guidance on Caretaker Conventions.* 2018. https://www.pmc.gov.au/sites/default/files/publications/guidance-caretaker-conventions-2018.pdf.

Canada. House of Commons Board of Internal Economy. *Members' Allowances and Services Manual.* 2019. https://www.ourcommons.ca/Content/MAS/mas-e.pdf.

–. Privy Council Office. *Guidelines on the Conduct of Ministers, Ministers of State, Exempt Staff and Public Servants during an Election.* Ottawa, 2019. https://www.canada.ca/en/privy-council/services/publications/guidelines-conduct-ministers-state-exempt-staff-public-servants-election.html#VIII.

–. Privy Council Office. *Open and Accountable Government.* Ottawa, 2015. https://pm.gc.ca/en/news/backgrounders/2015/11/27/open-and-accountable-government.

Cappe, Mel. "The Caretaker Convention in Canada." Memo for Workshop on Constitutional Studies, David Asper Centre for Constitutional Studies, University of Toronto, 2011. http://aspercentre.ca/wp-content/uploads/2017/06/Mel-Cappe-CARETAKER-CONVENTION.pdf.

Feldman, Charles. *Transition to the 42nd Parliament: Questions and Answers.* Background Paper, Publication No. 2015-56-E. Ottawa: Library of Parliament, 2015. https://lop.parl.ca/staticfiles/PublicWebsite/Home/ResearchPublications/BackgroundPapers/PDF/2015-56-e.pdf.

Marland, Alex. *Brand Command: Canadian Politics and Democracy in the Age of Message Control.* Vancouver: UBC Press, 2016.

New Zealand. Cabinet Office, Department of the Prime Minister and Cabinet. *Cabinet Manual.* 2017. https://dpmc.govt.nz/sites/default/files/2017-06/cabinet-manual-2017.pdf.

United Kingdom. Cabinet Office. *The Cabinet Manual: A Guide to Laws, Conventions and Rules on the Operation of Government.* 2011. https://assets. publishing.service.gov.uk/government/uploads/system/uploads/ attachment_data/file/60641/cabinet-manual.pdf.

Williams, Blair. "The Para-Political Bureaucracy in Ottawa." *Parliament, Policy and Representation,* edited by Harold D. Clarke, Colin Campbell, F.Q. Quo, and Arthur Goddard, 215–30. Toronto: Methuen, 1980.

Wilson, R. Paul. "A Profile of Ministerial Policy Staff in the Government of Canada." *Canadian Journal of Political Science* 48, 2 (2015): 455–71.

Zussman, David. *Off and Running: The Prospects and Pitfalls of Government Transition in Canada.* Toronto: University of Toronto Press, 2013.

3

Public Servants

Lori Turnbull and Donald Booth

The independent, non-partisan public service plays an essential role, albeit a behind-the-scenes one, during a federal election campaign and the transition that immediately follows. Whether an election results in a change of government or the return of the incumbent, federal public servants help to facilitate a smooth transition to ensure that there are no disruptions in service to Canadians, that government operations continue to run as seamlessly as possible, and that ministers of the Crown receive appropriate support in executing their legal responsibilities.

La fonction publique, indépendante et non partisane, joue un rôle essentiel dans les transitions gouvernementales au Canada, même en coulisse. Qu'une élection entraîne un changement de gouvernement ou le retour du gouvernement sortant, l'intervalle entre l'élection et l'assermentation du nouveau cabinet est une période très délicate au cours de laquelle une incertitude plane sur les carrières politiques, les relations de pouvoir et l'orientation des priorités du gouvernement. Le Bureau du Conseil privé, le ministère du premier ministre, ainsi que le Cabinet du premier ministre et l'équipe de transition dirigent les efforts afin de faciliter un processus de transition harmonieux sans interruption pour les Canadiens.

AN IMPARTIAL, PROFESSIONAL public service has been one of the pillars of Canada's system of government since the Public Service Commission was created in 1918 to enforce merit-based, non-partisan hiring. Today the federal public service is the most diverse workforce in the country. No other employer can boast of an employee complement of roughly 275,000 and well over seventy occupational categories. The workforce encompasses everything from law enforcement officials to entomologists to lighthouse keepers, with some degree of representation in virtually every community in the country.[1] Naturally, there are profound differences in the nature of the work, the professional backgrounds, and the day-to-day operational realities of those who populate its ranks. Yet there are certain shared principles that provide a common touchstone for federal public service employees, whether they are a deputy minister in Ottawa, a fisheries scientist in Prince Edward Island, or a correctional service worker in British Columbia.

These overarching principles, articulated in the *Values and Ethics Code for the Public Sector,* help to define expected behaviours as well as anchor the unique role of the civil service within our Westminster parliamentary system. It is no coincidence that "respect for democracy" is the first value outlined in the code's statement of values, with underlying commitments enumerated as follows:

a) respecting the rule of law and carrying out their duties in accordance with legislation, policies and directives in a non-partisan and impartial manner;

b) loyally carrying out the lawful decisions of their leaders and supporting ministers in their accountability to Parliament and Canadians; and

c) providing decision makers with all the information, analysis and advice they need, always striving to be open, candid and impartial.[2]

An election period, and the transitional phase that immediately follows election night, are highly sensitive political times that involve some degree of change at the centre of power. There are three types of transition: those that involve a change in the governing party, those that see a return of an incumbent government, and those in which there is a change in leadership of the governing party.[3] Any of these scenarios can create uncertainty. The permanent public service eases much of the tension by providing support and advice both to incoming and to outgoing leaders. Public servants help to ensure that the business of government is not disrupted as political events play out.

Duties in an Election Campaign

From a public service perspective, the election period can be more or less divided into three distinct phases: 1) pre-election planning, 2) the election/caretaker period, and 3) forming cabinet and launching the mandate.

For many in the public service, the election period is less about the campaign itself than about preparing for the days after the election. Generally speaking, pre-election planning is launched six months or more before the calling of an election. Advice is quietly prepared for an incoming government or a returning government that might wish to move in different directions or adopt a fresh start. This exercise can take many forms. Deputy ministers, for example, might begin by examining what works and what does not work in their portfolios and identify potential changes to the "machinery" for prime ministerial consideration. They also work to develop new policy proposals to complement the ideas and proposals that will make up the various parties' political platforms. Often these proposals touch on issues that might not get attention on the campaign trail given that they might not resonate with everyday Canadian voters, such as the need for investment in critical IT systems or the need to address potentially unpopular issues.

Once the election writ is issued, and Parliament is dissolved, government activity operates under the parameters of what is commonly referred to as the "caretaker convention." Constitutional conventions are political rules that guide actions.[4] They involve regular conduct in public administration that endures over time irrespective of which political party heads the government. The caretaker convention dictates that the government should act with restraint during an election campaign and, to the extent possible, confine itself to routine and necessary public business.[5] Ideally, this means avoiding taking action that could hinder a future government's ability to make decisions, such as signing large contracts or international treaties. In the twenty-first century, the practice has become more than restraint exercised simply as a matter of prudent good government, and successive governments have issued guidance specifically referring to the convention. Official public guidance was first issued in 2015, outlining the rules of engagement for ministers, political staff, and public servants. The guidance was subsequently updated and issued in advance of the 2019 federal election.[6] The caretaker convention, of course, is not law. Conventions are generally binding in a political but not a legal sense.[7] To paraphrase a senior Privy Council Office (PCO) official, the caretaker convention is a soft guardrail of our democracy.

The foundational principle behind the caretaker convention is simple but speaks to the core of our system of responsible government. For a government to have legitimacy, it must be able to demonstrate that it commands the confidence of the House of Commons. When a writ of election is issued, however, the House of Commons is dissolved, and there is no elected chamber to which the government can be held accountable. For this reason, and because one cannot presume which party will win the election, in order to respect democratic principles, a government should circumscribe its action. Equally important, the convention helps to uphold the impartiality and non-partisan character of the public service by minimizing the potential that public resources are used for partisan purposes.

The guidelines are pointed and prescriptive in some places. Yet, for the most part, they are pitched at the level of principle. This reflects the fact that, as noted, the day-to-day reality of the public service varies considerably depending on department, region, and occupation. To try to draft granular, detailed directions to capture and address all eventualities would be a fool's errand. It is impossible to anticipate all of the unexpected and unavoidable urgencies that can arise during a campaign. National security emergencies happen with no warning. Courts might force governments to respond to rulings. Sometimes commercial realities dictate that contracts must be signed. On the international front, the world does not stop because Canada has an election. Ultimately, it is a political decision whether or not something is consistent with the terms of the convention and whether or not something reaches the overall litmus test of routine or urgent business.

It is safe to say, for the most part, that the bulk of front-line civil servants do not see a great deal of difference in their daily work during an election period. Food continues to be inspected, cheques continue to be issued, and programs continue to be administered. However, the caretaker period is a time of escalating preparation for many in the upper echelons of federal departments and agencies, including for those who support them on policy development and related activities.

While the political campaign is being waged in public, senior federal officials work quietly behind the scenes to prepare for the eventual transition to an entirely new government or to a returning government with a refreshed and energized mandate. In this context, senior public servants spend much time watching the campaign unfold. They carefully scrutinize the various platform commitments of each political party to get a sense of which priorities a new government might pursue.

As noted, a department, under the close supervision of its deputy minister (the senior departmental civil servant), typically prepares advice for an incoming minister on policy ideas to consider within the portfolio. Officials will have reviewed the parties' election platforms and worked up strategies to implement the campaign promises, in part to demonstrate that they are aware of the political priorities and ready, willing, and able to implement them loyally. They also prepare materials to assist the new minister and staff to understand and navigate the sometimes unfamiliar world of Parliament and cabinet decision making.

Although departments have considerable autonomy to formulate the advice that they will provide to their incoming ministers, there is a significant degree of central coordination of briefing materials.[8] These materials are provided primarily by the PCO, often referred to as the "prime minister's department," led by the country's top civil servant, the clerk of the Privy Council. The PCO has a special role to play in ensuring that there is an appropriate degree of system readiness for transition across the federal family. This means ensuring that policy proposals are comprehensive, congruent, and mutually reinforcing. Equally crucial is ensuring that public service leaders are providing consistent advice.

Of course, for some public servants, like other Canadians, the election is also a time of personal engagement in the political process. It is hardly surprising, for example, to find that those attracted to careers in public administration might also want to serve their communities in more political ways. This fact is borne out in the long list of former public servants, from all levels of government, who have gone on to illustrious political careers.

Although public servants do not engage in partisan activities in the context of their work, as Canadian citizens they are entitled to run for office and to engage in political activities, within certain reasonable parameters.[9] The Public Service Employment Act explicitly recognizes and addresses this fact: "An employee may engage in any political activity so long as it does not impair, or is not perceived as impairing, the employee's ability to perform duties in a politically impartial manner."[10] This means that, when public servants are on their own time outside work hours, they can go door to door for candidates, put up yard signs, and volunteer for other campaign roles. The key here is *on their own time*.

Care needs to be exercised, particularly in light of digital social media, in which the lines frequently blur between private and professional selves. A senior official within the environment department, for example, might have a passion for the subject and strongly favour the platform of an opposition party. Although this official would be within her rights to campaign for that party, she would need to weigh doing so against her professional obligations. Could her advocacy affect not only her ability to be impartial but also the perception that she is being impartial? Ultimately, there is a large grey area, and decisions on this front tend to hinge on factors such as the nature of an individual's public service duties and personal visibility within the relevant organization. It can be of little surprise, therefore, that deputy heads are largely prohibited from engaging in any type of political activity other than voting. Their prominent profile and unique role within the public service ecosystem require nothing less.

Ultimately, an individual's right to seek office must be balanced against the need to preserve the impartiality of the civil service itself. For this reason, any federal civil servant who seeks to run for elected office must first seek permission from the Public Service Commission, which will assess the request. Depending on the nature of the individual's responsibilities, the commission might require the candidate to take a leave of absence without pay before and during the campaign. In rare cases, it might even reject the request if there is deemed to be a public interest in doing so.

Despite the excitement and energy of election night, a new government does not immediately take office, regardless of the result of the vote. Even if a government is defeated at the polls, ministers continue to serve until a new cabinet is sworn in. In practice, the period from election day to swearing in varies, though typically it has taken from ten to fourteen days and can take as long as a month.

During this period, the prime minister, or prime minister–designate, assumes the role of cabinet maker, determining the composition and structure of the cabinet and how the government should be organized to achieve its objectives optimally. Much of the technical work has traditionally been supported by the PCO's little-known and highly secretive Machinery of Government Secretariat. It is a small shop populated, as some have quipped, by "practitioners of the dark arts of the Westminster system." This is typically a quiet time in Ottawa as the city anxiously awaits decisions on cabinet formation. It is a tightly controlled and secretive process involving the highest levels of the Privy Council Office, the prime minister and the Prime Minister's Office (PMO), or, depending on the situation, the new prime minister–designate's trusted inner circle.

A prime minister or prime minister–designate will also appoint a transitional team to offer advice on cabinet formation, government priorities, strategies for engaging caucus members and other political parties, and the contents of the Speech from the Throne that will open the new session of Parliament.[11] Transitional team members might be experienced political advisers who have worked at various levels of the government. Therefore, they are equipped with first-hand knowledge about how to take the first steps of a new government's mandate or the return of an incumbent government. This team is disbanded once the transitional period is over, though often there are members of the team who go on to be appointed as political staff.

Once the prime minister or prime minister–designate has chosen the members of the cabinet, the new ministers are informed via a discreet meeting or telephone call and advised to prepare for the swearing-in ceremony. Arrangements are made between the PCO, the PMO, and Rideau Hall to determine the timing and details of the ceremony. Once new ministers are sworn in, they spend some time together as a new team prior to the new session of Parliament.

These early days are a time for a prime minister to engage with cabinet members and to impress on them the expectations of them as members of the executive team. In 2015, Prime Minister Trudeau released a document entitled *Open and Accountable Government,* which provided guidance to ministers and exempt staff on the meaning and significance of concepts such as responsible government, ministerial responsibility, and cabinet solidarity.[12] The document describes the relationship between public servants and political staff, and it identifies the prime minister's expectations for all public office holders, including standards of ethical behaviour. Prime

Minister Harper issued a similar document in 2006 called *Account-able Government: A Guide for Ministers*.[13] Early in the mandate, a prime minister will also issue to each minister a mandate letter outlining political expectations and priorities for the minister and portfolio.

These early days are a time for deputy ministers and their senior departmental staff to get to know their new ministers and their political staff. These first meetings are often seen as critical to forming the positive working relationship so important to delivering results for Canadians. Part of this relationship building is providing thoughtful and fearless advice. Another aspect is ensuring that appropriate "concierge services" are offered to both incoming and outgoing ministers and their offices. This means having office space, phones, and email ready on day one. It also means ensuring that matters of human resources, such as compensation issues, are dealt with quickly and efficiently.

Overcoming Obstacles

Each of the distinct phases outlined above is marked by different challenges faced and experienced by various parts of the public service. The pre-writ period can be particularly challenging, for example, for those public servants involved in government communications or in managing grants and contributions. Challenges arise because of the natural tendency of governments to ramp up activity dramatically as an election call looms, such as trying to tie up loose ends and deliver on priority commitments before Canadians go to the polls. Workloads suddenly increase, and timelines constrict. Equally, for many departments, the writ period itself can be a complex balancing act between providing support to a minister during a campaign and respecting the caretaker principles. For some senior officials, this can become a considerable preoccupation.

One of the most significant challenges is the degree of secrecy that typically cloaks the preparation of transitional materials. This is particularly true in the preparation for cabinet formation – one of the most secretive processes in the government. The need for discretion often means that this period is governed by a "need-to-know" culture. This runs counter to a political and public service environment that increasingly places a premium on openness and transparency and on cross-departmental collaboration. Often the need to preserve secrecy can become an impediment to carrying out thorough work on tight timelines. This is the inevitable price to be paid, however, to preserve both the public service's capacity to offer frank and honest advice and ministers' freedom to decide whether or not to take it.

Ultimately, an effective transition provides a strong argument in favour of the presence of a stable, impartial public service. In some systems of governance, for instance in the United States, it is typical for the top layers of the civil service to be replaced following a change in government. Although this approach assures a degree of ideological alignment between "political masters" and those entrusted to implement their wishes, this sudden change in leadership can result, at least temporarily, in paralysis from the resulting loss of institutional memory and the need to adjust to new personalities and leadership styles. Under the Westminster model, while talented political leaders and their staff often come and go depending on the will of the electorate, the public service as an institution provides continuity of expertise, knowledge, and service. As this chapter has shown, continuity is at the forefront regardless of which political party obtains the most seats in a federal election and goes on to form the government.

Notes

Note: The views and interpretations in this chapter are those of the authors and do not necessarily reflect the position of the government of Canada.

[1] Canada, Privy Council Office, *26th Annual Report to the Prime Minister.*
[2] Treasury Board of Canada Secretariat, *Values and Ethics Code for the Public Sector.*

3   Zussman, *Off and Running*, 14.
4   Jaconelli, "The Nature of Constitutional Convention"; Lagassé, "The Crown and Government Formation." Lagassé argues that the caretaker guidelines do not meet the test of a convention.
5   Lagassé, "Clarifying the Caretaker Convention"; Lagassé, "The Crown and Government Formation."
6   Canada, Privy Council Office, *Guidelines on the Conduct of Ministers*.
7   Aucoin, Jarvis, and Turnbull, *Democratizing the Constitution*.
8   Savoie, *Governing from the Centre*.
9   See Charter of Rights and Freedoms, sections 1–2.
10   Public Service Employment Act, section 113.
11   Walsh, "Ford's Transition Team Features Powerful Federal Conservative Duo."
12   Canada, Privy Council Office, *Open and Accountable Government*.
13   Canada, *Accountable Government*.

Bibliography

Aucoin, Peter, Mark Jarvis, and Lori Turnbull. *Democratizing the Constitution: Reforming Responsible Government*. Toronto: Emond Montgomery, 2011.

Canada. *Accountable Government: A Guide for Ministers*. Ottawa, 2006. http://publications.gc.ca/collections/Collection/CP22-73-2006E.pdf.

–. Privy Council Office. *Guidelines on the Conduct of Ministers, Ministers of State, Exempt Staff and Public Servants during an Election*. Ottawa, 2019. https://www.canada.ca/en/privy-council/services/publications/guidelines-conduct-ministers-state-exempt-staff-public-servants-election.html.

–. Privy Council Office. *Open and Accountable Government*. Ottawa, 2015. https://pm.gc.ca/en/news/backgrounders/2015/11/27/open-and-accountable-government.

–. Privy Council Office. *26th Annual Report to the Prime Minister on the Public Service of Canada*. Ottawa, 2019. https://www.canada.ca/content/dam/pco-bcp/documents/pdfs/ann-rpt-2019-eng.pdf.

Charter of Rights and Freedoms. https://laws-lois.justice.gc.ca/eng/const/page-15.html.

Jaconelli, Joseph. "The Nature of Constitutional Convention." *Legal Studies* 19, 1 (1999): 24–46.

Lagassé, Philippe. "Clarifying the Caretaker Convention." *Policy Options*, 9 October 2015. https://policyoptions.irpp.org/2015/10/09/clarifying-the-caretaker-convention/.

–. "The Crown and Government Formation: Conventions, Practices, Customs, and Norms." *Constitutional Forum* 28, 3 (2019): 1–18.

Public Service Employment Act. https://laws.justice.gc.ca/eng/acts/P-33.01/page-10.html

Savoie, Donald. *Governing from the Centre: The Concentration of Power in Canadian Politics*. Toronto: University of Toronto Press, 1999.

Treasury Board of Canada Secretariat. *Values and Ethics Code for the Public Sector*. 2011. https://www.tbs-sct.gc.ca/pol-cont/25049-eng.pdf.

Walsh, Marieke. "Ford's Transition Team Features Powerful Federal Conservative Duo." *iPolitics*, 8 June 2018. https://ipolitics.ca/2018/06/08/fords-transition-team-features-powerful-federal-conservative-duo/.

Zussman, David. *Off and Running: The Prospects and Pitfalls of Government Transitions in Canada*. Toronto: University of Toronto Press, 2013.

4

Leaders' Debate Coordinators

Brooks DeCillia and Michel Cormier

Leaders' debates offer Canadians a singular and valuable moment to evaluate the politicians hoping to lead our country. They are an unfiltered democratic exercise in which voters can compare leaders and their ideas side by side in real time. A healthy democracy requires healthy public debate. However, Canada's political parties and media organizations constantly wrangle about the terms of the leaders' debates, resulting in a debate about debates. The federal Leaders' Debate Commission was set up in response to those concerns. This chapter describes – and evaluates – Canada's first official debate commission.

Les débats des chefs offrent aux Canadiens un moment unique et précieux pour évaluer les politiciens qui espèrent de diriger notre pays. Il s'agit d'un exercice démocratique sans filtre où les électeurs peuvent comparer les dirigeants et leurs idées en temps réel. Une démocratie en santé nécessite un débat public sain. Cependant, les partis politiques et les médias canadiens se querellent constamment sur les termes des débats des chefs, ce qui occasionne un débat sur les débats. La Commission fédérale des débats des chefs a été créée afin de répondre à ces préoccupations. Ce chapitre décrit et évalue le travail de cette première commission canadienne officielle des débats des chefs.

IN A FRAGMENTED media environment, singular national "media events" have become increasingly elusive.[1] It usually takes a major sports event to capture the collective mediated attention of millions of Canadians at the same time. A staggering 16.6 million Canadians, for instance, watched the Olympic gold medal men's hockey game in Vancouver in 2010. Historically, the federal leaders' debates have risen to the level of a national media event and did so in the 2019 campaign when, for the first time, the Leaders' Debate Commission played a coordinating role.[2]

Canadians were first introduced to televised federal leaders' debates, beamed across the country from Parliament's Confederation Hall, in 1968. The studio lights dimmed for a few elections until they powered up again in 1979. The TV studio was empty again during the 1980 campaign because the parties and broadcasters could not agree to terms. From 1984 to 2011, federal leaders participated in televised debates organized and produced by a consortium of broadcasters. The consortium – CTV, TVA, Global, and CBC/Radio-Canada – negotiated privately with the political parties to determine the format, topics, and which politicians participated. Political strategists persistently call leaders' debates critical moments in election campaigns; political scientists are not so sure, stressing that the evidence is mixed when it comes to changing votes. These dramatic media spectacles – sometimes with knockout punches and gotcha moments – have affected how many Canadians vote.[3] Of note, however, party leaders have won debates and still lost elections.[4]

Far from the traditional face-off among three party leaders in the 1980s, the event has been altered in tangible ways in the 2000s by technology and changing politics. Among the changes are the increase of parties represented in the House of Commons and the new technology that disrupted the assumption that party leaders have to participate in debates to reach their supporters.[5] In 2008, the Green Party leader was excluded until the leaders of other parties and the broadcast consortium relented in the face of public backlash, yet in the next federal election she was deemed to be ineligible. These factors came to a head in 2015 when Prime Minister Stephen Harper refused to participate in the traditional consortium-produced English debate. Critics charged that Harper wanted to avoid the scrutiny that comes with the large audiences of the broadcast consortium debates. A fraction of Canadians watched the handful of debates compared with the 14 million who watched the consortium-organized debates four years earlier. The Institute for Research on Public Policy, in its consultations with academics, journalists, and democratic stakeholders, concluded that the hodgepodge of debates in that campaign did not serve democracy well.[6] As part of its democratic reform initiative, the federal Liberal government tasked an independent commission to organize a debate in each official language. It marked an attempt to reinvigorate the tradition of having larger regular debates. Presumably, an objective was to ensure that the democratic exercise would become an institution in which party leaders feel compelled to participate.

Led by former Governor General – and moderator of the 1979 debate – David Johnston, the commission had two significant roles: to organize the production, promotion, and distribution of the debates and to report to Parliament following the 2019 election on the lessons learned from producing the debates. Organizing the debates meant dealing with the thorny issue of determining which party leaders could participate on the stage.

Unlike other countries – including the United States, which has a long tradition of an independent commission – in Canada the people behind the first Leaders' Debate Commission often felt as if they were "building the plane while it was in the air." Making the debates happen – that is, formally designating an organizational partner that would be responsible for producing the events – comprised the biggest role and the most time for the commission. Consistent with federal procurement requirements, the Leaders' Debate Commission issued a request for interest and later a request for proposals from prospective media organizations or groups interested in producing the debates. Commission staff spent months detailing what they wanted from the debate producer and then negotiating with the media producers to put on the big show. A jury composed of two members of the commission and two independent experts then judged the submissions. The commission aimed to produce a journalistically rigorous debate that engaged millions of Canadians. In addition to making the debates free of charge to any group or individual who wanted to stream or distribute video and audio, the commission was determined to make the content as accessible and inclusive as possible. It aimed to reach the broadest audience on both traditional and social media.

Duties in an Election Campaign

Although the debates organized by the Leaders' Debate Commission happened two weeks before election day, a lot of the work required to make them happen occurred long before politicians started campaigning. The federal Liberal government appointed an independent commissioner to lead the institution. David Johnston then hired staff. In its early days, commission staff turned to experts and other debate organizers around the world with a mind to making "debates a more predictable, reliable, and stable element of federal election campaigns."[7] With values of democratic citizenship, civic education, and inclusion in the foreground, the commission consulted a wide cross-section of everyday Canadians and experts about how best to structure, deliver, and raise awareness about the debates. In its first few months, commission staff spent time researching and consulting with experts on how best to produce high-quality debates. To that end, the commission teamed up with like-minded civic groups to promote the debates. The commission also collaborated with the academically rigorous Canadian Election Study (CES) to conduct survey research before the debates to hear what Canadians wanted from them and afterward to hear if the debates delivered on their hopes.

In addition to consulting experts, the commission appointed a seven-member advisory panel – including former Liberal Deputy

Prime Minister John Manley, former Conservative MP Deborah Grey, and former New Democrat MP Megan Leslie – to act as a "sounding board" for the commission about everything from participating in the debates to getting more Canadians to engage critically with the debates. Commission staff met with forty experts and groups on issues ranging from accessibility and inclusivity to civic engagement and debate formats. Staff also met regularly with political party officials and news media executives in an effort to solicit their views and inform them of their ongoing work.

As noted above, debates are unfiltered and unedited national democratic events that offer brief opportunities for Canadians to hear directly from people who hope to lead the country. These opportunities infused the thinking and work of the commission. Mindful of the increasingly polarized Canadian electorate and the pernicious tactics of misinformation that currently mark politics internationally, commission staff hoped that the debates might combat nefarious foreign and domestic forces that want to influence the outcomes of elections and propagate dissension and distrust in democracy.[8] Moreover, the public servants behind the debates wanted the events to penetrate the pervasive confirmation biases and filter bubbles that have people seeking information and news media that substantiate their views.[9] Commission staff aspired to give Canadians a trusted political discourse free of partisan manipulation. They wanted to produce a real-time, unfiltered, democratic space where everyone gets to assess all the party leaders and their ideas on one stage at the same time.

In the months before the election campaign, the Leaders' Debate Commission asked media companies to bid on a contract to produce the English and French debates. Tendering and bidding on federal government contracts comprise a complicated and arguably daunting process. The request for proposals prepared by commission staff for the federal leaders' debate was a forty-two-page document of exacting requirements and mandatory evaluation criteria.[10] Ultimately, nine media outlets teamed up to form the Canadian

Debate Production Partnership (CDPP) that won the $1.5 million contract to produce the two events. The official request for proposals from media companies did not require them to team up to bid on the contract to produce the debates. Nevertheless, the commission recommended such a course, recognizing that the requirements for audience reach and broadcast quality indicated a media partnership.

The Leaders' Debate Commission issued some clear requirements for the CDPP; chief among them was that the media companies disseminate the debates widely at no cost. In the past, the consortium of broadcasters zealously guarded control of the debates. The commission changed the traditional consortium's exclusive broadcast and rebroadcast rights, requiring the CDPP to distribute the debates as widely as possible across the country on TV, radio, and digital media. Cineplex theatres live-streamed the debates on nearly two dozen of its megasized, high-definition screens free of charge. The CDPP made the debates more accessible than previous debates with American and Quebec Sign Language, closed-captioning, and described video. In addition to English and French instant translation, the CDPP offered multilingual simulcasts of the debates in Arabic, Cantonese, Inuktitut, Italian, Mandarin, Ojibwe, Plains Cree, and Punjabi. As well, the Leaders' Debate Commission, in its official request for proposals, asked the debate producers to produce events that allowed the leaders to have consequential and intelligent conversations about issues and topics that reflected the cultural, economic, and demographic diversity of Canada. Other than that stipulation from the commission, the partnership of media companies in charge of the debates had complete journalistic independence to produce the events, including format and questions.

In the days before the election campaign officially began, the CDPP announced that the two official debates would cover five topics: affordability and economic insecurity; national and global leadership; Indigenous issues; polarization, human rights, and immigration; and environment and energy. The CDPP relied on publicly available poll data and issues dominating the news media to determine the topics and questions for the two debates. The Leaders' Debate Commission asked the CDPP to engage with Canadians about the debates' potential topics and questions. Almost nine thousand Canadians submitted questions to the CDPP through its many news media companies. From those thousands of responses, ten questions made it into the two debates. Both the English debate and the French debate were held at the Canadian Museum of History in Gatineau, Quebec, facing Parliament Hill before a live audience. An all-female cast of five prominent news anchors and political journalists were chosen as moderators of the English debate by the media organizations that made up the CDPP. The commission had no input into who were chosen as debate moderators. A CDPP spokesperson said that the moderators were chosen based on their journalistic skill and experience and their roles within their respective media organizations, not because of their gender.

In the weeks leading up to the debate, the commission mounted an extensive online public awareness campaign, encouraging people to watch the debates. It collaborated with groups to organize several watch parties across the country. The commission produced videos and memes for Facebook, Twitter, and Instagram to publicize the debates and raise awareness about how to watch them. The commission's website featured a "top ten" list of reasons that people should watch the leaders' debates. As well, the commission produced videos of David Johnston being questioned by his grandchildren on topics ranging from why people should watch the debates if they already knew whom they planned to vote for to the consequences of leaders saying untrue things during the debates. The commission also offered an online education tool for how to engage with the debates critically.

In the days leading up to the English debate, the commission made headlines for barring two right-wing media outlets from obtaining accreditation to cover the debates with the rest of the news media inside the Museum of History. Accreditation was necessary for reporters to speak with party leaders and their surrogates at the debates' venue after the events. In its accreditation policy, and mindful of its responsibility to uphold high journalistic standards, the commission decided that only professional media organizations would be allowed to attend the debates and the media availability with the party leaders. *The Rebel Media* and the True North Centre for Public Policy were denied accreditation because the commission determined that they engaged in political activism that went beyond the norms of responsible journalism. The two media organizations' websites notably ran petitions and fundraising operations aimed at putting pressure on the prime minister to resign or to combat the carbon tax. True North and *The Rebel Media* petitioned the Federal Court to gain access, accusing the commission of acting in bad faith. A federal court justice agreed, ruling that the two media companies would suffer if they were not granted accreditation. In its court filing, True North claimed that blocking its access to the debates was tantamount to censorship. Lawyers for the commission argued, however, that there was nothing preventing the two organizations from reporting on the debates because they were broadcast freely online and on television and radio. Both news organizations were ultimately given access to the debates' venue. The lawsuit – and the public debate that it sparked – raised normative questions about who is a "professional" journalist and the role of advocacy in the news media. Supporters of *The Rebel Media* and True North wondered aloud about the *Toronto Star*'s participation in the debate given the newspaper's public commitment to a progressive mission and so-called Atkinson Principles.[11] The lawsuit also exposed the larger issue of nascent Canadian media organizations that provocatively test values regarding democracy, race, and gender.[12]

The debates drew big audiences. The English-language debate, with a reach of more than 14 million, penetrated the minds of almost four in ten Canadians. The French-language debate had a reach of almost 5 million. Beyond the conventional television audience, 4.3 million Canadians watched the debates through social media such as YouTube, Facebook, and Twitter. In comparison, this reach far surpassed the numbers of Canadians who watched and listened to the handful of independent debates organized in the previous campaign. Although the debates organized by the commission drew big audiences, they also attracted the usual critiques from commentators and pundits about their format, topics, and questions.

As in other elections, the events' participants, format, questions, moderators, busy stage, and freewheeling contest among politicians received plenty of criticism. Historically, punditry about debates has been critical of the so-called gotcha moments, knockout punches, grandstanding, catcalling, and crosstalk. These perennial critiques persisted in 2019, including concerns about the seriousness of the debates and questions about whether TV's demand for conflict outweighs the public interest.[13] In addition, much of the analysis of the English debate suggested that six leaders sharing a stage – and the tight time limits required by that many leaders – made it hard for politicians to convey their ideas meaningfully or to engage in substantive debates with their counterparts. Some commentators wondered why Maxime Bernier, as the leader of a small party, and Bloc Québécois leader Yves-François Blanchet, a Quebec nationalist, had places on the English debate stage. With a mere forty-five seconds to make their points, leaders ended up with only about twenty minutes to speak during the entire debate. Concerns about length were compounded by the considerable crosstalk among the leaders, producing a frustrating and hard-to-comprehend cacophony at times. The leaders frequently pivoted from the questions posed by the moderators to other topics and talking points. Other criticisms focused on the quality and diversity of the questions and how the five moderators in the English-language debate moved quickly from question to question. Critics suggested that there were too many moderators and that they could have been stricter, reining in the leaders when they strayed from the topic or talked over one another. The French-language debate rectified some of these concerns somewhat by dimming the lights over leaders when they were not eligible to speak, which helped to quell the side talk. Despite these usual critiques, many viewers watched for more than fifty minutes, suggesting that they found the debates worthwhile.

After the debates, commission staff turned their attention to producing a report for Parliament, detailing key findings, lessons learned, and recommendations. The head of the commission acknowledged the prevalent dissatisfaction with the format of the English debate, suggesting that the post-mortems would likely contain suggestions for improvement.[14] Commissioner Johnston even welcomed the criticism, calling it "important."[15] He floated the idea of hosting additional debates with fewer moderators and leaders, perhaps featuring only the main contenders for prime minister. Anticipating inevitable criticisms, the commission engaged political scientists with the CES to ask Canadian voters what they got out of the debates and what they liked and did not like about the format and topics. Most of this type of commentary about the debates is arguably subjective. The commission wanted data addressing the long-standing criticisms about the debates' format and questions. The CES findings will inform the commission's final report and recommendations.

Overcoming Obstacles

By far, the most prickly issue that the Leaders' Debate Commission faced during the campaign was determining whether or not the leader of the People's Party of Canada (PPC) would be allowed to participate in the two debates. When it established the commission, the federal Liberal government dictated that a party must meet two of three criteria in order to be part of the debates:

1 elected at least one MP under the party's banner;
2 intend to field candidates in 90 percent of the country's ridings; and
3 received at least 4 percent of the vote in the previous federal election or have a legitimate chance, taking into account the recent political context, of electing candidates in the upcoming election.

The third factor was difficult for the commission because it is more subjective. Initially, the commission did not invite Maxime Bernier to the debates. Stressing that the decision was not final, Commissioner Johnston asked him to provide more information to bolster his case for participation. Specifically, the PPC was invited to suggest three to five ridings where it thought it had a chance of winning.

The commissioner wanted a reasoned, deliberative, and transparent process to determine the basis for Bernier's inclusion or exclusion. Participation affords party leaders considerable media exposure, and the decision can have positive or negative effects on the campaign. Therefore, the commission was determined to interpret and apply the federal government's criteria for participation fairly. The question about participation triggered considerable discussion within the commission and plenty of work for the staff. The weight of the decision was tangible. The commissioner sought the advice of experts and the commission's seven-member advisory panel about applying the participation criteria. Ultimately, though, the final decision rested with the independent commissioner.

Unable to rely on national polls that showed the PPC polling from 1 to 5 percent, the commission hired EKOS Research Associates to conduct surveys in three ridings in Ontario and one in Manitoba where the PPC said it had a chance of winning. The random bilingual surveys, using interactive voice response, asked people how likely they were to vote for the People's Party of Canada. Mindful of not wanting to influence voters, the commission did not ask the traditional horse-race question about vote intention. In each riding, four to five hundred voters were surveyed. The results were weighted using Statistics Canada data about age, gender, and education to approximate a representative sample. The riding-level poll results suggested that between 24.5 percent and 34.1 percent of respondents might vote for the PPC. A historical analysis of voting conducted by the polling firm Nanos Research for the commission concluded that it is possible to win a riding with a quarter of the vote. Ultimately, the PPC received 1.6 percent of the total vote share, and none of its candidates was elected. Bernier himself was not re-elected. This information was obviously not available before the debates.

The commission also looked at the political context, identifying ten indicators to measure the PPC's organizational strength and prominence. In addition to looking at the party's membership, fundraising, and ability to attract candidates, the commission considered media penetration. Commission staff was keen to know whether or not the PPC's ideas on issues such as climate change, immigration, and fiscal responsibility had currency beyond its political base. Based on polling numbers and its evaluation of the political context, three weeks before the debates the commissioner decided that the PPC met two of the three criteria for participation. As expected, the inclusion of Bernier sparked controversy. His exclusion likely would have also triggered dissent. After the election, Johnston conceded that the six leaders made for a busy stage and that the bar for participation might have been too low.

Canada's first Leaders' Debate Commission arranged two official debates that reached millions more Canadians than the mishmash of small independent debates in the previous election. The commission produced a collective media event for voters to evaluate the politicians hoping to lead Canada. Whether the debates had any significant influence on voters' decisions remains a puzzle for political science. Yet the efforts of the commission did prove that there is a different way for Canada to organize how its leaders debate one another. Moreover, the research commissioned by the commission about the format of the debates could offer useful data for addressing perpetual critiques of these important democratic events. Ultimately, MPs will decide whether or not the Leaders' Debate Commission becomes a fixture of Canadian democracy.

Notes

1. Katz and Dayan, "Media Events."
2. The campaign also featured two leaders' debates hosted by *Maclean's*/Citytv and Quebec's TVA. Prime Minister Trudeau did not participate in the *Maclean's*/Citytv debate, which drew an audience of 1.6 million people. The TVA debate attracted 1.2 million viewers. These debates were outside the mandate of the commission and therefore are not examined in this chapter.
3. Blais and Boyer, "Assessing the Impact of Televised Debates."
4. Johnston et al., *Letting the People Decide;* Blais et al., "Campaign Dynamics in the 1997 Canadian Election"; Nevitte et al., *Unsteady State.*
5. Institute for Research on Public Policy, "Creating an Independent Commission for Federal Leaders' Debates."
6. Ibid.
7. Leaders' Debate Commission, "Mandate and Roles."
8. On the polarized electorate, see Johnston, "Affective Polarization in the Canadian Party System 1988–2015."
9. Warner and Ryan Neville-Shepard, "The Polarizing Influence of Fragmented Media."
10. Government of Canada, "Debates Producer Request for Proposals."
11. Joseph Atkinson was a long-time publisher of the *Toronto Star* who espoused progressive editorial principles that remain the basis for its "intellectual foundation," including "a strong, united and independent Canada; social justice, individual and civil liberties, community and civic engagement; the rights of working people; and the necessary role of government." *Toronto Star,* "The *Star* Mission and Atkinson Principles."
12. Adams, "Who Is a Journalist?"
13. Paas-Lang, "Viewership Up, but Format Questions Remain for Leaders' Debates."
14. Wright, "Debates Commissioner David Johnston Suggests Separate Debate for Main Contenders."
15. Ibid.

Bibliography

Adams, Paul. "Who Is a Journalist?" *Policy Options,* 17 October 2019. https://policyoptions.irpp.org/magazines/october-2019/who-is-a-journalist/.

Blais, André, and Martin Boyer. "Assessing the Impact of Televised Debates." *British Journal of Political Science* 26, 2 (1996): 143–64.

Blais, André, Richard Nadeau, Elisabeth Gidengil, and Neil Nevitte. "Campaign Dynamics in the 1997 Canadian Election." *Canadian Public Policy* 25, 2 (1999): 197–205.

Government of Canada. "Debates Producer Request for Proposals. (35035-182821/B)." Public Works and Government Services Canada, 2019. https://buyandsell.gc.ca/procurement-data/tender-notice/PW-CX-010-76809.

Institute for Research on Public Policy. "Creating an Independent Commission for Federal Leaders' Debates: Round Table Report." 2018. https://irpp.org/research-studies/creating-independent-commission-federal-leaders-debates/.

Johnston, Richard. "Affective Polarization in the Canadian Party System 1988–2015." Paper presented at the Canadian Political Science Association Conference, Vancouver, 4–6 June 2019. https://www.cpsa-acsp.ca/documents/conference/2019/334.Johnston.pdf.

Johnston, Richard, André Blais, Henry E. Brady, and Jean Crete. *Letting the People Decide: Dynamics of a Canadian Election.* Montreal and Kingston: McGill-Queen's University Press, 1992.

Katz, Elihu, and Daniel Dayan. "Media Events: On the Experience of Not Being There." *Religion* 15, 3 (1985): 305–14.

Leaders' Debate Commission. "Mandate and Roles." 2019. https://debates-debats.ca/en/about/mandate-and-roles/.

Nevitte, Neil, André Blais, Elisabeth Gidengil, and Richard Nadeau. *Unsteady State: The 1997 Canadian Federal Election.* Toronto: University of Toronto Press, 2000.

Paas-Lang, Christian. "Viewership Up, but Format Questions Remain for Leaders' Debates." *National Post,* 8 October 2019. https://nationalpost.com/pmn/news-pmn/canada-news-pmn/viewership-up-but-format-questions-remain-for-leaders-debates.

Toronto Star. "The *Star* Mission and Atkinson Principles." 2019. https://www.thestar.com/about/aboutus.html#c3.

Warner, Benjamin R., and Ryan Neville-Shepard. "The Polarizing Influence of Fragmented Media: Lessons from Howard Dean." *Atlantic Journal of Communication* 19, 4 (2011): 201–15.

Wright, Teresa. "Debates Commissioner David Johnston Suggests Separate Debate for Main Contenders." CBC News, 12 November 2019. https://www.cbc.ca/news/politics/debates-for-top-leaders-johnston-1.5356825.

5

News Editors

Colette Brin and Ryan MacDonald

In national news media, senior editors supervise and coordinate the election-related work of journalists on the ground and in the newsroom. They determine the attribution of resources and priority topics before and during the campaign. The drive for independence from partisan strategies and the desire to provide relevant content for the audience, in a highly competitive environment and with dwindling resources, lead them to adopt a more proactive role. Their position requires them not only to respond rapidly but also to adopt a broader perspective on the news of the day in order to focus attention on major issues beyond campaign controversies and mishaps.

Les responsables de la couverture électorale dans les médias nationaux supervisent et coordonnent le travail des journalistes sur le terrain et dans la salle de rédaction. Ils décident de l'attribution des ressources et des sujets prioritaires avant et pendant la campagne. La volonté d'indépendance à l'égard des stratégies partisanes et le souci de servir l'intérêt public, dans un contexte de forte concurrence et d'effectifs réduits, les amènent à adopter un rôle plus proactif. Leur fonction exige une grande réactivité, mais impose aussi de prendre du recul face à l'actualité, pour ramener l'attention sur les enjeux du scrutin au-delà des incidents de parcours.

UNDERSTANDING THE WORK of a news editor requires thinking beyond old notions of how newsrooms operate and the definitions of traditional roles in election campaign coverage. In its most conventional sense, the title of news editor encompasses a variety of roles and tasks, from assigning stories to editing copy to deciding how each news item will be "played" in the final output at the end of the day – newscast or newspaper, website or app. In the digital age, the editor's job is changing to reflect a general pressure on newsrooms to innovate and adapt to the changing media environment.

At a time of declining advertising revenues and reduced staff levels, especially for newspapers, media companies are faced with a series of labour-intensive challenges. They include the continuous news cycle and immediacy of social media;[1] the reorganization of newsrooms around multimedia production; a growing need to connect and collaborate with audiences; and a diversity of competitors, including magazines and other specialized or niche media, as well as American companies with a Canadian presence, such as *Huffington Post* and the *New York Times*. Alternative or partisan news sites, from *Rebel News* to the *National Observer*, play a marginal role in the Canadian media ecosystem.[2] In early 2019, the government under Prime Minister Justin Trudeau announced a subsidy program for Canadian journalism, providing $600 million over five years to qualifying organizations through a labour tax credit, a non-profit component, and a tax credit for subscriptions to online news services. The program was not yet in place when the election was called, but it raised questions about newsroom independence. Would this promise "buy" favourable coverage for the outgoing Liberal government? In Quebec, where the provincial government provided discretionary support for newspapers in 2017, there was ample criticism of the incumbent party in the coverage of the 2018 campaign; however, the provincial Liberals were not returned to office.

As editorial structures shrink and become more strategic, many newspapers are vying to become subscriber businesses rather than focusing solely on obtaining revenue through advertising. To stake out this ground and to convince readers to pay for online news content, they strive to offer value-added content – exclusive stories as well as unique insights into and perspectives on issues that matter to Canadians. In this context, editors are often tasked with many considerations and decisions that fall outside the field of journalism: audience, metrics, revenue, and marketing among them.[3] Editors often play several roles, including developing products and acting as project managers.[4] They might make a new kind of judgment call: namely, determining what information is worth purchasing.

Whereas editors were once generalists for the most part, there is now a strategic move to put them into topic areas such as health and economics where they can showcase their expertise. This is not entirely new, but it has taken on added relevance in an age of disinformation. In an election, the overseeing editor can be a specialist, with experience in and knowledge of politics, but can also draw on the experience of other specialists in the newsroom. A news editor might be responsible for making many important decisions for the product, be it digital, print, television, or radio, but a specialist editor who has experience and expertise in a particular area will bring that specific knowledge set to a topic. This form of specialization might compensate in part for the decline in beat reporting because of diminishing newsroom resources. However, research suggests that media rely more and more on external expertise from sources and contributors, such as on-air analysts and op-ed writers, than on substantive expertise within the newsroom.[5] Social media also offer a cheap and continuous source of political news.

Preparation for a federal election begins at least a year in advance in a newsroom, with budgets allocated for travel, polling, freelance contributions, and so on. The actual planning of election stories and content starts six months prior to voting day with initial "showcase" assignments. For the *Globe and Mail,* these are intensive and exhaustive profiles of the federal leaders at five thousand words or more. Senior editors from news bureaus across the country along with business and feature sections are involved in these discussions.

The timing for delivery and publication of these stories will be determined later as well as editing and photography – access to leaders being a key consideration.

As the election call approaches, cross-functional team meetings are held in which the opportunity to grow readership through engagement (i.e., interaction with online content) and the potential for new subscribers are discussed. The meetings include revenue, marketing, and subscription acquisition managers with editorial providing the lion's share of input and the other departments reacting to and adapting plans.

During national election campaigns, news media play an assertive, proactive role in "pushing" stories and setting the news agenda, while also dealing with parties' communication strategies, which include data harvesting and social media in addition to the threat of online disinformation.[6] In this context, editors face a significant challenge: they must work to define their organization's vision, strategy, and road map for the campaign. Then they must make it happen – and be willing to throw out all those plans as the campaign develops and changes.

The media are campaigning, in a sense, to establish or maintain their own credibility and legitimacy in the eyes of their audiences and the public. Indeed, academics and political analysts regularly criticize the media's biases, blind spots, and framing of issues such as gender and race during election campaigns.[7] As well, the media are taken to task for treating election campaigns like sports events – a horse race or boxing match for leaders' debates – rather than as an opportunity for substantive discussion of Canadians' concerns and priorities.

During an election campaign, some might expect the media to limit their role to that of stenographer or neutral observer, leaving the campaign to the parties and politicians. But news editors appear to be more and more comfortable embracing an active watchdog function – which includes independent investigation, fact-checking, and critical analysis – even during this period when the stakes are high.[8]

Duties in an Election Campaign

Our primary focus in this chapter is on national news media organizations such as broadcasters CBC/Radio-Canada, CTV, TVA, and Global; newspapers *Globe and Mail, National Post, Toronto Star,* and *La Presse;* and national news agency Canadian Press.[9] Although local newsrooms do provide coverage of local issues, designated ridings, and leaders when they are in town, they typically have fewer resources to cover the campaign as a whole in a systematic fashion, and their resources are dwindling more rapidly.[10]

The largest national newsrooms usually appoint a senior editor as the "election overseer," whose responsibilities include not only advance planning for the campaign but also coordination between reporters and editors working full time on the campaign and those on other beats, such as business, energy, environment, and so on, who might contribute specialized perspectives. Generally, an overseeing editor will be a senior manager in the organization – someone who can work with editors in all departments to assign tasks if necessary and always to be nimble to what arises during the campaign.

The establishment of fixed-date elections in Canada over a decade ago has provided news editors with more time to plan their campaign strategies. Key topics and potential swing and bellwether ridings are identified; regular contributors and analysts are booked; and features for weekend editions, fact-checking units, live coverage of debates, and of course the election night itself are put together.[11] This is naturally more precarious in a minority government when there is uncertainty about the election date. Editors also coordinate investigative and other in-depth stories that can be released before and during the campaign. However, during the five weeks or so between the issuing of the writ and election day, many editorial decisions have to be made on the fly, for unexpected events within or outside the political bubble can intervene in the campaign agenda.

Covering simultaneously the electoral campaigns of numerous political parties is a delicate and deliberate balancing act. The importance of each political party and its leader in the overall coverage is determined by a combination of factors. Beyond the news organization's commitment to fairness, this assessment encompasses each party's perceived strength throughout the country, measured by seats in Parliament at dissolution and potential gains in the election as indicated by voting intentions and seat projections provided by polls and aggregators. Editors are attentive to shifts in public opinion as the campaign progresses, especially after the leaders' debates and in the last few days before the vote. French-language media, whose audiences are concentrated in Quebec, cover the Bloc Québécois as intensively as the Liberal and Conservative Parties.

Some editors decide not to send reporters on the leaders' tours, which are expensive. In 2019, the price was $11,500 for a seat on the Conservative plane, $27,000 for the Liberal plane, and $55,000 for the NDP plane. Following the tours provides, in their view, a low-quality form of journalism and little added value for their audiences. For some organizations, getting on the ground allows for stories to be defined by citizens in different parts of the country, to get a more authentic sense of voters' concerns, as opposed to allowing politicians to frame issues in daily news briefings.

Despite some distrust of public opinion polls within newsrooms, the data and analysis provided by a pollster or aggregator are often too tempting to pass up as sources of news independent of partisan strategies, especially in a context of limited staffing. For budgetary reasons, many organizations enter into cooperative agreements with a polling company, such as *Globe and Mail*–CTV–Nanos or TVA-Léger. Newspaper editors must also decide which party to endorse at the end of the campaign – or whether to publish an endorsement. Editorial endorsements are generally the purview of senior management and considered an opportunity to show leadership as well as to understand what audiences believe is important. However, they are polarizing and can backfire. Alternatively, an editorial board can engage in a series of critiques or assessments of political positions and platforms and offer judgments without endorsing a particular leader or party.

In retrospect, there are missed opportunities in every campaign. At the *Globe and Mail,* one of them was not identifying the resurgence of the Bloc Québécois earlier in the 2019 campaign. However, in an election that turned out to reveal regional divisions in Canada, there was a substantive discussion about Alberta in the *Globe and Mail* and other media outlets.

If media focus only on the ridings that can lead to victory, then they are buying into the strategy of the politicians. Bringing to the fore issues not addressed by the parties and leaders themselves is possibly the most important contribution of media coverage during an election. A significant part of the editor's job is to ensure that the media lead the coverage and do not simply follow the priorities of parties. Editors strive to establish a constructive agenda around policy issues outside those that politicians want to discuss. In some cases, such as third-party registration and campaign funding, journalists questioned whether existing legislation is sufficient.

The threat of disinformation is a growing concern in election campaigns, largely because of the political climate in the United States and the role of social media, especially Facebook, and Google in disseminating news. Several news organizations assign reporters to verify politicians' statements and to debunk hoaxes, conspiracy theories, and other types of false content circulating online. At mid-campaign, it appeared that the volume of so-called fake news was relatively low in Canada.[12]

In the final weeks of the campaign, the overseeing editor begins planning election night coverage by establishing an early schedule of stories and resources and then discusses the plan with other senior editors. The plan evolves over time with these conversations as stories and additional reporting and editing resources are added.

The overall challenge of an election for a news editor is one of organization. Reporters in the field require adequate support at their home bases so that assumptions and policies can be tested and questioned with up-to-date, comprehensive, and accurate information. Committing other resources to things such as in-depth profiles of the leaders requires planning several months in advance to allow journalists to gain access as well as to dig deeply into the biographies of politicians, especially party leaders.

Elections also bring business opportunities, which necessitate cross-functional planning among teams – from editorial to marketing to revenue. On the product side, new distribution channels, such as pop-up newsletters, can be launched to allow greater exposure to content through the election period and help to drive engagement, a key metric for most media companies. In the digital economy and especially on social media, "engagement" includes any type of user interaction with content: clicks, likes, shares, comments, and time spent. For publications such as the *Globe and Mail,* which increasingly focuses on digital subscribers for revenue, free content can drive engagement, whereas paywalled content serves to retain and attract subscribers. Senior editors rely on instinct and intuition to make decisions on subscriber-only content; in other cases, the decisions are algorithmic. Exclusive stories naturally go behind the paywall; stories that encourage a broad debate on policy can be accessed for free.

Overcoming Obstacles

A major challenge for news editors is to keep a broader view of the campaign as it evolves beyond the daily stories and incidents that often constitute distractions rather than useful information for voters. News editors have a responsibility to filter the noise and resist the urge simply to echo and amplify what other media might be reporting or whatever is drawing the most attention.

At the midway point of an election campaign – as the initial jolt of adrenalin begins to subside and the reality of the many weeks of coverage sets in – an existential angst begins to take hold in the news editor's mind. Is our coverage fair? Is it important to

Canadians? Are we setting the agenda? Does our coverage matter? Do people care? Journalism can be a lonely pursuit, even more so for those tasked with making key decisions that can affect political campaigns. Whereas reporters are tasked with finding stories and reporting them, editors decide whether to publish them and when to do so. The decision to publish a contentious story requires discussion of a central question: is it relevant to the election and in the public interest? This discussion takes place within a mini-cabinet – the editor-in-chief, the deputy editor, the elections editor, and the Ottawa bureau chief. Other senior editors might be surveyed for their opinions and observations.

In the 2019 federal election, two examples of past actions by party leaders, and the implications for their leadership and character, are worth considering. Both, it could be argued, were hiding in plain sight for Canadian journalists. However, they also raise the question of the media's role in conducting and vetting opposition research on candidates.

The first case was Justin Trudeau's decision to wear brownface and blackface multiple times before becoming an MP and his admission during the campaign that they comprised racist acts. The story broke on social media the night of 18 September. *Time* magazine published it, and Trudeau quickly confirmed the story. For the *Globe and Mail,* there was no doubt that the decision of a federal leader to act in this manner was newsworthy – the discussions ranged from a front-page, above-the-fold story without a picture to showcasing the picture as main art. As the story quickly evolved, and it was revealed that Trudeau had worn makeup to change his skin colour three times (and could not recount how many more times), the decision was clear. All available pictures would be published, and the story would lead all platforms. The story and first photograph originated from the yearbook of a private school in Vancouver – something that Canadian media could have readily obtained had they been tipped off or curious enough to investigate Trudeau's time as a teacher. The incidents raised questions for many organizations about how much reporters really cared to dig into his past. As eventually revealed, it was not a Canadian journalist who discovered the photograph but a member of the school community who released it to an American periodical.

The second case was less explosive but illustrates the kind of journalism that could have exposed the Trudeau brownface and blackface incidents and subsequent stories. Early on, while *Globe and Mail* journalists were researching an extensive profile of Conservative leader Andrew Scheer, it became clear that one of the few professional credentials that he highlighted was questionable. Two reporters took several weeks to research his past in an attempt to understand Scheer. He had spent almost his entire adult life in politics, and it was unclear what experience he had outside politics. Did Scheer really sell insurance in Saskatchewan – and, if he did, was he licensed? Ultimately, the answer was unclear, became less clear during the campaign, and eventually became a meme used against him. The question for *Globe and Mail* editors was whether or not, in a five-thousand-word profile, this bit of information should be pulled out as a stand-alone story. In an election defined by constant "drive-by assassinations," the decision was to allow readers to absorb this detail within the context of the broader story. Other media picked up the story, however, and criticism of other aspects of Scheer's political career brought forward by Liberals on social media, such as his prior statements on abortion and same-sex marriage, was widely covered as well.

However, questions remain about the Canadian journalism community's insufficient research on Trudeau's past and, more generally, the importance of investigating the details of the lives of party leaders and other candidates, whether incumbents or challengers. Did the media effectively play their watchdog role, "monitoring and holding the powerful accountable," as opposed to the undiscerning aggressiveness of the attack dog and the unwavering loyalty of the lapdog?[13]

Suspicions of partisan bias in the media often arise from different points of the political spectrum – a fact sometimes cited by journalists as proof that their work is balanced. Canadian journalists hold a strong professional commitment to impartiality and believe that they are insulated from political pressures, at least in international comparison.[14] A recent expert survey on the Canadian media system suggests that most organizations tend to lean right on economic issues, with more pluralism on social matters, specifically on religious diversity.[15]

The media's proactive role in elections raises the eternal debate of accountability and regulation, without limiting press freedom. The Canadian public broadcaster is independently monitored to ensure that its coverage is fair and accurate,[16] and the Canadian Radio-television and Telecommunications Commission provides guidelines for election coverage based on the Broadcasting Act and other regulatory documents. Moreover, the National NewsMedia Council and Conseil de presse du Québec, as well as ombudspersons and public editors in certain organizations, receive and respond to complaints regarding ethics in journalism. However, as this chapter attests, national news editors continue to play a significant role in defining the campaign agenda, despite their newsrooms' limited resources and the fact that Canadians consume news increasingly, for free, on social media.

Notes

1   Hermida, "Twittering the News."
2   Taylor Owen et al., *Polarization and Its Discontents* found that consumption of partisan sources is low in Canada, even among heavy users of social media.
3   On metrics, see Blanchett Neheli, "News by Numbers."
4   Duffy, "Out of the Shadows"; Hollifield, "Newsroom Management."
5   Reich and Godler, "The Disruption of Journalistic Expertise."
6   Blumler and Esser, "Mediatization as a Combination of Push and Pull Forces"; Cushion and Jackson, "Introduction to Special Issue about Election Reporting."
7   "The Media and Canadian Elections."
8   On the watchdog function, see Nai, "Watchdog Press."
9   Timmons, "How the Canadian Press Is Using Bots to Build the Future of Election Coverage."

10 Lindgren, "What the Death of Local News Means for the Federal Election."
11 On fact-checking units, see Graves, *Deciding What's True.*
12 Flamini, "Canadian Fact-Checkers Are Pleasantly Surprised."
13 Nai, "Watchdog Press."
14 Rollwagen et al., "Just Who Do Canadian Journalists Think They Are?"
15 Thibault et al., "Assessing Politicization in Media Systems."
16 The Centre d'études sur les médias has conducted this research for federal and provincial Quebec elections since 2006.

Bibliography

Blanchett Neheli, Nicole. "News by Numbers." *Digital Journalism* 6, 8 (2018): 1041–51.

Blumler, Jay G., and Frank Esser. "Mediatization as a Combination of Push and Pull Forces: Examples during the 2015 UK General Election Campaign." *Journalism* 20, 7 (2019): 855–72.

Duffy, Andrew. "Out of the Shadows: The Editor as a Defining Characteristic of Journalism." *Journalism,* 30 January 2019. https://doi.org/10.1177/1464884919826818.

Flamini, Daniela. "Canadian Fact-Checkers Are Pleasantly Surprised by a Low Amount of False Electoral Content." Poynter, 7 October 2019. https://www.poynter.org/fact-checking/2019/canadian-fact-checkers-are-pleasantly-surprised-by-a-low-amount-of-false-electoral-content/.

Graves, Lucas. *Deciding What's True: The Rise of Political Fact-Checking in American Journalism.* New York: Columbia University Press, 2016.

Hermida, Alfred. "Twittering the News: The Emergence of Ambient Journalism." *Journalism Practice* 4, 3 (2010): 297–308.

Hollifield, C. Ann. "Newsroom Management." In *International Encyclopedia of Journalism Studies.* Hoboken, NJ: John Wiley and Sons, 2019.

Lindgren, April. "What the Death of Local News Means for the Federal Election." *The Walrus,* 24 April 2019, updated 22 August. https://thewalrus.ca/what-the-death-of-local-news-means-for-the-federal-election/.

"The Media and Canadian Elections." *Policy Options,* 26 August 2019. https://policyoptions.irpp.org/magazines/august-2019/the-media-and-canadian-elections/.

Nai, Alessandro. "Watchdog Press." In *International Encyclopedia of Journalism Studies.* Hoboken, NJ: John Wiley and Sons, 2019.

Owen, Taylor, Peter Loewen, Derek Ruths, Aengus Bridgman, Robert Gorwa, Stephanie MacLellan, Eric Merkley, Andrew Potter, Beata Skazinetsky, and Oleg Zhilin. *Polarization and Its Discontents.* Digital

Democracy Project, Research Memo #3, September, 2019. https://mcgill.
ca/maxbellschool/files/maxbellschool/ddp-research-memo-3-sept2019.
pdf.

Reich, Zvi, and Yigal Godler. "The Disruption of Journalistic Expertise."
In *Rethinking Journalism Again: Societal Role and Public Relevance in a Digital Age,* edited by Chris Peters and Marcel Broersma, 64–81. London: Routledge, 2016.

Rollwagen, Heather, Ivor Shapiro, Geneviève Bonin-Labelle, Lindsay Fitzgerald, and Lauriane Tremblay. "Just Who Do Canadian Journalists Think They Are? Political Role Conceptions in Global and Historical Perspective." *Canadian Journal of Political Science* 52, 3 (2019): 461–77.

Thibault, Simon, Frédérick Bastien, Colette Brin, and Tania Gosselin. "Assessing Politicization in Media Systems: A Canadian Perspective." Paper presented at the European Communication Research and Education Association (ECREA) Journalism Studies Conference, University of Vienna, 14 February 2019.

Timmons, Lucas. "How the Canadian Press Is Using Bots to Build the Future of Election Coverage." J-Source, 30 July 2019. https://j-source.
ca/article/how-the-canadian-press-is-using-bots-to-build-the-future-of
-election-coverage/.

6

Pollsters

André Turcotte and Éric Grenier

The role of pollsters has evolved over the years. Although the main responsibilities continue to focus on providing and recording the voices of voters, technological advances have led to an increased level of sophistication in how the job is done. As a result of a shift from traditional polling to market intelligence, pollsters have become integrated within the daily strategic apparatus of a campaign. Their advice has shifted from the general and national to the narrow and local. Consequently, a new polling instrument – poll aggregators – is the latest innovation in this constantly evolving field.

Le rôle des sondeurs a évolué au fil des ans. Bien que leurs principales responsabilités soient toujours axées sur la mesure et la présentation des intentions de vote, les transformations technologiques ont permis une sophistication accrue des méthodes de travail. À la suite d'un passage des sondages traditionnels vers l'analyse de marché, les sondeurs se sont intégrés à l'appareil stratégique quotidien d'une campagne. Leurs conseils sont passés de généraux et nationaux à précis et locaux. Par conséquent, les agrégateurs de sondage constituent la plus récente innovation dans ce domaine en constante évolution.

IN A QUOTATION attributed – maybe apocryphally – to Albert Einstein, the scientist once told a young man to become a public opinion pollster. Einstein apparently suggested that the young man would never be unemployed as a pollster because tall tales rule people, and therefore rulers must always try to find out what they can get away with. One can find other negative references to pollsters. The origin of the term goes back to a book by Lindsay Rogers entitled *The Pollsters*, published in 1949.[1] It evoked Frederic Wakeman's polemical work against modern advertising, *The Hucksters*, not a complimentary reference.[2] Despite unflattering comments, pollsters have emerged as very influential actors in the political process. In this chapter, we focus on political polling in general and political pollsters in particular, the individuals who provide public opinion data to political parties. However, it is difficult to avoid references to media pollsters – the individuals who provide public opinion data to the media – because the roles intersect, especially during election campaigns. This overlap occurred right from the inception of the field of public opinion research and occurs even more so in today's twenty-four-hour mediated political environment.

How polling came to play such a prominent role in elections has been well documented. A then unknown university professor named George Gallup used his doctoral thesis on sampling techniques to help his mother-in-law become the first woman to hold the position of secretary of state in Iowa in 1932. Three years later Gallup, as well as Archibald Crossley and Elmo Roper, began conducting polls on a regular basis. Roper was the first of the media pollsters. In July 1935, he released the findings of a study of three thousand American adults about their attitudes toward a range of current affairs issues in *Fortune* magazine. He would repeat this exercise on a quarterly basis and discuss his findings under the rubric of "The *Fortune* Survey."[3] A few months later, in October 1935, Gallup started releasing his survey results in a weekly column entitled "America Speaks."[4] For his part, Crossley also developed a regular poll entitled "The Crossley Political Poll" for the newspapers of the Hearst Corporation.[5] The first big test of this new way of measuring public opinion came during the 1936 US presidential election. The young upstart Gallup publicly challenged the venerable *Literary Digest* and claimed that it would be unable to predict accurately the outcome of the election because of inherent flaws in its methodology. As it turned out, his own prediction in that election was off by 7 percent.[6] However, unlike the *Literary Digest,* Gallup correctly predicted Roosevelt's victory, and with that the polling industry was born.

Although the details of the profession have evolved, the general job profile of a pollster has not changed much since the 1930s. On the surface, a pollster is the "neutral recorder" of the opinions of a particular population. The role of a pollster has been instrumental in entrenching the need to give citizens a voice and have them play a role in the political process in general and policy making in particular. As Gallup wrote in *The Pulse of Democracy,* "the kind of public opinion implied in the democratic ideal is tangible and dynamic. It springs from many sources in the day-to-day experience of individuals who constitute the political public, and who formulate these opinions as working guides for their political representatives."[7] This conceptualization of public opinion serves as a justification for using surveys and polls to measure it.[8]

The job has not changed much over the years. However, technological advances have led to an increased level of sophistication in how it is done. As the industry grew in size and influence, the best practitioners became perceived as "seers," those with the ability to understand the general mood of an electorate.[9] Then pollsters realized that, not only could they tell what people are thinking, but also they could provide advice on how to influence the way that people are thinking and, maybe more importantly, what they are thinking about. This realization had a significant impact on the duties of a pollster during an election campaign.

Duties in an Election Campaign

Through the influence of a second wave of pioneers – Richard Wirthlin, Peter Hart, Pat Caddell, and Allan Gregg, among others –

pollsters learned that not every voter is to be given equal attention and that a successful campaign needs to identify and consolidate its base of support and understand the relatively few voters who make a difference between winning and losing. This is generally described as an evolution from traditional polling to market intelligence. The campaign duties of a pollster are a reflection of this evolution.

This progression toward market intelligence is documented in the growing literature on political marketing. According to the main tenets of this discipline, market intelligence focuses on the behaviour of voters and how their needs, wants, attitudes, and priorities influence their behaviour.[10] The discipline treats the electoral landscape as a political marketplace, essentially a forum in which buyers and sellers – or voters and candidates – have open entry and exit and competition exists to enable information to be extended to consumers (voters). The concept of a marketplace is well accepted in economics; however, it has been seen in negative terms in the field of voting behaviour. The main criticism is that opinion polling is incompatible with the rational exchange of arguments essential for a well-functioning democracy. Accordingly, a political marketplace influenced by opinion polling cheapens the act of voting and reduces it to a transaction between politicians with short-term goals and a fickle electorate.[11] Despite the criticism, it remains true that the practitioners of the political craft have adopted this conception of voting behaviour because it is very effective in providing a road map to electoral victory.

The key duties of pollsters during an election campaign start with an understanding that party strategists no longer look at the electorate homogeneously but adopt strategic segmentation techniques that allow for policies and communications to be designed for targeted groups. The time required to develop a thorough understanding of a segmented electorate means that, in many ways, the campaign duties of the pollster begin several months before the writ is dropped. Very early on in the pre-election–preparedness phase, the pollsters conduct large-scale benchmark polls to collect data on every relevant aspect of the campaign, from issues to leaders' favourability and impression, messaging, and potential segments of the electorate likely to determine the outcome of the election. This polling is typically supplemented by focus groups. They are habitually used to deepen and refine the findings from the more robust quantitative phase. The results of the pre-election study are dissected by the senior leaders of the campaign and help in the development of the campaign strategy. At this stage, the pollster often becomes fully integrated into the command structure of the campaign and is part of every key discussion about both strategies and tactics. Contacts with the campaign evolve from several times a week before the writ is dropped to daily, if not several times a day, during the election campaign.

In line with these pre-campaign functions, the pollster spends time and resources to develop and refine the voter segments that will be the focus of the campaign efforts. Segmentation has become a key element of party polling. Market intelligence allows for the identification of very narrow segments of the electorate that make a difference between winning and losing an election. In specific terms, "segmentation tries to identify common characteristics. It helps to create new and more precise groupings and can help to provide new understanding where traditional political labels no longer apply or work effectively."[12] This approach is largely inspired by the ways in which business marketing campaigns are designed with a focus on potential consumers and represents a departure from the more sociological and anthropological parameters that dominated early voting research.

Once the writ is dropped, polling focuses solely on supporting execution of the campaign strategy. Although there can be adjustment and refinement, a realignment of strategy is ill-advised at this stage. Another key departure from previous practice is that the market intelligence function favours reliance on a more varied set of instruments to gather information. The accumulation of market intelligence now depends on more than surveys and polls and taps into the potential of other formal as well as informal means.

The campaign relies on a wide range of market intelligence tools to comprehend the campaign dynamics affecting the segmented electorate. More than before, the collection and interpretation of market intelligence data are multilayered. They range from ad hoc and unscientific data – such as canvasses, volunteer phone banks, and interactive voice response – to highly technical and mathematically sophisticated tools such as telephone and online campaign tracking polls, focus group testing, voter ID tracking programs, mathematical modelling, and data analytics. The responsibilities of the pollsters are not only to execute these multifaceted research designs but also, more importantly, to digest all this information and communicate the results to the campaign in a concrete and actionable way.

A major development in the duties of the pollster is that the commissioning of national polling during the campaign has become increasingly irrelevant because of this narrowly focused strategy based on segments of the electorate. Although this practice occurs partly because of changes in campaign financing legislation, political parties tend to focus their resources on battleground areas and rely on the numerous polls released almost daily by media outlets to get a sense of how the national campaign is evolving.[13] They also use national polls to supplement their internal analyses.[14] This new reality has added novel campaign duties for the party pollster, now required to navigate the interface between the media narrative influenced by the media pollsters and the internal narrative focused on narrow segments of the electorate. The last section of this chapter examines interactions among media polling, party polling, and media reporting, and it looks at how they contribute to framing the election campaign. Specifically, it shows how polling results affect media coverage as well as party leaders' activities and messages. This campaign dynamic leads to an interaction between public data and party data in a fight for capturing the public campaign narrative. The pollster is in the middle of this high-stakes drama.

Overcoming Obstacles

One of the consequences of the migration from traditional polling to market intelligence is the need for a reliable source for a national outlook of vote choice that can supplement the more granular party-based data. Poll aggregators have emerged to fill that need. Poll aggregation is not particularly new – "polls of polls" were compiled as early as the 1970s in the United Kingdom. However, they became particularly ubiquitous following the popularity of Nate Silver's FiveThirtyEight.com, in which Silver used a statistical model based on polling and other factors to predict Barack Obama's victory for the Democratic presidential nomination and subsequently the US presidential election in 2008. Aggregators have also existed in Canada for some time, Barry Kay's work with the Laurier Institute for the Study of Public Opinion and Policy being one notable example. Aggregation became more widely cited beginning in the 2011 federal election, when some aggregators – including one of the authors – worked directly with media organizations.

The literature on this topic so far has focused on the development of poll aggregators.[15] Little has been written on the mechanics of this practice and the rationale behind it. There are various methods used in poll aggregation. The basic concept is the same: an average of all voting-intention polls, with weights applied to each poll, often based on when the fieldwork was done, how many people were sampled, and a track record rating for the polling organization. Many overlook the weighting process and the judgment and evaluation that go into the development of the poll aggregators. Moreover, though party-based reasons exist for the emergence of poll aggregators, it is important to note that reduced newsroom budgets have made it more difficult for media organizations to afford commissioning individual surveys. The value of these surveys has been questioned because of the greater number of surveys being published, often self-commissioned by polling firms without a formal relationship with a media outlet, and the lack of certainty that the commissioned polls will prove to be accurate, regardless of how much they cost. This torrent of polling information makes aggregations more digestible, both for the average news consumer and for journalists covering election campaigns. Perhaps more importantly, an average of polls has historically performed better than most individual polls. For instance, the Poll Tracker in 2019 accurately identified the probability of the Liberal victory, the likelihood of a minority government, and the party standings.

The impact of this emergence is still unfolding. Some polling firms have accepted – grudgingly or otherwise – this new reality and have cooperated with aggregators to make their data accessible and available, and they provide additional information when asked. Others have raised objections to the use of their data without permission, and as a result they have made their complete data tables available only by subscription or the signing of a terms of service contract, prohibiting the use of their data in any aggregation model. In most cases, polling firms – despite their objections – are unwilling to forgo the media publicity associated with being part of poll aggregators. The growing influence and prevalence of aggregators in elections held around the world suggest their impact on the polling industry is worthy of deeper study.

As we discussed in the previous section, poll aggregators influence how political parties do their polling. Parties and politicians keep an eye on the poll aggregates and seat projections, particularly local candidates who do not have their own poll data for their riding. Parties with smaller budgets for polling rely in part on these publicly available poll aggregates to monitor the national and regional voting trends, opting to spend their resources on polling of target regions or groups of ridings instead of national surveys.

It is unclear what impact poll aggregations – despite their popularity – have on voters. For example, CBC's Poll Tracker has consistently attracted thousands of page views daily in every election since its launch. It is also a popular Internet destination between election campaigns. Whether the aggregation has more or less of an impact on voters than the individual polls reported by other media outlets is impossible to assess, but it does seem that the emphasis on seat projections has an influence on how voting intentions are discussed. In the past, unless they have their own seat projection models, pollsters have spoken in more general terms about whether their numbers indicate a majority or minority government for one party or another. Presenting seat estimates with the aggregates appears to give journalists more confidence in discussing the practical implications of what poll data suggest could be the outcome of an election, fraught with risk as that might be.

Poll aggregation does face some challenges going forward, including how willing pollsters will be to make their poll data accessible to both aggregators and the public. There is also the risk posed by incorrect election calls. The promise of poll aggregation is increased accuracy, but the aggregation is only as good as the polls included in it. Even in elections in which some polls are accurate, a few bad polls can make the entire aggregate – and thus "the polls" as understood by the public – less accurate. As well, there is the challenge of using poll data to make seat projections or probability estimates of electoral outcomes, adding a second potential for error to the risk of error that already exists in public opinion research. Nevertheless, the increasing presence and popularity of aggregators suggest that they meet a public need for more digestible and practical information during an election campaign. If it presents an opportunity to show the value of public opinion research and the capability of individual polling firms, then pollsters and aggregators can complement each other's work in making it accessible to a wider audience.

Notes

[1] Rogers, *The Pollsters*.
[2] Wakeman, *The Hucksters*.
[3] Blondiaux, *La fabrique de l'opinion*, 158.
[4] Ibid.
[5] Micheau, *La prophétie électorale*, 29.
[6] Warren, *In Defense of Public Opinion Polling*, 87.

7   Gallup, *The Pulse of Democracy,* 8.
8   Glynn et al., *Public Opinion,* 14.
9   Turcotte, "Polling as Modern Alchemy," 207.
10 Lees-Marshment, *Current Issues in Political Marketing,* 10.
11 Bruckweh, *The Voice of the Consumer,* v.
12 Lees-Marshment et al., *Political Marketing,* 64.
13 On campaign financing legislation, see ibid., 88.
14 Ibid.
15 Silver, *The Signal and the Noise;* Issenberg, *The Victory Lab.*

Bibliography

Blondiaux, Loic. *La fabrique de l'opinion.* Paris: Seuil, 1998.

Bruckweh, Kerstin, ed. *The Voice of the Consumer.* Oxford: Oxford University Press, 2011.

Gallup, George. *The Pulse of Democracy.* New York: Simon and Schuster, 1940.

Glynn, Carroll J., Susan Herbst, Mark Lindeman, Garrett J. O'Keefe, and Robert Y. Shapiro. *Public Opinion.* 3rd ed. Boulder, CO: Westview Press, 2016.

Issenberg, Sasha. *The Victory Lab.* New York: Broadway Books, 2013.

Lees-Marshment, Jennifer. *Current Issues in Political Marketing.* New York: Routledge, 2006.

Lees-Marshment, Jennifer, Brian Conley, Edward Elder, Robin Pettitt, Vincent Raynauld, and André Turcotte, eds. *Political Marketing.* 3rd ed. London: Routledge, 2019.

Micheau, Frédéric. *La prophétie électorale.* Paris: Les Éditions du Cerf, 2018.

Rogers, Lindsay. *The Pollsters: Public Opinion, Politics and Democratic Leadership.* New York: Alfred A. Knopf, 1949.

Silver, Nate. *The Signal and the Noise.* New York: Penguin Books, 2012.

Turcotte, André. "Polling as Modern Alchemy." In *Election,* edited by Heather MacIvor, 199–217. Toronto: Emond Montgomery, 2010.

Wakeman, Frederic. *The Hucksters.* New York: Grosset and Dunlap, 1946.

Warren, Kenneth F. *In Defense of Public Opinion Polling.* Boulder, CO: Westview Press, 2001.

PART 2
Campaign Offices and the Campaign Trail

7

Party Fundraisers

Erin Crandall and Michael Roy

Many things are needed for a successful election campaign, but arguably none is more essential than money. Fundraising has always been a necessary feature of campaigning for votes. In this chapter, we explore the duties of party fundraisers. Changes to fundraising tools, communication technologies, and regulations have transformed the profile and skills of party fundraisers over the past half-century. Today's party fundraisers are trained professionals with skills in direct marketing, brand positioning, and digital marketing who work to build and maintain relationships with donors across multiple fundraising channels.

Même si de nombreux éléments sont nécessaires à la réussite d'une campagne électorale, l'argent demeure l'élément le plus essentiel, le nerf de la guerre. La collecte de fonds a toujours été un aspect incontournable des campagnes électorales. Le présent chapitre porte sur le travail et les fonctions des collecteurs de fonds d'un parti. Les changements apportés aux outils de collecte de fonds, aux technologies de communication, et à la réglementation ont modifié le profil et les compétences des collecteurs de fonds au cours des cinquante dernières années. Les collecteurs de fonds d'aujourd'hui sont des professionnels qualifiés qui possèdent des compétences en marketing direct, en positionnement de marque, et en marketing numérique, et qui travaillent à établir et à maintenir des relations avec les donateurs provenant de divers réseaux de collecte de fonds.

A GREAT IDEA is priceless. A great campaign to share that idea comes with a big price tag. Elections cost money, making fundraisers integral to any successful political party. The profile of party fundraisers, the tools and technologies that they use, and the regulations that they must follow have changed over time, but the basic objective remains the same: to create and foster relationships with supporters while raising funds for the party.

Although unimaginable today, fundraising fell to federal party leaders until after the First World War.[1] Removing fundraising from the purview of party leaders helped to insulate them from fundraising-related scandals.[2] It also gave rise to a specialized group of fundraisers, commonly referred to as bagmen. For the Liberal and Conservative Parties, these men were prized for their close connections to top firms in Montreal and Toronto. With no regulations on party donations, a few well-connected bagmen could raise a significant portion of party funding. In 1957, the Liberal Party raised most of its campaign funds from three to four hundred donations alone.[3] These types of close relationships and the social occasions that fostered them, such as fundraising dinners, meant that few donations came from outside the world of business. For example, in 1953, 50 percent of the national party income for both major parties came from industrial or commercial firms, 40 percent from executives closely associated with particular companies, and only 10 percent from individuals.[4] Bagmen were not the norm for all federal parties, however. When the Co-operative Commonwealth Federation was founded in 1932, it adopted a grassroots approach to fundraising, focusing on small donations from individual citizens. However, the practical difficulties of this approach in an age before the raising of money through systematic direct mail or phone campaigns meant that the party was nearly always short of funds.[5]

The 1970s brought major changes to the world of party fundraising. Accessibility to computerized direct mail lists and a generous tax credit for party donations, introduced in the 1974 Election Expenses Act, meant that targeting small donations from individual citizens became a lucrative strategy for party fundraisers.[6]

Individuals quickly became the most important source of revenue for candidates of all parties, constituting about 40 percent of candidate financing.[7] Business contributions still played a critical role well into the early 2000s. During the 2000 election cycle, the Liberals raised approximately six of every ten dollars and the Progressive Conservatives half of their funds from corporate contributors, whereas the New Democrats received one-third of their funding from trade unions.[8]

In 2003, major reforms to federal party finance regulations placed significant caps on individual, corporate, and union donations. A per-vote subsidy that served to offset the revenue loss created by these changes was also introduced for eligible parties. In 2006, corporate and union donations were banned altogether. By 2015, the per-vote subsidy had been phased out. As a result, party fundraisers of all political stripes must now target small donations from individuals to raise funds. This grassroots approach to fundraising is ultimately about bringing in a large number of donors rather than cultivating a select group of supporters with deep pockets. Corporate affluence, union money, and personal connections still play a role in fundraising, but that role has been modified so that business and union leaders, rather than businesses and unions themselves, donate to parties. At times, this is a source of controversy, particularly when the governing party hosts fundraising events attended by the prime minister and/or ministers, leading to allegations of so-called cash for access.[9] By bundling a group of individual donations in a networked approach to fundraising, political parties can still fundraise large sums from organizations while operating within regulatory parameters. In 2019, Canadians were permitted to donate up to $1,600 to each registered political party.

Fundraising tools such as direct mail, phone, and email campaigns designed to target individual supporters illustrate how success for party fundraisers is no longer predicated on leveraging personal connections. Rather, fundraisers must know how to communicate effectively a personalized message on a mass scale to potential supporters. Parties have made significant investments in data infrastructure to support their fundraising work. They use sophisticated online marketing tools, donor relationship databases, and increasingly predictive analytics to identify fundraising prospects, target their appeals, and ensure that all prospects and donors have positive experiences and long-term relationships with the party that they support.[10] Although the upfront costs are significant, the investment in digital tools yields clear financial benefits. The use of data analytics permits a party to differentiate among donors, which in turn allows it to raise more money with fewer phone calls and letters. With so many tools available to fundraisers, the integration of these channels to communicate effectively with as many supporters as possible is now the gold standard for fundraisers.

Whereas the bagmen of earlier decades were an informal network recruited by parties for their personal connections, top party fundraisers are now trained professionals who bring diverse skills in direct marketing, brand positioning, and digital marketing. Fundraising directors and their sizable teams are skilled practitioners who deploy significant financial and staff resources to build and maintain relationships with donors across multiple fundraising channels. Today's political fundraisers combine backgrounds in communications, marketing, and data analytics to design and execute programs that have to deliver between $30 and $40 million per election cycle. Fundraising year round is necessary to help ensure that the party can obtain resources to run its operations between elections and fund its campaign come election time. A further impetus is that every three months the media and the parties routinely treat the fundraising data reported to Elections Canada as a competitive barometer of success.[11] Generating data on supporters for party databases is therefore a major impetus of party communications. Visitors to party websites are asked to submit their contact details; people are urged to add their names to digital petitions and participate in surveys that generate information associating citizens with issues of concern; and data collected on doorsteps by candidates, MPs, and volunteers are input into digital consoles. Database marketing has become a major priority of year-round campaigning and fundraising.[12] In addition to fundraising, it assists with other forms of targeted communication, such as get-out-the-vote efforts.

Duties in an Election Campaign

The work of a director of fundraising is always an essential part of a political party's operations, though the stakes are necessarily higher during an election campaign. Although the focus of the work is reasonably constant before an election, the intensity and scrutiny of the work ramp up considerably during the campaign. A general election is by far the largest expense that a party undertakes. Therefore, planning for the fundraising component of the campaign necessarily begins months in advance and is a critical part of the duties of a director of finance. The director starts by looking at the election calendar, the party's fundraising goals, and available resources – such as lists of party members, voters and sympathizers, and potential private fundraising vendors – to support the effort. Once these goals and resources are established in a plan for election fundraising, the focus turns to timing and the design and implementation of the outreach strategy.

The party's database is a formidable resource for informing targeted fundraising efforts. In the lead up to the election, fundraising through telemarketing, direct mail, and especially digital appeals increases in frequency. Additional fundraisers – either in house or through fundraising contractors – are engaged, and the amount of contact time is increased. Telemarketing typically continues in high intensity throughout the campaign, targeting both past donors and new prospects identified through voter outreach efforts. A number of direct mail fundraising appeals are generally sent during the campaign, and they are planned and written in advance. Where possible, they tie into campaign themes or policy announcements; however, this is often difficult to coordinate given the secretive and last-minute nature of campaign policy announcements. The vast majority of campaign emails contain fundraising appeals.

Timing is a major factor in terms of resources and strategies. As election day draws closer, fundraising efforts start to shift away from monthly donations and toward one-time donations. This change in strategy occurs because one-time donations generally yield more money in the short term. It is typical for 50 percent of the fundraised revenue in an election cycle to be raised in the ninety days leading up to election day. For that reason, it is critical that the pre-election and election fundraising plans ramp up all fundraising efforts, with an eye to ensuring that high donors give the legal maximum for the year. The focus on one-time donations, rather than monthly donations, is valuable given that a successful fundraising campaign relies not just on party members but also on party sympathizers. For example, digital technologies have helped the New Democratic Party (NDP) to confirm that party members and sympathizers donate at comparable levels, making the distinction between the two types of donors increasingly meaningless for fundraising purposes.[13] Timing is also helpful in creating conditions that can prompt prospective donors to take action and donate to a party. An election presents a number of useful deadlines that can help a fundraising team to create a sense of urgency. Three of the most notable dates are the start of the election, the end of the quarter when financial data are publicly reported, and election day itself.

During the official campaign period, party fundraisers are regularly debriefed so that they can get an idea of which messages are resonating and what feedback the party is getting from its core supporters about the campaign. Fundraisers are regularly briefed on policy proposals and the latest updates from the campaign as tools to engage supporters better. As already noted, however, policies are frequently secretive until they are announced, which leaves relatively little preparation time for drafting fundraising messages. Like all members of the campaign team, fundraisers must act and adapt quickly in a dynamic political environment so that fundraising messages continue to reach the right people, at the right time, using the right medium of communication.

For modern political campaigning, the standard is to have as many positions operating in house as possible.[14] This places fundraising staff in the same headquarters as other members of the election campaign team, such as war room, tour, administration, digital, products/research, policy/platform, organization, and targeted ridings. The extent to which traditional fundraising and digital fundraising are integrated varies by political party. The NDP, for example, splits fundraising between these two teams, which generally run their activities independently. The digital team, in particular, integrates field and communication outreach closely with election fundraising appeals.

Some factors that build a successful election fundraising campaign are beyond a fundraiser's control. A potential donor's perception of a party's likelihood of electoral success can affect the decision to donate to that party and what amount. The more positive momentum a party can build during an election campaign, the easier it is for fundraisers to meet or even exceed fundraising goals.

Overcoming Obstacles

All political parties, and indeed all fundraising organizations, face a common challenge when it comes to fundraising: recruiting new donors at a reasonable cost. One of the ironies of fundraising is that it can be very expensive. A successful fundraiser is not simply a person who raises a lot of money but also does so in a cost-effective way. These numbers matter. Although the past couple of decades have seen the Conservative Party consistently raise more money than other federal parties, it has also spent the most money to do so. For example, the Conservatives raised $24.2 million from 104,000 donors in 2018 compared with the Liberals, who raised $15.9 million from 66,000 people.[15] The Conservatives, however, spent $8.5 million to raise their amount, whereas the Liberals spent $3.4 million, cutting the actual fundraising gap between the two parties by more than half.[16] This fine balance between money raised and money spent motivates party fundraisers to refine and renew their fundraising techniques.

The task of recruiting new donors has changed dramatically over time. Whereas early fundraisers relied on leveraging personal relations for large donations, technological developments mean that this type of approach is no longer essential, and more importantly today's donation limits mean that large donations are no longer permissible. In the latter half of the twentieth century, the challenge of recruiting new donors at a reasonable cost was addressed mainly by exchanging lists with other organizations or reaching out to the public in the hope of attracting new donors. This latter process, however, is generally costly, with organizations paying more than $150 for each new donor acquired through telephone or direct mail prospecting. In the digital era, list exchanges are still a part of new donor acquisition, but targeted online ads have increasingly become the norm. They are designed to encourage prospective supporters, for example by signing an online petition, so that the party can then acquire their email addresses. Once on the list, they receive fundraising appeals in an effort to make them donors.

For the NDP, one solution to the new donor acquisition challenge has come with a modern twist on two old ideas: contests and dinner with the party leader. For years, direct mail fundraising firms have used contests (e.g., "win a trip to Hawaii if you donate!") as a means to entice donors. And, for as long as there has been political fundraising, political leaders have invited supporters to pay for dinners with them. Such dinners vary from large ticketed banquets to intimate meals for high-dollar donors. The twist on these time-tested tactics was to ask supporters to chip in as little as a few dollars and offer them a chance to win an exclusive experience with the candidate. The NDP ran a number of these contests in both 2015 and 2019. One saw a young woman from Nova Scotia attend a Montreal Canadiens hockey game with the party leader, and another had the two winners join the party leader on the campaign plane during the election itself. The "Jet with Jagmeet" Contest offered the winner the chance to fly on the plane for a day during the election campaign.[17] These contests attracted thousands of new donors to the NDP's campaign at a relatively low cost.

Inevitably, a party's momentum contributes significantly to a fundraising campaign. Whether an effort to acquire new donors or motivate long-time supporters, nothing is better for fundraising than momentum. So what does one do when the overwhelming view is that the party does not have it? This was the challenge faced by the NDP going into the 2019 election campaign. For the party's digital fundraising team, a narrative on momentum was deployed in three phases over the course of the campaign: the possibility of momentum, achieving momentum, and protecting momentum.

Momentum is always possible even if not immediately apparent. In the first half of the campaign, when poll numbers for the NDP showed relatively little movement, emails to supporters focused on an "energy of possibility," according to Oliver Paré, the NDP's digital director for fundraising for the 2019 election.[18] As positive recognition of NDP leader Jagmeet Singh built over the campaign, particularly following the English-language leaders' debate, the fundraising narrative was able to change accordingly, from the possibility of momentum to illustrations of momentum in action. For example, when Singh did an impromptu walk-through at Ryerson University the day after the leaders' debate and was swarmed by student supporters, the digital fundraising team quickly sent out an email describing the event and asking for support.[19] Another organic experience that contributed to the party's fundraising momentum occurred while Singh was visiting Grassy Narrows, a First Nations community in Northern Ontario that for decades has grappled with unsafe drinking water and mercury poisoning.[20] When asked by a reporter if the NDP was simply writing a "blank cheque" for the problems of all Indigenous communities, Singh responded that the same question would not be asked if the problem of unsafe drinking water was in Vancouver or Edmonton.[21] This response went viral and garnered considerable media attention. As election day drew near, the party introduced a final email campaign, the

Fight Back Fund, in which the focus was on how supporters could help the party to respond to attacks from the other parties. This shift in framing from achieving momentum to protecting momentum was designed to sustain supporters' motivations to donate to the NDP. Thus, momentum was always part of its fundraising narrative, but inevitably fundraising picked up as the party's poll numbers improved.

A chapter focused on fundraisers might leave the impression that money is the sole factor that wins elections. This is certainly not the case. Although fundraising, securing bank loans, and managing debt are critical parts of an election campaign, they are not determinative. Nonetheless, a party is unquestionably much worse off without a strong fundraising team that can create and foster relationships with supporters while raising funds for the party. After all, a great election campaign is never priceless.

Notes

1 Paltiel, *Political Party Financing in Canada.*
2 McMenamin, *If Money Talks, What Does It Say?*, 38.
3 Paltiel and Van Loon, "Financing the Liberal Party 1867–1965," 170.
4 Ibid., 169.
5 Paltiel, *Political Party Financing in Canada*, 48.
6 Stanbury, *Money in Politics*, 252.
7 Padget, "Large Contributions to Candidates in the 1988 Federal Election," 321.
8 Cross, *Political Parties*, 146.
9 Cotton, "Little Reason to Believe."
10 Giasson and Small, "Online, All the Time"; Marland and Mathews, "'Friend, Can You Chip in $3?'"
11 Vigliotti, "Liberals, Tories Claim Record-Breaking Q2 Fundraising Figures."
12 Patten, "Databases, Microtargeting, and the Permanent Campaign."
13 McGrane, *The New NDP*, 78.
14 Ibid., 71; Flanagan, "Political Communication and the Permanent Campaign," 137; Patten, "Databases, Microtargeting, and the Permanent Campaign," 53.

15   Canadian Press, "Tory Fundraising Almost $8 Million More than Liberals' in 2018."

16   Ibid.

17   Moss and Lapointe, "Air Singh."

18   Paré, interview with Crandall.

19   *CityNews,* "Jagmeet Singh Visits with Students on Ryerson University Campus"; Paré, interview with Crandall.

20   Paré, interview with Crandall.

21   Canadian Press, "NDP's Singh Promises $1.8B to Provide Clean Drinking Water in Indigenous Communities."

Bibliography

Canadian Press. "Tory Fundraising Almost $8 Million More than Liberals' in 2018 According to Financial Returns." *National Post,* 3 July 2019. https://nationalpost.com/news/politics/parties-financial-returns-show-tories-topped-liberals-in-2018-fundraising.

–. "NDP's Singh Promises $1.8B to Provide Clean Drinking Water in Indigenous Communities." Global News, 5 October 2019. https://globalnews.ca/news/5994764/jagmeet-singh-grassy-narrows/.

CityNews. "Jagmeet Singh Visits with Students on Ryerson University Campus." 8 October 2019. https://toronto.citynews.ca/video/2019/10/08/jagmeet-singh-visits-with-students-on-ryerson-university-campus/.

Cotton, Christopher. "There Is Little Reason to Believe that Changes to Political Fundraising Rules Will Do Much to Curb the Influence of Big Donors." *Policy Options,* 2 February 2017. https://policyoptions.irpp.org/magazines/february-2017/the-impact-of-trudeaus-cash-for-access-fundraising/.

Cross, William P. *Political Parties.* Vancouver: UBC Press, 2004.

Flanagan, Tom. "Political Communication and the Permanent Campaign." In *How Canadians Communicate IV: Media and Politics,* edited by David Taras and Christopher Waddell, 129–48. Edmonton: Athabasca University Press, 2012.

Giasson, Thierry, and Tamara A. Small. "Online, All the Time: The Strategic Objectives of Canadian Opposition Parties." In *Permanent Campaigning in Canada,* edited by Alex Marland, Thierry Giasson, and Anna Lennox Esselment, 109–26. Vancouver: UBC Press, 2017.

Marland, Alex, and Maria Mathews. "'Friend, Can You Chip in $3?' Canadian Political Parties' Email Communication and Fundraising." In *Permanent Campaigning in Canada,* edited by Alex Marland, Thierry

Giasson, and Anna Lennox Esselment, 87–108. Vancouver: UBC Press, 2017.

McGrane, David. *The New NDP: Moderation, Modernization, and Political Marketing*. Vancouver: UBC Press, 2019.

McMenamin, Iain. *If Money Talks, What Does It Say? Corruption and Business Financing of Political Parties*. Oxford: Oxford University Press, 2013.

Moss, Neil, and Mike Lapointe. "Air Singh: NDP Offering Spot on Campaign Plane for a Day." *Hill Times*, 2 September 2019. https://www. hilltimes.com/2019/09/02/air-singh-ndp-offering-spot-on-campaign -plane-for-a-day/213162.

Padget, Donald. "Large Contributions to Candidates in the 1988 Federal Election and the Issue of Undue Influence." In *Issues in Party and Election Finance in Canada,* edited by F. Leslie Seidle, 319–67. Toronto: Dundurn Press, 1991.

Paltiel, Khayyam Z. *Political Party Financing in Canada*. Toronto: McGraw-Hill, 1970.

Paltiel, Khayyam Z., and Jean Brown Van Loon. "Financing the Liberal Party 1867–1965." In *Committee on Election Expenses, Studies in Canadian Party Finance,* edited by Khayyam Z. Paltiel, 147–256. Ottawa: Queen's Printer, 1966.

Paré, Oliver. Interview with Erin Crandall. 16 November 2019.

Patten, Steve. "Databases, Microtargeting, and the Permanent Campaign: A Threat to Democracy." In *Permanent Campaigning in Canada,* edited by Alex Marland, Thierry Giasson, and Anna Lennox Esselment, 47–66. Vancouver: UBC Press, 2017.

Stanbury, W.T. *Money in Politics: Financing Federal Parties and Candidates in Canada*. Vol. 1 of the report of the Royal Commission on Electoral Reform and Party Financing. Toronto: Dundurn Press, 1993.

Vigliotti, Marco. "Liberals, Tories Claim Record-Breaking Q2 Fundraising Figures." *iPolitics,* 30 July 2019. https://ipolitics.ca/2019/07/30/ liberals-tories-claim-record-breaking-q2-fundraising-figures/.

8

Party Platform Builders

Jared Wesley and Renze Nauta

Drafters of campaign platforms face many conflicting demands. They must consider competing requests from various corners of the party. Their decisions must balance good policy goals with staying within tight fiscal limits. Their determination to win through bold policy proposals must align with the necessity of setting an achievable agenda for governing. Platform directors also serve as their parties' policy leads, providing moment-to-moment answers to journalists about their own policy commitments and those of their opponents. In this chapter, we explain the strategic objectives and challenges involved in building major party platforms in Canada.

Les rédacteurs doivent composer avec de nombreuses demandes contradictoires lorsqu'ils élaborent des plateformes électorales. Ils doivent tenir compte des demandes concurrentes des divers partis et leurs décisions doivent assurer l'équilibre entre de bons objectifs stratégiques et le respect de limites budgétaires serrées. Leur détermination à gagner par des propositions de politiques audacieuses doit s'harmoniser avec la nécessité d'établir un programme de gouvernance réalisable. Les directeurs de plateformes assument également le rôle de responsables politiques de leur parti; ils fournissent des réponses instantanées aux journalistes au sujet de leurs propres engagements politiques et de ceux de leurs adversaires. Ce chapitre explique les objectifs stratégiques et les difficultés liés à l'élaboration des programmes des grands partis canadiens.

A PARTY'S PLATFORM is among its most coveted documents. Leaks can derail an entire campaign since they expose the party's plans to scrutiny before they are ready.[1] For these reasons, only select people have access to the full platform as it is being developed. The platform director, also known as the policy director, is at the centre of this group, helping to guide the document through various stages of drafting and approval. This leader is typically an expert drawn from within political parties, academia, or the bureaucracy. Few platform directors are eager to reveal the trade secrets involved in their craft. On-the-record interviews with them have been rare. As a result, we must mine memoirs and insiders' accounts for glimpses of the world of platform design.[2]

Alongside advances in political marketing, platform drafting became more professionalized.[3] The 1993 Liberal Red Book set the modern standard in this regard.[4] Manifestos are no longer crafted by cadres of elites walled off from the influences of public opinion. There is a recognition that even the most artful political advertising cannot sell an unpopular suite of policies. Rather, platform directors must work with public opinion and communication specialists to determine which issues matter the most to voters and, of those issues, which ones voters trust their party the most to handle. The platform is a tool to highlight those issues. Properly crafted, it allows the party to "ride the wave" of public opinion and capitalize on "issue ownership."[5]

The platform director holds the pen on early drafts of the document. Platform directors do not work alone, however. Given time and resources, they often consult from within and outside the party to gain input and buy-in on the document. Their primary responsibility is to ensure that the party's core commitments align with the priorities of its accessible voters and stakeholders. This issue landscape is identified through polling and on-the-ground intelligence from party volunteers and candidates.

Election platforms are central to modern campaigns. They are compendiums of policy commitments and can serve as plans for governance. They allow voters to assess parties based on how well their promises and priorities align with their own preferences and to provide the winning party with an agenda to govern. This might be an idealized view. The media gloss over much of the platforms' contents in favour of stories focused on personality and gamesmanship, and voters' social media feeds are unlikely to feature high-minded debates about public policy. Few voters base their decisions on specific policy initiatives on offer, and even fewer review the platforms themselves. For this reason, it is tempting to dismiss platforms as inconsequential.

Yet they serve another set of purposes for the parties that release them. A platform is a key part of the party's brand or personality. It binds campaign teams together and connects them to key groups of supporters.[6] When well constructed, a platform helps a diverse collection of people and organizations to gel around a common set of objectives and policy aims. The expected and desired reactions of stakeholders place a constraint on the coherence and workability of policies. Strong support from one stakeholder, elicited by a commitment to a particular side on a given issue, might evoke strong opposition from another. In contrast, a more nuanced position might satisfy a broader range of stakeholders but fail to energize either side. In this sense, the reality that one cannot be all things to all people provides a natural limit on the ability of the party to say anything to win votes.

Platforms are key tools for internal party management and external communication. They can bind the party's various factions, providing a common rallying point and keeping everyone on message. This is a tall order for national parties whose bases are divided along ideological, generational, regional, ethnic, and other lines. At the same time, the platform serves as the central thread of the party's campaign communication. The platform captures all forms of messaging – about the leader, policy, contrast to opposition, and so on. The cover page is emblazoned with the party's campaign slogan. Different section headings announce the party's key priorities.

Photos of the leader, images, and other visual elements convey the tone that the party wishes to set. Daily press releases build on, and in some cases contribute to, the platform's contents.

Prior to the campaign, the platform director consolidates input from throughout the party apparatus. The range of people who need to be consulted in designing platforms has widened over time. As late as the 1980s, the leader and cabinet (or senior critics) shared control over the platform with the party's executive, supported by the campaign manager. Today's platform directors often engage with a variety of people at various stages. Party members and executives are usually organized into working groups for this purpose. The platform director also consults elected officials, including candidates, caucus, and critics or members of the cabinet. Allied interest groups and stakeholders are likewise involved. For a party in government, public servants are also engaged in the process. The platform director might also work with academics, think tanks, policy experts, economists, and public finance experts to refine the policy instruments included in the document. Public opinion and marketing experts are engaged to ensure that the platform resonates with the target audiences, measuring any progress against the baseline polling conducted at the outset of the campaign.

This product development stage can last anywhere from a few years to a few months before the campaign begins. Fixed election dates have helped to make the timing somewhat more predictable. Changes in leadership and the possibility of snap elections can speed up the process.

Duties in an Election Campaign

As the campaign nears, platform directors begin assembling the platform document. It must be a living text consistent with the party's brand and campaign strategy. Platforms need to be flexible enough to adapt over the course of the campaign. For this reason, the platform team's work must be integrated into the broader campaign structure. The platform director must work with the campaign manager, the communications director, the leader's chief of staff, and others to ensure that the platform aligns with other elements of the party's strategy.

Platform directors do not work with a blank canvas. Previous commitments made by the party in past elections often act as a foundation for the party platform. So does the leadership campaign platform of the leader if he or she was selected since the previous general election. Parties in government often construct throne speeches and budget documents with an eye to the next election campaign. Policy announcements at the end of a government's term also provide ingredients for the party's platform. Platform directors must also keep the party's policy manuals and declarations in mind. They are usually produced through resolutions passed by party members or delegates at conventions midway between elections. Policy resolutions that align with the campaign narrative can make their way into the final platform, whereas those deemed not to align might be excluded. In this sense, the platform is a meeting point among the party's grassroots policy declarations, the leader's prerogatives, and the broader electorate's priorities.

At the same time, the platform director must assemble a coherent set of workable policies. The party must be able to deliver on most of these promises if elected. This includes providing realistic costing for policies, which the platform director oversees with the help of economists and experts in public finance. The costing of a platform places a natural check on a political party, which could otherwise propose policies without limits. The adoption of fiscal constraint is the choice of the party itself, subject to expectations of the public and the party's base (e.g., a balanced budget, a declining debt-to-GDP ratio, etc.). In some instances, parties might choose to muddy, distort, or ignore the cost of implementing their proposed policies. The electorate's expectations for costing can vary from election to election. Nevertheless, the accepted norm of including a detailed fiscal plan as part of the platform places a limit on the party's ability to make promises.

The costing process is iterative. The fiscal costs of desired policies are estimated and then tailored according to the available fiscal room. A political party can create fiscal room through proposals that increase revenues or decrease expenditures; however, the downside of these typically unpopular proposals has to be weighed against the upside of the policies made possible by them. The platform ultimately presented to voters is the party's best determination of the collection of policies that will appeal to them. For the first time in 2019, the Parliamentary Budget Office (PBO) was available to support federal political parties that wished to refer their own campaign proposals for independent costing. It too was an iterative process with a lot of back and forth between the PBO and the parties as the platforms were developed and finalized. Important questions remain about how each party availed itself of this service. The PBO's mandate is likely to evolve in future elections.

Building a platform is not like assembling a catalogue or an inventory of promises. The days of assembling a series of leaders' statements and policy commitments in an incoherent document have long since passed.[7] Care needs to be taken to determine the order and amount of space devoted to the various policy planks. Promises that appear the earliest in the platform tend to carry more weight, whereas those at the end of the document are less central to the party's desired ballot question. To be successful, the party has to align its priorities with those that the public trusts it the most to address. It is not possible to play only to the party's strengths in a platform. The document must cover the entire issue landscape. It cannot leave entire areas of public policy in abeyance, particularly when the public might trust its opponents more to handle them. If a party owns a stable of social policy issues but is weaker on the economy, it still needs to mention the latter. In most cases, the platform director mentions but downplays the issues that the public does not trust the party to handle. Downplaying occurs by giving certain issues less space and placing them near the end of the platform. On other occasions, the platform director might take a more proactive approach. It involves taking the public's side on issues traditionally unfavourable to the party. This strategy of inoculation counters charges that the party has a hidden agenda or is out of step with mainstream public opinion on the issues. The approach runs the risk, however, of alienating members of the party's base.

A platform director can do nothing without the support of a high-quality communications team. Once the issues are determined in consultation with the leader and chief of staff, the platform director works with communication experts to determine the right rhetoric and imagery to convey the party's position. This type of wordsmithing is crucial to the party's success. The style will differ if the party wishes to project itself as competent and steady, for instance, rather than visionary and path breaking.

Once the platform team develops the policy content, the scripting team reworks the document to ensure consistency with the campaign narrative and to improve its readability when drafting news releases and backgrounders. Some parties use online tools such as Flesch–Kincaid or Hemingway to ensure that their writing is simple and understandable. Various drafts are passed back and forth between the platform and scripting teams in yet another iterative process until a final version is released.

The platform team becomes the party's de facto policy shop over the course of the campaign. Indeed, the group is often called the policy team. As the platform items are announced, the platform director and the policy team become the authorities on the details of platform commitments. The platform director responds to questions from the communications team about the objectives, costs, and benefits of various promises. A significant amount of time can be spent ensuring that the media and public policy experts understand the policies and what is or is not included in a given promise. As well, the director leads research on opponents' platforms by fact-checking them or drawing contrasts. A significant amount of time is therefore devoted to comparing one's own promises with those of opponents and helping the communications team to draw those contrasts in the media. Quick responses are required, especially in a fast-paced news cycle.

Strategists continue to market-test the platform until weeks or days before its official release. This product refinement phase involves a combination of focus groups, surveys, and – more recently – crowd sourcing.[8] The Liberal Party entered the last domain in 2015 with its myPlatform app. The tool allowed users to browse different parts of the party's platform. They could also assemble their own collection of favourite policies. The party used these data to determine which of its planks was the most popular. This allowed the Liberals to refine their platform before its official release. Other parties use data analytics on their websites and social media feeds to collect similar data. All parties rely on feedback from candidates and party volunteers on what accessible voters are saying at the doorstep or on the street. However, once the leader has signed off on the platform following this product refinement stage, there is little room for input from outside the leader's inner circle.

One of the more artful decisions confronting the campaign team concerns the timing of the platform's release. The choice between the two approaches – releasing it early in the campaign or closer to election day – depends on many factors, including the party's competitive position and overall narrative. Releasing the platform before the writ is dropped, or in the opening days of the campaign, conveys a sense of confidence and openness. However, an early release can reduce the impact of announcing a new policy every day during the campaign, expose the party to prolonged scrutiny, and risk that other parties might adopt or steal ideas. Early release also means that the party cannot adapt to changing circumstances during the campaign.

Releasing the platform late holds those advantages. It allows the party to test the popularity and resonance of its core commitments. It can refine its style and tone before firming them up in the final document. Releasing the platform later in the campaign also allows the party to maximize its message potential. Issuing the document before or at the outset of the campaign removes the mystery, rhythm, and momentum of daily policy releases. However, it is risky to release a platform too late. Critics can allege that parties fail to provide voters with adequate time to scrutinize their policy commitments, especially if the platform is released after the leaders' debates. Such charges can feed into a narrative of the party having a hidden agenda. Nevertheless, there is little to no direct evidence of voters penalizing parties for late platform releases.

After a successful campaign, some platform directors play key roles in the transition to government. They might be appointed to senior roles in policy, such as in the Prime Minister's Office. This helps to ensure that campaign promises are properly translated into policy plans in the new government. In other cases, platform directors play no part in the transitional process and return to partisan duties or work outside the government.

Overcoming Obstacles

Commentators often remark on the similarities among political parties when it comes to their campaign pledges. The 2019 campaign demonstrated this, for the Conservatives and Liberals released policies that bore striking resemblances. A look at how the Conservative campaign responded to these developments provides an interesting window into the day-by-day activities of a policy director.

The Liberal and Conservative campaigns converged on parental benefits in particular. As first announced by the Conservative leader during his 2017 leadership campaign, the Conservatives pledged to make Employment Insurance (EI) benefits for maternity and parental leave tax free. This had been the subject of Andrew Scheer's private member's bill in 2018. At the time, the party announced that, if not enacted into law, the policy would become a plank of the Conservative platform in 2019. The Liberals had voted against the bill in the House of Commons. They joined public policy experts who criticized the complexity of a tax credit offering the possibility of deferral to future years.

It therefore came as a significant surprise to the Conservative campaign when, about a week into the election period, the Liberals themselves announced that they, too, would make EI maternity and parental benefits tax free. The Liberals promised a simpler mechanism so that parents could receive the benefits immediately. Instead of a tax credit, they pledged to remove EI benefits from the definition of taxable income. Thus began a fight about whose policy mechanism was better.

As early as 2017, the Conservative policy team had put together the finer points of how its proposed tax-free maternity and parental benefits would work. The team considered how the credit would benefit the poor versus the rich and how the timing of a pregnancy in the calendar year would change how it applied to parents. The policy developers built in a few key features to target it at those who needed it the most, make it fair for all parents, and inoculate it from criticism. Because the Conservatives had put a lot of thought into the details of the policy before the campaign, the platform team was ready to respond to the Liberals' surprise counterproposal.

That is not to say that the Conservatives expected it. Quite the contrary, Justin Trudeau's announcement of the Liberal policy surprised the Conservative war room. It quickly became clear that, by proposing tax-free parental benefits, the Liberals were proposing a similar outcome, but their policy mechanism was unknown initially. The Conservative platform team huddled together to figure out what the Liberals were proposing and to brainstorm a response. The team agreed that the Liberal policy benefited from having a simpler explanation of how parents would receive their tax benefits immediately. At the same time, the Conservative team realized that its policy provided larger proportional benefits to lower-income parents compared with higher-income parents. The platform team gave that information to the communications team, which then took the message to the media. The communication battle lasted a few days as the Conservatives attempted to explain the salient details of the EI system and the Income Tax Act.

This episode highlights the importance of several key roles of the platform director. First, it is crucial to develop a sound policy up front that can withstand the criticism of experts and alternative proposals from other parties. A policy that lacks a sound basis will leave a gap that will be filled by an opponent. Second, platform directors must understand the fundamental points of various government systems so that they can quickly grasp the differences among competing policy proposals from various parties. It is not sufficient to understand one's own policies; one has to be prepared to respond to counterproposals from one's opponents. Third, platform directors and their teams must work seamlessly with their parties' communications teams to package policies in easy-to-understand language and get the message out. A policy proposal can be the best idea in the world, but if it is too complicated, or if people fail to hear why it is great, then it will not secure votes.

In sum, platform building is a complex and challenging craft. Platforms are more than simply collections of policy proposals. Observers are right to dive deeply into the costs and implications of a party's plans for the future. However, as central campaign documents, platforms are rightly viewed as strategic tools. They symbolize the compromises required to unite disparate groups of supporters and stakeholders behind a common vision. They represent an attempt to market that vision to a broader pool of accessible voters. A party's success or failure is not solely attributable to the strength of its platform. Yet the challenges faced by platform directors during a campaign can provide good insight into the party's performance in other areas covered in this volume.

Notes

[1] Flanagan, *Harper's Team*, 154–55.
[2] See Esselment, "Designing Campaign Platforms"; and Flynn, "Rethinking Policy Capacity in Canada."
[3] Paré and Berger, "Political Marketing Canadian Style?"
[4] Esselment, "Designing Campaign Platforms."
[5] Miljan, *Public Policy in Canada*, 85.
[6] Walters, "Platforms as Political Process," 438.
[7] For a compendium of early federal party platforms, see Carrigan, *Canadian Party Platforms 1867–1968*. For platforms since then, see the Poltext Project website.
[8] Flynn, "Rethinking Policy Capacity in Canada."

Bibliography

Carrigan, D. Owen. *Canadian Party Platforms 1867–1968*. Urbana: University of Illinois Press, 1968.

Esselment, Anna. "Designing Campaign Platforms." In *The Informed Citizens' Guide to Elections: Electioneering Based on the Rule of Law,* edited by Gregory Tardi and Richard Balasko, 179–92. Toronto: Carswell, 2015.

Flanagan, Tom. *Harper's Team: Behind the Scenes in the Conservative Rise to Power.* 2nd ed. Montreal and Kingston: McGill-Queen's University Press, 2009.

Flynn, Greg. "Rethinking Policy Capacity in Canada: The Role of Parties and Election Platforms in Government Policy-Making." *Canadian Public Administration* 54, 2 (2011): 235–53.

Miljan, Lydia. *Public Policy in Canada: An Introduction.* 7th ed. Don Mills, ON: Oxford University Press, 2018.

Paré, Daniel J., and Flavia Berger. "Political Marketing Canadian Style? The Conservative Party and the 2006 Federal Election." *Canadian Journal of Communication* 33, 1 (2008): 39–63.

Poltext Project. Département de science politique, Université Laval. https://www.poltext.org/en/part-1-electronic-political-texts/electronic-manifestos-canadian-provinces.

Walters, Ronald W. "Platforms as Political Process." *PS: Political Science and Politics* 23, 3 (1990): 436–38.

9

National Campaign Directors

David McGrane and Anne McGrath

Most observers agree that the actions of national campaign directors are consequential for the success or failure of political parties in Canadian federal elections. Yet little is known about what they do on a day-to-day basis. In this chapter, we argue that campaign directors play four important roles in national campaigns. They make strategic decisions about the allocation of resources and how to react to changing campaign dynamics, constantly monitor the overall strengths and weaknesses of the party's campaign, consult with a wide array of important political actors inside and outside the party, and solve large and small problems that threaten the progress toward the party's electoral success.

La plupart des observateurs s'entendent pour dire que les actions des directeurs de campagne sont étroitement liées au succès ou à l'échec des partis politiques lors des élections fédérales canadiennes. Pourtant, on sait peu de choses sur leurs activités au quotidien. Ce chapitre soutient que ces acteurs centraux jouent quatre rôles déterminants dans les campagnes nationales. En plus de prendre des décisions stratégiques au sujet de l'affectation des ressources et de la façon de réagir à l'évolution de la dynamique de la campagne, ils surveillent constamment les forces et les faiblesses globales de la campagne du parti; ils consultent un large éventail d'acteurs politiques importants à l'intérieur et à l'extérieur de leur parti; et ils résolvent de petits et grands problèmes qui menacent la progression de celui-ci vers le succès électoral.

CAMPAIGN DIRECTORS APPEAR fleetingly in academic accounts of Canadian party history. With the exception of the work of Tom Flanagan, the University of Calgary political scientist who has managed a number of Conservative Party campaigns, the role of the campaign director is generally mentioned only in passing when political scientists discuss the successes and failures of political parties.[1] For example, in the chapters on the campaigns of federal political parties in the Carleton University–led series of studies, the names of national campaign directors usually appear with their dates of appointment and their backgrounds.[2] Little additional information is given.

Campaign directors themselves have authored much of what has been written about the role. They ascend to the apex of Canadian party politics only after years of working in a large number of roles for their respective party through which they acquire deep knowledge about their party's culture, develop extensive networks, and understand thoroughly the organization of national and local campaigns. Canadians who follow politics were probably first introduced to the existence of national campaign directors through media accounts of Senator Keith Davey – the Liberal Party's "rainmaker" – who managed the party's successful campaigns from the beginning of the 1960s to the middle of the 1980s. At the end of his career, Davey wrote a political memoir entitled *The Rainmaker: A Passion for Politics,* which describes the strategies of the campaigns of the Liberal Party during his time as national campaign director.[3] A few campaign directors from other political parties have followed suit.[4] A common element of these books is that they concentrate on the pivotal events of the campaigns in which these men were participants. The reader gets a good sense of what went on in the back rooms and how these operatives reacted to the twists and turns of the campaign. However, their books lack a basic description of the duties that national campaign directors are expected to perform and how those duties fit into the larger organizational structure of a national Canadian campaign.

In recent elections, campaign directors have been thrust either willingly or unwillingly into the media spotlight. They have gained a public media profile as large as that of cabinet ministers and much larger than that of most MPs. For instance, in the lead up to the 2015 federal election, several newspapers and magazines ran stories highlighting that the national campaign directors for all three contenders for the government were women (Jenni Byrne, Conservative; Katie Telford, Liberal; and Anne McGrath, New Democratic Party) and exploring their personalities and life stories. Consequently, Byrne was the subject of much media speculation that she had been demoted when she stopped travelling with Prime Minister Stephen Harper on his tour plane in the middle of the campaign and returned to work in the war room in Ottawa. The party denied the rumour.

Overall, in the Canadian public and media, and to a lesser extent in academia, there is a sense that national campaign directors play a formidable role in Canadian federal elections. They are judged as having a significant amount of political power. Furthermore, their actions are seen as consequential for the outcomes of elections. They are like the head coach of a hockey team in that they play the leading role in devising the party's overall strategy and plan to win the election. Therefore, they are often held accountable for just about everything that happens during the party's campaign. Just like a head coach at the end of the season, a national campaign director will be proclaimed a genius if the party wins the election but, along with the party leader, will take most of the blame if the party loses it.

Duties in an Election Campaign

To examine the activities of campaign directors, we draw on the experiences of Anne McGrath and Jennifer Howard, the national campaign directors, respectively, for the 2015 and 2019 federal campaigns of the New Democratic Party (NDP). The duties of campaign directors vary by party and election. Therefore, the description that follows is not intended to be definitive or to fit every case. Drawing on the recent experiences of these two operatives, we argue that national campaign directors have four primary duties: strategic decision making, consultation, monitoring, and problem solving.

As in life, in a campaign not all decisions are equally consequential. Every day during a campaign, volunteers, staff, and candidates make thousands of decisions with limited consequences. A campaign manager in a local riding will decide to send a candidate door knocking in one area of the riding and decide to ignore another area. Although such a decision could be important for the success of that local campaign, it is not a "make or break" decision for the party's national campaign. Campaign directors are frequently involved in making "strategic decisions."[5] Such decisions are complex and thus made at the top of the organization. They have great impacts on the performance of an organization because they shape its general direction, commit large amounts of resources, and are not easily reversible.

Within days of their appointment, campaign directors have to start making a variety of strategic decisions. One of the first and most important decisions involves human resources management. They need to build a team of senior staff, which necessitates hiring new people, keeping some people in their existing positions, and moving other people to new positions. They are particularly interested in hiring directors for each of major departments at party headquarters such as digital outreach, finance, and fundraising. Another task that needs to be undertaken immediately is the creation of a formal campaign strategy document that broadly outlines the main elements of the campaign. Once this document is in place, the campaign director collaborates with the directors of each department to create the campaign budget and formulate specific plans for areas such as platform development, communication with the media, organization within local ridings, candidate recruitment, and the leader's tour. Like the pieces of a large puzzle, the strategy document, the budget, and the plans in these specific areas set the general direction of the party's campaign long before voters start to cast their ballots. As the campaign approaches, these documents are constantly refined by the campaign director and their senior staff.

After the writ drops, strategic decision making continues to be an important duty of campaign managers. However, decisions have to be made more quickly, and their consequences are much more immediate. Every day of the official campaign period campaign directors are involved in making decisions about which events the leader will attend, how to react to unforeseen events making headlines, and when and how to criticize opponents as the dynamics of the campaign develop. Given the extensive planning that has gone into the campaign, strategic decisions about altering the allocation of resources and organizational structures are more difficult to carry out during the writ period, though small changes in the leader's schedule and some shifting of resources to ridings where the party is in trouble are possible. The stakes are high, and there is always risk and reward involved. The campaign director's strategic decisions about how to respond to the fast-moving and ever-changing campaign environment and about where to make last-minute organizational adjustments can have large impacts on the overall performance of the party on election day.

It would be a mischaracterization to suggest that campaign directors make these strategic decisions in isolation in their offices, far removed from others. Consultation is a process that campaign directors must engage in daily. They have to consult with and report to a plethora of people. In the pre-writ period, they interact daily with the directors of the departments of party headquarters and speak frequently to party staff spread throughout the country. Formal reporting occasions establish relationships of accountability between the campaign director and the people in the party who fight on the front lines of the elections. They have frequent meetings with the leader of the party and the leader's staff to discuss election preparations and possible election themes. They report to the party's executive and hold conference calls with candidates and local campaign managers.

Informal consultations are also part of their daily activities as they speak one on one or in small groups with the party president, senior MPs, representatives of citizens' groups and industrial associations, members of the media, and prominent pundits. These conversations allow a campaign director to get a sense of the feelings and thoughts of important party members and influential people in Canadian politics. The interactions are also opportunities to influence the thoughts and actions of these people. During the election, campaign directors generally continue to consult the same individuals and groups that they consulted prior to the election period. The difference is that, because of time constraints and events happening quickly, they can consult a much smaller group of people before acting. Ultimately, efforts to consult as widely as possible before making decisions can help the campaign director to make the best decision, whether a small decision with short-term consequences or a strategic decision that might prove to be decisive for the outcome of the campaign.

As mentioned, campaign directors have directors working under their supervision who are responsible for specific elements of the campaign (e.g., digital outreach or managing the media). Although these staff concentrate exclusively on their responsibilities, the campaign director must constantly monitor all areas of the campaign to discern where strengths and weaknesses are emerging. In short, a campaign director always tries to get a sense of the big picture.

In the pre-election period, the day begins with both traditional media and social media scans to see which issues are emerging within Canadian politics and whether there is any immediate role for party headquarters to play. Next the campaign director looks at the daily reports coming in from the various departments that track the party's fundraising, organization, spending, and communication. These reports give an overall sense of the party's performance in these areas. The information indicates how close these departments are to meeting the goals and internal deadlines set out in the strategy documents of the campaign. These reports are crucial for understanding the party's overall performance and the areas where the campaign director needs to intervene to improve it. The rest of the day is filled with face-to-face meetings and conference calls with a variety of people from party staff to vendors to stakeholders. The slate of people scheduled for each day changes, but the goal of all the meetings is always to monitor the party's election readiness – though a campaign director never thinks that the party is 100 percent ready for an election or that there is nothing more that can be done.

Once the writ is dropped, monitoring duties become even more important. If campaign directors are stationed in Ottawa and not on the leaders' tours, then they arrive at party headquarters early to prepare for the day. Sometime before 9 a.m., they hold a daily strategy meeting with their staff to monitor all of the key metrics of the campaign (e.g., polling, fundraising, canvassing) and to review the "message of the day" that war room staff have formulated. The directors of each department are then given instructions to follow at the end of that meeting. With the morning strategizing done, the rest of the campaign director's day and evening consists of meetings to get updates on particular aspects of the campaign. Campaign directors make decisions about what direction to take in these areas and the planning required in preparation for the next day of the campaign. Between these meetings, they are present and visible outside their offices as they check with their senior staff to see how they are progressing on instructions given to them at the beginning of the day. They are also in communication with personnel on the leader's plane. They speak with staff on the plane and possibly the leader at least twice a day. Their day ends after the leader's last event, the time of which varies depending on the time zone, but normally it is about 9 p.m. After a final round of emails and phone calls once back at home, campaign directors hopefully will be in bed about 11 p.m. They cope with the sleep deprivation by the adrenalin that fuels their work in a hectic, stressful environment.

Campaign directors' monitoring role sets up their final important duty: problem solving. The general rule both before and after the writ of election is dropped is that areas of the campaign running smoothly and meeting expectations get less attention from campaign directors. For example, if their daily monitoring indicates that candidate recruitment is running ahead of schedule, then they can turn their attention to other areas of the campaign that might be struggling. Another rule is that, the more difficult the problem, the higher the likelihood that campaign directors will be called on to deal with it. Some of the problems brought to their attention are challenging but can be dealt with relatively quickly and easily. For instance, if candidates in a certain region are struggling to get media attention, then campaign directors will instruct the director of communications to organize media training for them. However, the campaign director does not have the time to solve every problem that arises during a campaign. They have to trust their senior staff to figure out which problems do not require their attention and which problems do.

Occasionally, a crisis explodes and will require all of the campaign director's immediate attention. The emergence of such a serious problem usually necessitates quick strategic decision making that can be decisive for the election results. For instance, a gaffe by the leader or an issue that divides the party can throw the entire campaign off message and cause polling numbers to plunge. In these types of situations, almost all of the central resources of the campaign are consumed with dealing with it, and the campaign director is called on to take a leadership role in coordinating all parts of the campaign to get it back on track as soon as possible. It is their job to keep everyone focused, unified, and working together to solve the problem at hand.

Overcoming Obstacles

Over the course of one evening, all four duties of the NDP's campaign director in 2019 came into play: monitoring, consultation, problem solving, and strategic decision making. With little time to reflect, she had to act quickly concerning an issue that turned out to be decisive for the success of the party's campaign.

As was her duty, the campaign director was monitoring a town hall meeting that NDP leader Jagmeet Singh was holding in a racially diverse riding in Toronto. As he was speaking, the campaign director was made aware that a photo of Justin Trudeau in blackface had surfaced and that the news story was going viral on social media. Singh had not seen the photo, nor had he been briefed on what to say about it. As at every town hall meeting during the campaign, the NDP leader was scheduled to take questions from the media after he had responded to questions from the public. The NDP staff on the leader's tour immediately called the campaign director to consult with her on how to solve this problem. With the clock ticking down before the leader started to take questions, the campaign director was faced with a strategic decision. Would it be best to pull the leader awkwardly off the stage before he was asked a question about the blackface photo so that he could be briefed? Or would it be better to allow him to speak from the heart and get his response out into the public realm as soon as possible? Considering that Singh was the first person from a racialized minority background to lead a major Canadian political party and the only non-white party leader in the campaign, everyone in the country would be interested in his reaction. Indeed, it would instantly become one of the top new stories of the day.

In consultation with the NDP staff on the leader's tour, the campaign director decided to let the event continue as planned. Once the decision was made, she thought to herself: "Am I really doing the best thing for my leader?" However, she had often talked with him about his personal experiences with racism that he had faced growing up in Canada. She therefore had confidence that he could handle the impromptu situation.

A reporter put a question to Singh about the photo and said that the Liberal campaign had confirmed its authenticity. The NDP leader stopped to think. He responded that he had not seen the photo but that it was "insulting" and "troubling" and that the prime minister would have to answer for it. He then spoke about how the act of dressing in blackface makes a mockery of racialized minorities. The room of supporters, many of whom had often experienced racism themselves, erupted in applause. Given these difficult circumstances, Singh had performed admirably, and many news media, pundits, and citizens began to praise his answer on social media.

The NDP campaign director was then informed that the prime minister would hold a press conference on the blackface photo that evening. Another challenge immediately emerged: Should the NDP leader address the issue that night now that he had seen the photo, or should he wait to do so until the next day? Over the phone, the campaign director held a meeting with Singh and staff on their bus as it travelled to a hotel in Mississauga, where an event was scheduled for the next day. Singh had already received a large number of messages and phone calls from racialized people that he knew personally telling him about how the blackface photo was bringing back painful memories of discrimination and bullying. After consultation among the campaign director, the leader, and his staff, the strategic decision was made to have Singh address the media that evening soon after Trudeau had finished speaking. There were few racialized minority voices commenting in the media on the story, and Singh felt a responsibility to racialized minorities in Canada to speak up as soon as possible. Although there could be a general conversation on what the leader would say, there would be no time to develop a precise message, write comprehensive speaking notes, or rehearse lines.

Without an appropriate backdrop for television, Jagmeet Singh held a hastily organized press conference in a poorly lit hotel room about one hour after Justin Trudeau spoke. The campaign director held her breath because she had no idea exactly what Singh would say. It was the NDP leader speaking directly to Canadians on a major issue of the campaign with almost no preparation. It was a risky proposition. Fortunately, Singh effectively communicated that he wanted to focus not on Trudeau's actions but on the people who were hurt by them. Talking to young racialized minorities, he said "You might feel like giving up on Canada. You might feel like giving up on yourselves. I want you to know that you have value. You have worth. And you are loved. And I don't want you to give up on Canada, and please don't give up on yourselves."[6] The campaign director considered Singh's reaction to the blackface photo his finest moment in the campaign. His popularity in internal polling and public domain polling began to rise after his address.

These events offer an excellent example of how a campaign director must monitor, consult, problem-solve, and make strategic decisions – sometimes all within a few hours. Technology can force a campaign to pivot quickly amid fast-moving circumstances. There is no time to think through a response when an immediate reaction is required. In the days of Keith Davey and other campaign directors of yesteryear, political operatives carefully planned their media interactions and then waited to see the headlines on the evening news or in the morning newspaper. In today's hybrid and fast-paced media system, a party leader and senior staff receive instant responses to what is happening on the campaign trail. They rapidly exchange information by phone and take cues from social media reactions. Pressure grows to address the press without sufficient preparation. It is a lesson that communication technologies can shape campaign decision making. As politics speeds up, campaign directors will be compelled to harness all of their expertise as they inject a measure of strategic calm into hectic, high-stakes situations.

Notes

1   Flanagan, *Harper's Team;* Flanagan, *Winning Power;* Jeffrey, *Divided Loyalties,* 24–28; McGrane, *The New NDP,* 47–60; Marland, *Brand Command,* 147–48.
2   See Pammett and Doran, *The Canadian Federal Election of 2015,* 30, 63, 86.
3   Davey, *The Rainmaker.*
4   Flanagan, *Harper's Team;* Flanagan, *Winning Power;* Lavigne, *Building the Orange Wave;* Laschinger, *Leaders and Lesser Mortals;* Laschinger, *Campaign Confessions.*

5 Wilson, "Strategic Decision Making."
6 Quoted in Zimonjic, "Trudeau Says He Is 'Deeply Sorry.'"

Bibliography

Davey, Keith. *The Rainmaker: A Passion for Politics*. Toronto: Stoddart, 1986.
Flanagan, Tom. *Harper's Team: Behind the Scenes in the Conservative Rise to Power*. 2nd ed. Montreal and Kingston: McGill-Queen's University Press, 2009.
–. *Winning Power: Canadian Campaigning in the 21st Century*. Montreal and Kingston: McGill-Queen's University Press, 2014.
Jeffrey, Brooke. *Divided Loyalties: The Liberal Party of Canada, 1984–2008*. Toronto: University of Toronto Press, 2010.
Laschinger, John. *Campaign Confessions: Tales from the War Rooms of Politics*. Toronto: Dundurn Press, 2016.
–. *Leaders and Lesser Mortals: Backroom Politics in Canada*. Toronto: Key Porter Books, 1992.
Lavigne, Brad. *Building the Orange Wave*. Madeira Park, BC: Douglas and McIntyre, 2013.
Marland, Alex. *Brand Command: Canadian Politics in the Age of Message Control*. Vancouver: UBC Press, 2016.
McGrane, David. *The New NDP: Moderation, Modernization, and Political Marketing*. Vancouver: UBC Press, 2019.
Pammett, Jon H., and Christopher Dornan, eds. *The Canadian Federal Election of 2015*. Toronto: Dundurn Press, 2016.
Wilson, David. "Strategic Decision Making." In *Wiley Encyclopedia of Management*. Vol. 12. https://doi.org/10.1002/9781118785317.weom120115.
Zimonjic, Peter. "Trudeau Says He Is 'Deeply Sorry' He Appeared in Brownface at School Gala in 2001." CBC News, 18 September 2019. https://www.cbc.ca/news/politics/trudeau-brownface-arabian-nights-1.5289165.

10

National Campaign Director of Communications

Stéphanie Yates and John Chenery

A national campaign's director of communications is responsible for developing the communication strategy following the party's brand. This strategy serves as the backbone to devise a slogan, determine key messages, orient media reach, and work out the campaign calendar, in collaboration with the senior campaign management team. During the campaign, the director of communications oversees all communication activities – providing communication assets for candidates and the media at every tour stop – and works closely with local campaigns. The director is also part of daily meetings with the rapid response team to determine the daily policy message as well as how to respond to problematic issues or attacks. Moreover, the director collaborates with the digital manager to reach out to the party's supporters through social media platforms. Yet even the most carefully crafted communication strategy cannot always overcome structural components that influence an election outcome, such as strategic voting.

Le directeur des communications d'une campagne nationale est chargé d'élaborer la stratégie de communication en fonction de l'image de marque du parti. Cette stratégie sert d'assise à la conception d'un slogan, à la détermination des messages clefs, à l'orientation des relations médias et à la préparation du calendrier électoral, en collaboration avec l'équipe de la haute direction de la campagne. Pendant la campagne, le travail consiste à superviser toutes les activités de communication, à fournir des ressources de communication aux candidats et aux médias à chaque étape de la tournée, et à travailler en étroite collaboration avec les campagnes locales. Le directeur des communications participe également aux réunions quotidiennes avec l'équipe d'intervention rapide pour déterminer les messages politiques quotidiens et la façon de réagir aux problèmes ou aux attaques. De plus, il ou elle collabore avec le directeur de la campagne numérique pour rejoindre les partisans du parti par l'entremise d'outils web et des médias sociaux. Toutefois, même la stratégie de communication la plus sophistiquée peut ne pas permettre de surmonter des facteurs structuraux qui influencent le résultat électoral, comme le vote stratégique.

THE ROLE OF A PARTY'S director of communications is to promote and protect the party brand. The individual bearing this title must ensure that the vision, mission, and policies of a party align with its corporate identity and brand, which itself "evokes emotional connections to specific images and stimulates loyalty among target audiences."[1] To do so, the director of communications must frame the content of the electoral platform, ensuring that campaign commitments are attractive and understandable, while still faithfully reflecting the party's brand image and, more generally, expressing the world views commonly associated with this political body.[2]

More specifically, the director of communications is responsible for embedding and anchoring election commitments – and the vision thereby offered by a party – in an overarching communication strategy for a national political campaign. This strategy will serve as the backbone to devise a slogan and determine key messages, based on the general theme of the campaign. Various iterations of the key messages are then created to cater to different segments of the electorate.[3] With this communication strategy, the director of communications targets voters as well as secondary audiences.[4] Party members, for instance, must be mobilized and invested in the campaign: critical efforts will thus pinpoint their queries and grievances. This remains true even if technological practices have become paramount in fundraising.[5]

The director of communications starts to work on drafting the communication strategy a few months before the election, for instance in the spring for a fall election. The strategy takes into account lessons learned during the previous campaign, information gathered during the political term, as well as the themes likely to take centre stage during the upcoming campaign. The process can repeat itself many times as circumstances evolve. The final decision on the campaign slogan generally happens one or two months before the launch of the campaign, with key messages following. At this stage, online surveys or focus groups are usually conducted to test different slogan ideas. Key messages are developed internally in conjunction with key stakeholders who provide valuable input at every step: the leader, deputy leaders, campaign working group, members of the cabinet, and senior staff. The campaign working group is composed of the campaign manager, deputy campaign managers, director of communications, executive director, and policy director.

One of the fundamental goals of the communication strategy is media reach, which first includes advertising through traditional media (i.e., television, radio, print, "out-of-home" displays such as billboards and transit ads). In conjunction with a media placement agency, the director of communications collaborates with the national campaign manager and other senior members of the campaign team to plan media buys, often focusing on districts where the party has strong chances to achieve political gains, thus optimizing spending. Social media and other digital advertising platforms are also firmly entrenched in election campaign strategies.[6] However, in 2019, the decision by Google to exclude political advertising from its platforms during the official campaign period forced parties to re-evaluate their digital advertising strategies, to the point of reinvesting resources in traditional media. Facebook's advertising rules, which stipulate that partisan ads must go through an approval process before being published, is also a time-sensitive factor. Advertising strategies on that social media platform need to be planned earlier on, and iterations aimed at reacting quickly to events or a party's attacks can no longer be done instantaneously.

As the start of the campaign approaches, the team that the director of communications oversees grows significantly with the hiring of short-term contract personnel to fulfill various functions, including graphic design, video editing, social media content, writing, and editing. At all times, the director of communications works closely with the senior campaign management team (i.e., the national campaign manager and deputy managers). With the leader's input, the senior campaign team devises the campaign calendar. This essential campaign component includes the timing and location of the campaign launch, platform launch, and announcements of various policies that it contains – these elements are broken down into a weekly time frame. In preparation for the campaign, the director of communications determines the outreach strategy and main talking points related to the different announcements. The specific material that will accompany each campaign announcement (e.g., one-pager, fact sheet, press release) is finalized as the campaign unfolds, allowing for adjustments when needed. Several external factors are considered when developing the campaign calendar, particularly the dates and locations of the televised leaders' debates. Moreover, scheduling takes into account the specific interests of voters in each electoral district, media availability, and the party leader's itinerary, while also remaining flexible to handle unforeseen events and seize opportunities as campaigning evolves.

Duties in an Election Campaign

As is the case with most of the positions involved in political campaigns, the pace of work of a national campaign's director of communications drastically accelerates once the campaign is officially launched. The job entails overseeing all communication activities and working closely with other teams – mobilizing squad, leader's tour team, policy group – from the beginning of the campaign to election day. Communication assets for candidates and the media must be ready and available at every tour stop. The director of communications watches the volume and tone of media coverage as it happens through a proprietary media monitoring and distribution platform. The director ensures that advertising deadlines are met and that the multi-platform ad campaign stays on track.

Traditionally, a director of communications works from the party headquarters for most of the national campaign, collaborating closely with the team that accompanies the leader on tour. Indeed, the person ensuring the leader's liaison with the media also liaises with headquarters to gather strategic feedback on the campaign. This allows the director of communications to collect insights and adapt the key messages accordingly.

Whereas the overall election communication strategy is developed and finalized some time in advance of the campaign, a daily policy message – also known as a script message – is determined for every campaign day. The national campaign manager and the director of communications generally agree on this message the day before, depending on the schedule of campaign events and announcements. Delivering this message to the national campaign team and local campaign teams by 7:30 a.m. Central Time is crucial. Doing so allows candidates in eastern Canada to prepare their messages for the day.

That being said, and despite the strategy planned beforehand, a director of communications and the team must be ready to adapt quickly to the news cycle. The big challenge is to maintain focus and stay on message while working with campaign management and the rapid response team – that is, the war room – to deal with negative storylines generated by the flood of "oppo," research supplied to the media by opposing parties and their surrogates.[7] To this end, the director of communications takes part in daily meetings with the rapid response team. The director participates in early morning discussions about the day's news cycle to determine how to respond to problematic issues, mostly involving attacks by other parties or their affiliates.

These attacks can take many different forms, from offensive or embarrassing episodes in the lives of party leaders to inappropriate social media content posted by otherwise unknown candidates. All political parties struggle to varying degrees with the challenge of vetting their election candidates. Their opponents go to great lengths to identify and capitalize on any misstep. Adversaries do so because critiquing an opponent's weaknesses serves several objectives: generating negative media coverage of the opposing party, potentially eroding public support for it, and forcing the opposing leader and campaign team to expend precious time and effort responding to the exposé. Research shows that negativity in political campaigns can indeed increase voter turnout, depending on timing and circumstances.[8] In every instance, the team must determine whether and how the party should comment or refrain from doing so, knowing that in some cases commenting on or responding to an attack can fan the flames. Similar discussions occur about attacks against a party's policies – whether stated directly, through social media, or as part of a rival party's advertising strategy.

Per the team's decisions and leader's input, the director of communications works with the rapid response team to craft the message: that is, the line that the party will take on any given issue. Ideally, the national campaign manager makes the final decision on a response, even if this level of approval is not always reachable given the fast pace of a campaign's decision-making process. In urgent situations, there is no time to follow the chain of command, and the highest available person in the campaign hierarchy can be asked to make an immediate decision.[9] It is up to the director of communications to ensure that the response is communicated externally, via the media, and internally to staff, candidates, and their campaign teams by sending them timely information and talking points to help them deal with local inquiries. Through all of this, the communications team must make every effort to ensure that these frustrating episodes do not prevent them from delivering on the objectives of the campaign communication strategy.

Another task of the director of communications during the campaign is to collaborate with the digital manager to reach out to the party's supporters through social media platforms. With the intention of ensuring consistency across the national campaign initiatives, the director will oversee the posting calendar, tactics, monitoring process, and stakes involved. Although the digital manager is given a free hand to create social media graphics and messages related to context and platform, all content is subject to approval by the national campaign manager before being posted online. Digital platforms offer a dynamic range of messaging options, from posts that simply reinforce the daily platform announcement or key message to short videos (either custom made or shared from other sources) to various memes. The digital manager routinely shares and retweets content from the social media feeds of the leader and other supportive individuals and organizations.

Finally, the director of communications works with local campaigns to ensure that their activities are consistent with the national campaign and party brand. The director works closely with candidates, local campaign directors, and campaign communication leads, sharing the latest updates on the national campaign and providing them with tools and the best advice to increase their efficiency, for instance proposing design templates for signs and brochures and offering advice on local advertising and media outreach. The director also prepares a series of visual assets designed for digital media tactics, along with guidelines on what to post, when, and how often. Instructions are provided on how to respond to and when to ignore online trolls or unfavourable comments. Yet, for the most part, the day-to-day management of local campaigns and digital media is in the hands of local teams – aside from key ridings, where the national communications team is more deeply involved in matters of campaign materials, messages, and strategies.

Overcoming Obstacles

For the director of communications, the overall tone of the election campaign can present both opportunities and obstacles. In the campaign of 2019, the famous misquotation of former Prime Minister Kim Campbell – "an election is no time to discuss serious issues" – could have been the shared slogan of the main parties.[10] Many veteran political commentators said that it was among the nastiest campaigns in memory and bemoaned the fact that the relentless attacks and counterattacks left little room for anything else, including serious discussion on issues and policies. The parties blamed each other, but there was plenty of blame to go around.

The following anecdote illustrates the type of climate that prevailed. An acclaimed documentary about the 1992 Clinton campaign's communications team has made "the war room" shorthand for the teams that work long into the night at party headquarters trying to stay one step ahead of, or at least trying not to get run over by, the news cycle. Mostly, these operatives are anonymous, but in the 2019 campaign at least one party decided that its war room warriors needed to stand out. From various parts of downtown Ottawa came reports of young men and women walking the streets wearing jackets emblazoned with the Conservative Party logo and underneath the words *War Room* – a term that applies, for this party, to the whole national campaign office. Working on an election campaign can feel a lot like going through a war. In 2019, some of the campaign soldiers had a uniform.

In this context and in common with the other parties, the Green Party had to deal with a number of different controversies, primarily the product of meticulous opposition research on its candidates' social media histories going back a decade or more. A few candidates withdrew from the election and were replaced by the party, but most of them apologized, disavowed past positions, and resumed campaigning. As Churchill himself put it, "politics are almost as exciting as war and quite as dangerous. In war you can only be killed once, but in politics many times."[11] This complicated game of "gotcha" involved many players – the party workers who unearthed the damaging material, the media that ran with it, the social media amplifiers who made sure that it reached the widest possible audience, and the unfortunate targets, most of whom suddenly found themselves in the eye of a storm created by words that they had typed years ago and forgotten. For the Green Party, the severity and frequency of the attacks were new terrain. They were somewhat expected given that the Greens went into the campaign with their best-ever poll numbers, record fundraising, strong membership growth, and a general sense that a breakthrough was in the offing.

As frustrating and distracting as these attacks were, they were not the Green Party's biggest communication challenge. That came, as it does in every election cycle, during the last weeks of the campaign as the party struggled to prevent its support from bleeding away to strategic voting. Canada's first-past-the-post electoral system rewards parties that can convince voters to choose them as the lesser of two or more evils. It was predictable, therefore, that Justin Trudeau would use the last week of the campaign to warn voters repeatedly about the consequences of not voting Liberal: a Conservative majority government. NDP canvassers used the same message on doorsteps to move Green Party votes to their side.

In 2019, it looked as if the Greens might weather the storm. The party stressed that a citizen's vote was no less than a citizen's voice; thus, it was paramount to vote according to individual will and beliefs. The party also insisted on the idea that it could hold the balance of power in a minority government.

Through the final week of the campaign, the time when Green support historically starts to slide, daily poll numbers were holding steady at just under 10 percent. The bad news came in the last poll before election day – 6.5 percent. In light of these results, it appears that the work of a national campaign director of communications remains at the mercy of such elements. Even the most carefully crafted communication strategy cannot always overcome structural components that influence an election outcome.

In conclusion, even if the role of the director of communications during a national campaign might be more encompassing in a party with a small organization, such as the Green Party, one can draw useful general insights into the position. First, the chapter has highlighted the multiple tasks overseen by a director of communications and the collaborative relationships that individual has with other members of the national campaign team. Second, it has provided a detailed account of a campaign communication strategy's timeline. And third, it has enlightened the process allowing the determination of the script message of the day and a party's reaction to the news cycle.

Notes

[1] Burton and Shea, *Campaign Craft;* Marland, *Brand Command,* 36.
[2] Arbour, "Issue Frame Ownership."

3   Baines, "Political Public Relations and Election Campaigning."
4   Ibid.
5   Johnson, *Campaigning in the Twenty-First Century.*
6   Lilleker, Tenscher, and Štětka, "Towards Hypermedia Campaigning?"
7   On the war room, see Kinsella, *The War Room;* on oppo, see Pitney, *The Art of Political Warfare.*
8   Krupnikov, "How Negativity Can Increase and Decrease Voter Turnout."
9   Maarek, *Campaign Communication and Political Marketing,* 186.
10   Ferreira, "'An Election Is No Time to Discuss Serious Issues.'"
11   Quoted in Hayward, *Churchill on Leadership,* 29.

Bibliography

Arbour, Brian. "Issue Frame Ownership: The Partisan Roots of Campaign Rhetoric." *Political Communication* 31 (2014): 604–27.

Baines, Paul. "Political Public Relations and Election Campaigning." In *Political Public Relations: Principles and Applications,* edited by Jesper Strömbäck and Spiro Kiousis, 115–37. New York: Routledge, 2011.

Burton, Michael J., and Daniel M. Shea. *Campaign Craft: The Strategies, Tactics, and Art of Political Campaign Management,* 4th ed. Santa Barbara, CA: Praeger, 2010.

Ferreira, Victor. "'An Election Is No Time to Discuss Serious Issues': Five Comments that Sank Canadian Political Campaigns." *National Post,* 12 August 2015. https://nationalpost.com/news/politics/an-election-is-no -time-to-discuss-serious-issues-five-comments-that-sank-canadian -politicians-during-elections.

Hayward, Steven F. *Churchill on Leadership.* Rocklin, CA: Forum/Prima, 1997.

Johnson, Dennis W. *Campaigning in the Twenty-First Century: A Whole New Ballgame?* New York: Routledge, 2010.

Kinsella, Warren. *The War Room: Political Strategies for Business, NGOs, and Anyone Who Wants to Win.* Toronto: Dundurn Press, 2007.

Krupnikov, Yanna. "How Negativity Can Increase and Decrease Voter Turnout: The Effect of Timing." *Political Communication* 31, 3 (2014): 446–66.

Lilleker, Darren G., Jens Tenscher, and Václav Štětka. "Towards Hyper-media Campaigning? Perceptions of New Media's Importance for Campaigning by Party Strategists in Comparative Perspective." *Information, Communication and Society* 18, 7 (2015): 747–65.

Maarek, Philippe J. *Campaign Communication and Political Marketing.* Chichester, UK: Wiley-Blackwell, 2011.

Marland, Alex. *Brand Command: Canadian Politics and Democracy in the Age of Message Control.* Vancouver: UBC Press, 2016.

Pitney, John J. *The Art of Political Warfare.* Norman: University of Oklahoma Press, 2000.

11

Senior Adviser to the Leader on Tour

Mireille Lalancette with Marie Della Mattia

In this chapter, we explore the role of the senior adviser to the leader – also called the political lead – in image management during the campaign. Political leads need to have experience in all aspects of campaigning: strategy, polling, targeting and messaging, fundraising, media relations, and social media. They are constantly thinking about the impact of every word and action on the candidate's image and voters' perceptions. Advisers play an important role in communication strategies of the leader before, during, and after the campaign. They prepare the leader for the long journey of a political campaign and participate in strategic choices that will help the leader to look her or his best among the public and in the media eye.

Ce chapitre explore le rôle du conseiller principal en gestion de l'image auprès du chef pendant la campagne. Ces conseillers, qui accompagnent les leaders au quotidien sur leurs tournées, doivent avoir de l'expérience dans tous les aspects de la campagne: stratégie, sondages, ciblage des message, collecte de fonds, relations avec les médias traditionnels et numériques. Ils réfléchissent constamment à l'impact que peut avoir chaque mot, chaque action sur l'image du candidat et sur la perception des électeurs. Les conseillers principaux jouent un rôle important dans les stratégies de communication du chef avant, pendant et après la campagne. Ils préparent le chef au long cheminement d'une campagne politique et ils contribuent aux choix stratégiques qui aideront le leader de parti à se présenter sous son meilleur jour devant le public et les médias.

IN MOVIES ABOUT political campaigning, we often see a character who whispers in a politician's ear, providing strategic advice about what to say to the media and/or making decisions about what information to conceal from the leader. Who are these skilled strategists? In Canadian politics, special advisers to leaders are often called political leads and go on tour with the leaders. They play a key role in a political campaign.

The political lead is the last voice in the leader's head before events and media scrums while on tour. The lead reports to the campaign director and travels with the leader at all times, providing constant feedback to keep the leader focused and on point. Image management takes up a substantial part of the lead's time. The job is all about making sure the leader successfully implements the campaign strategy while on tour. Since image encompasses every public utterance, movement, and interaction, a political adviser must evaluate choices about how to present the politician to voters and the media.

Image management requires strategic mobilization of symbolic devices – visual and verbal – to provide shorthand cues to voters. Branding, marketing, public relations, advertising techniques, and polling are then used to sell the candidate.[1] Research shows that citizens look for specific leadership qualities when electing a politician for office. Image and personality traits are significant determinants of vote choice.[2] During and between election campaigns, every aspect of a leader's life is leveraged to manage image, including style, character, public life, and private life.[3] Voters assess leadership abilities by looking for qualities such as honesty, intelligence, friendliness, sincerity, responsiveness, and trustworthiness.[4] Political advisers play a crucial role in helping the leader to project these qualities.

Political advisers need to have experience in all aspects of campaigning: strategy; research/polling; audience and targeting; messaging; and tactics such as voter contact, fundraising, media relations, and social media. They constantly consider a number of questions. Is our message coming through in our leader's images and words? What are audiences hearing from us, and is it resonating? What accomplishes our goals of defining ourselves and defining our opponents? What helps us to define what the election is about? They use the answers to these questions to give continuous feedback to the leader.

What does it take to become a political lead? The campaign director in consultation with the leader usually selects the political lead well before the writ of election is issued. Political advisers need plenty of experience to get the job. It is among the most senior roles of a campaign. Years of experience managing people and understanding the psychology of leadership are key elements of a political lead's acumen. That experience might include working for years as a local campaign organizer, as a staffer to elected politicians, as a communication or advertising person, and/or as a staffer for leaders on their campaign buses. Studying politics in university does not specifically prepare someone for this job, but academic studies do help political leads to acquire the tools to analyze what makes politicians successful. They can also develop the necessary skills by examining past Canadian and American campaigns to find examples of what works and why. Those curious about voters' desires and concerns will be able to connect better with them and understand how they see the choices that governments make. Drawing on that experience helps the political adviser to earn the trust of the leader and campaign director.

Political advisers know what drives successful communications. They are good at breaking down politics and campaign strategies and explaining how things work. Their knowledge enables other personnel to build their own messages more successfully and achieve their communication goals. Like a tennis coach getting a player ready for a match, political advisers often participate in preparations for special events such as debates. They perform in the shadow of the politician, working behind the scenes so that the leader can shine in the limelight.

It is a powerful position in terms of having influence on the leader's headspace and performance. Being a political adviser is not about knowing the most about policy or breaking news; the job is more about relationship and confidence. Political leads must understand the leader's mindset and have the discernment to know the right time to talk about each subject. They must embody the campaign message since they are the liaison among the war room, the leader's tour, and the leader. Advisers accompanying the leader's tour relentlessly ensure that the leader is delivering the campaign message to reporters and voters every day. They might also talk to reporters in the background. In short, they serve primarily as the leader's guide through the strategic training necessary to be the best and win the competition.

Duties in an Election Campaign

When whispering in the leader's ear, political leads are always thinking about managing impressions and the leader's "presentation of self."[5] The overall goal of political image making is to generate, maintain, sharpen, and strengthen favourable perceptions among the public in order to affect their personal political attitudes and, by extension, decision making in strategic ways.[6] This special adviser is responsible for all aspects of the leader's performance. A political adviser's duties during an election campaign can be presented on a timeline with three major stages: before, during, and after the campaign.

Before the campaign, the political adviser must provide the leader with the confidence that each day will go as planned so that there will be no second-guessing the decision-making process. Political advisers and the rest of the strategy team work together to manage impressions and craft a strong message about the strengths of their leader. Image management helps to generate confidence and highlight the leader's best features. A good guideline is that "you can't create something if there is nothing underneath." A political lead works to polish the leader's brand during the campaign. Politicians have their own styles. Each has a unique background, communication skill, and motivation for being in politics. The political adviser must factor in this information when planning the leader's tour and contemplating how to highlight the leader's strengths.

The leader's attributes are thoroughly studied by the campaign team before the campaign begins. In focus groups up to two hours long, citizens are invited to say what they think about the leader. This information offers a distilled look at the public's view of what the leader has to offer. It generates impressions of the perceived strengths and weaknesses of both the leader and opponents. Current advice suggests that leaders lean into what makes them different. The political adviser must keep the contrasts in mind when presenting the leader and trying to shift citizens' perceptions. During this crucial period, the adviser and the campaign team find a strategy for using the leader's strengths to shape the story of the campaign. The adviser tries to make both the team and the media see the election in a certain way, within a frame that works for them. This strategy is in line with the adoption of political marketing tactics in recent campaigns in order to modernize the party's brand.[7]

The activities intensify after the writ is dropped. The political lead supervises and coaches the leader to be at their best. The lead is responsible for the leader's preparation and performance and can influence what the politician wears; how the politician comes off the bus; what the politician says and does at events, interviews, and scrums; and how the politician interacts with citizens and the media while on tour. During the campaign, the political adviser works with the other members of the team to prepare the leader and think through questions: What is the message? How are we defining the choice for voters? Are we connecting with people on what they care about? Are we supporting the leader to be authentic and true to that individual's values, not scripted? Political advisers play a crucial role in "shaping and recalibrating campaign messages, selecting campaign tour stops, making sure their candidates put their best foot forward – and sometimes cleaning up when they put out the wrong foot."[8] On the campaign trail, every detail is considered, from the politician's words in speeches to the locations visited or the features of the politician's private life shown to the public.

Politicians, along with their advisers, devote time, money, and energy to present themselves in the best possible light. Collectively, they try to offer voters an appealing package without revealing how it was crafted strategically.

When planning events, the political lead asks certain questions repeatedly: What is the best way to tell our story? Whom is the leader with? What issues are we profiling? What places should we visit? How do we showcase our strengths? The three modes of persuasion – ethos, logos, and pathos – are continuously appraised and, if necessary, reoriented to offer an engaging discourse and image to voters.[9] The ethos is tied to the character and credibility of the political actor. The logos relates to policy and reliability in speeches. And the pathos is connected to the ability to foster emotions and a certain frame of mind to connect with voters.

A political lead's job is complex. It entails making decisions in attempts to convince voters to elect the party leader. Filtering information to let leaders operate at their best, the lead continually asks: "Do they need to know this, or would sharing the information distract the leader from focusing on performing?" The adviser keeps the chaos of campaigning out of the leader's thoughts, removing the leader from the campaign's daily vicissitudes. Leaders rely on their teams to deal with both small and big matters, so they do not need to be concerned with every aspect of the campaign along the way, such as the discovery that a candidate posted something controversial on social media. The job of the senior political adviser is to maintain focus and simplicity. This is challenging even in our daily lives – imagine what it is like during an election in which attacks are coming from every direction and the media are covering the campaign as if it was a boxing match. Social media platforms amplify this impression. In this context, leaders need not be in the thick of everything. They must be free to focus in order to perform well. During the campaign, their attention should be on connecting with the audience during a talk and answering journalists' questions calmly, confidently, and, most of all, clearly. The political adviser's coaching makes the leader feel secure in the message – which, in turn, makes the leader appear to be authentic, an important aspect of modern politics.[10] The senior political adviser is responsible for fostering authenticity and having the leader internalize the message and campaign strategy. At some point, the leader must live and breathe the campaign message. The politician must deliver it every day of the campaign, whether on a talk show or during a town hall event.

Political advisers also participate in debate preparation. The team works with the leader to focus on what the audience should take away from the debate and believe about the leader and the opponents. As with any other job, overconfidence is a problem. Undermining confidence can be an even bigger problem. Coaching the leader to be at her or his best can be a long process in which things get worse before they get better. Why? Because being a political leader is different from being a local elected representative. Leaders continuously receive intense doses of feedback from all directions, including colleagues, media, and people on the street, even when they are not looking for it. They rely on strategists such as political advisers to sort out the often confusing and contradictory opinions about image and performance that can weaken a leader's confidence. Leaders are also coached to improve their focus and discipline. Since they interact with the media daily, there is a high risk that the campaign can be derailed if the leader says something wrong. Consequently, the management of message and image is a key concern throughout the campaign.

After the votes are counted, political advisers celebrate if their party is successful, or they roll up their sleeves to help the next leader get ready for the next election. During this period, they consider lessons that can be learned from the experience: What are the takeaways? How much of the result is due to context, and how much is due to something that we did? Learning from this intense experience is crucial; the adviser knows that there will be other leaders to coach and other strategies to develop.

Overcoming Obstacles

During the campaign, the political adviser prepares the leader to be noticed in a favourable manner during key moments. For example, if a leader is widely dismissed by commentators, the adviser and the communication team must work to rehabilitate the leader's image and rise above expectations. Advisers must prepare leaders to exploit opportunities and be prepared for criticisms. This includes performing in the leaders' debates, answering questions about specific issues (or perhaps an unplanned event), reacting to false information, or simply interacting with voters while walking down the street.

In the 2019 campaign, race was a factor for Jagmeet Singh, leader of the New Democratic Party (NDP), as the first racialized leader to run for prime minister. His very identity made him different from the other leaders. To some Canadians, this raised a barrier to understanding. He and his team had to overcome preconceived notions of who he was and what he believed. Political advisers are mindful that the fundamentals of campaign strategy are about exploiting strengths and overcoming weaknesses. How can a desired image be conveyed, especially in a context of systemic racism?[11] During the campaign, questions such as "is Canada ready for a Sikh prime minister?" were often raised. As with sexism, these kinds of questions are insidious.

The NDP knew that Singh would be a tough sell in Quebec since the province had just passed Bill 21, which stipulates that public servants in positions of authority – such as teachers, judges, and police officers – are prohibited from wearing religious symbols. Following focus group research, the NDP saw that the panel members evaluated Singh's values positively, but party strategists needed to demystify "the turban and the religious orthodoxy they felt it represented."[12] To do that, and in line with image management strategies, Singh followed the practice of a number of leaders of opposition parties by publishing a memoir.[13] It allowed him to present and demystify himself as a person – telling the story of his family, his trials, and his resilience. The book demonstrated that his values were aligned with those of his party and many Canadians. Profiling his political ideals – including that Singh is pro-choice – was part of the party's message during the campaign, particularly in Quebec, where people assumed that the opposite is true because he wears a turban. The NDP team worked to make his differences a strength, not a weakness. They became part of the party's messages and ads. Want a different result? Make a different choice. The political lead and the strategic communication team worked during the campaign to frame his difference as a force that would do politics differently. Also, the party created an ad that starts with a shot of Singh without his turban and shows how he puts it on. This is followed by scenes of him in a boxing ring and out in nature. The ad's message is that Singh wants to fight for Canadians in the same way that he has had to fight all his life. The ad shows that he is more than his turban and that it does not define him. This was an important strategic move: it allowed the NDP leader to frame the question before he was framed by it.

This is an important takeaway for all campaign strategists: refuse to be defined by a campaign's weaknesses. Every leader and every campaign face perceived risks, but they can be reframed as opportunities and used against opponents. Seizing control of the message changes the conversation. As all good tennis coaches would say, if a player's backhand is a weakness, teach the player to have a better backhand. A player cannot win the match if his opponent can successfully target his weakest point.

After the campaign, political advisers and other campaign operatives engage in post-mortems to examine successes and failures. They look at how they presented issues to voters and evaluate which tools were useful and what kind of framing resonated or not with targeted voters.[14] They assess the accuracy of their assumptions during the campaign. They analyze the polls and see whether their projections were right or not.[15] Was talking about affordability the best way to reach some citizens in specific ridings? Would a different narrative have helped? Could the image of the leader have been shaped differently in order to counter stereotypes? Political advisers take notes so as not to repeat mistakes in future elections. Sometimes they share their insights with journalists trying to interpret the results and assess what happened behind the scenes. Anonymity is often guaranteed so that the staffer does not experience repercussions for disclosing inside information.

As they did before and during the campaign, political advisers reflect on perceptions of their leaders. This helps them to make sense of what could have been done to shape the leader's image differently to win more votes. They reflect on communication strategies more broadly. They contemplate the strengths and weaknesses of how they reached out to and connected with the electorate. Political leads reflect on both the tools used for (e.g., traditional media, advertising, social media platforms) and the packaging of the message. They consider how they were able to reach specific segments of the population, such as the success that Singh enjoyed by lip-synching on TikTok, a social media video app.[16] Media fragmentation, regionalism, and the diversity of opinion and population are among the many reasons that it is challenging to convey a desired message to targeted audiences. Thinking about communication strategies means evaluating narratives and how they reach – or fail to reach – specific parts of the population. Using humour shapes the narrative in a different way and can grab the media's attention.[17]

In this sense, image management does not stop at the end of the campaign. Lessons learned from analyzing the campaign data help to make adjustments for the next campaign. Senior advisers on the leader's tour prepare for the next campaign by considering the responses to how messages were framed and delivered. The next time that they whisper in the leader's ear, their guidance will be grounded in their most recent campaign experiences and lessons learned, providing yet another source of counsel from the leader's retinue of image managers.

This chapter has shed light on the central work of the senior adviser to the leader – also called the political lead on tour with the leader – before, during, and after the campaign, as well as a the adviser's role in image management strategies. It has shown how the senior adviser and campaign team work together to highlight the leader's qualities and try to turn weaknesses into strengths. Voters have specific expectations of leaders, so much work must go into crafting the leader's image in a socio-political context in which there are challenges and in which a campaign is simultaneously a short period and a long period to manage issues, images, and events.

Notes

1. Marland, *Brand Command.*
2. Bittner, *Platform or Personality?*
3. Lalancette and Raynauld, "The Power of Political Image."
4. King, "Do Leaders' Personalities Really Matter?"
5. Goffman, *Presentation of Self in Everyday Life.*
6. Strachan and Kendall, "Political Candidates' Convention Films."
7. Marland, *Brand Command;* McGrane, *The New NDP.*
8. Hunter and Bailey, "Inside the Campaigns for the BC Election." See also Shaw and Zussman, *A Matter of Confidence.*
9. On the modes of persuasion, see Flanagan, *Winning Power.*
10. See Enli, *Mediated Authenticity.*
11. For more on how the media cover racialized politicians in Canada, see Tolley, *Framed.*
12. Raj, "How Justin Trudeau Didn't Lose the 2019 Election."
13. Singh, *Love and Courage.*
14. See Gurney, "Election Post-Mortem, Part 1."
15. See ibid.; and Gurney, "Election Post-Mortem, Part 3."
16. See Gurney, "Election Post-Mortem, Part 2."
17. See ibid.

Bibliography

Bittner, Amanda. *Platform or Personality? The Role of Party Leaders in Elections.* Oxford: Oxford University Press, 2011.

Enli, Gunn. *Mediated Authenticity: How Media Constructs Reality.* New York: Peter Lang, 2015.

Flanagan, Tom. *Winning Power: Canadian Campaigning in the 21st Century.* Montreal and Kingston: McGill-Queen's University Press, 2014.

Goffman, Erving. *Presentation of Self in Everyday Life.* New York: Doubleday Anchor Books, 1959.

Gurney, Matt. "Election Post-Mortem, Part 1: A Conservative Insider Explains How His Party Got It So Wrong." TVO, 23 October 2019. https://www.tvo.org/article/election-post-mortem-part-1-a-conservative-insider-explains-how-his-party-got-it-so-wrong.

–. "Election Post-Mortem, Part 2: Why Did the NDP Get Blown Out? A War-Room Strategist Explains." TVO, 24 October 2019. https://www.tvo.org/article/election-post-mortem-part-2-why-did-the-ndp-get-blown-out-a-war-room-strategist-explains.

–. "Election Post-Mortem, Part 3: Why Doug Ford Had Toronto Seeing Red." TVO, 25 October 2019. https://www.tvo.org/article/election-post-mortem-part-3-why-doug-ford-had-toronto-seeing-red.

Hunter, Justine, and Ian Bailey. "Inside the Campaigns for the BC Election." *Globe and Mail,* 1 May 2017. https://www.theglobeandmail.com/news/british-columbia/bc-election-backroom-whoswho/article34871078/.

King, Anthony. "Do Leaders' Personalities Really Matter?" In *Leaders' Personalities and the Outcomes of Democratic Elections,* edited by Anthony King, 1–43. Oxford: Oxford University Press, 2002.

Lalancette, Mireille, and Vincent Raynauld. "The Power of Political Image: Justin Trudeau, Instagram, and Celebrity Politics." *American Behavioral Scientist* 63, 7 (2019): 888–924.

Marland, Alex. *Brand Command: Canadian Politics and Democracy in the Age of Message Control.* Vancouver: UBC Press, 2016.

McGrane, David. *The New NDP: Moderation, Modernization, and Political Marketing.* Vancouver: UBC Press, 2019.

Raj, Althia. "How Justin Trudeau Didn't Lose the 2019 Election: From Scandals, Spin and Slams to a Minority Government." *Huffington Post,* 5 November 2019, updated 17 November 2019. https://www.huffingtonpost.ca/entry/justin-trudeau-canada-election-how-did-they-win_ca_5dcod8c1e4bobedb2d519a3d.

Shaw, Rob, and Richard Zussman. *A Matter of Confidence: The Inside Story of the Political Battle for BC.* Toronto: Heritage, 2018.

Singh, Jagmeet. *Love and Courage: My Story of Family, Resilience, and Overcoming the Unexpected.* Toronto: Simon and Schuster, 2019.

Strachan, Cherie J., and Kathleen E. Kendall. "Political Candidates' Convention Films: Finding the Perfect Image – An Overview of Political

Image Making." In *Defining Visual Rhetorics,* edited by Charles A. Hill and Marguerite Helmers, 135–54. Mahwah, NJ: Lawrence Erlbaum Associates, 2004.

Tolley, Erin. *Framed: Media and the Coverage of Race in Canadian Politics.* Vancouver: UBC Press, 2016.

12

Political Advertisers

Vincent Raynauld and Dany Renauld

The Canadian mass media environment has expanded and diversified significantly, particularly with the proliferation of digital technologies. In this chapter, we look at how political advertisers are leveraging the characteristics, properties, and reach of electronic mass media channels (e.g., radio, television, digital media) to develop, roll out, and deliver political ads. We also examine how political advertisers are isolating and reaching out to specific targets within the public, sometimes even individuals, in order to craft messages appealing to their narrow interests, preferences, and objectives.

L'environnement canadien des médias de masse a pris de l'expansion et s'est considérablement diversifié, particulièrement avec la prolifération des technologies numériques. Ce chapitre examine de quelle façon les publicitaires politiques tirent parti des caractéristiques, des propriétés et de la portée des médias électroniques de masse (radio, télévision, médias numériques) pour élaborer, déployer et diffuser des publicités politiques. Il examine également de quelle façon ces publicitaires isolent ou rejoignent un public cible, parfois même des individus, afin de rédiger des messages qui répondent à leurs aspirations, leurs intérêts et leurs préférences.

WORLDWIDE, POLITICAL advertising is a mainstay in voter outreach by political parties and candidates during elections. In Canada, federal political parties' advertising activities during general elections have intensified and diversified greatly over the past decade. For example, the previous four federal electoral campaigns were generally marked by a rise of major political parties' advertising expenditures.[1] The expansion of the mass media landscape and the fragmentation of audiences have led to changes in how political ads are conceived and delivered to the public.[2] In this chapter, we shed light on these dynamics by exploring the role of political advertisers and the implications of their work on election campaigns.

Political advertisers are marketing specialists who participate in packaging and selling political parties, candidates, and their ideas to the electorate through wide-ranging media platforms.[3] In other words, their role is to amplify political parties' and candidates' messages so that they can resonate with different audiences. In Canada, political advertisers usually work for advertising firms that have long-standing relationships with specific political parties. Leaders of these firms – who have expertise in the advertising of political products – tend to be aligned ideologically with the political parties that they work for during campaigns. Furthermore, these firms have extensive resources enabling them to provide committed services to political parties and candidates throughout the campaign cycle.

Political advertisers contribute to campaigns in three key areas. First, they can help to pinpoint and cluster voters with shared preferences, interests, and goals. In doing so, they can isolate slices of the electorate – or "target universes" – and, in some cases, individual voters deemed likely to be receptive to and persuaded by specific genres of political appeal. Market research insights from pollsters and other public opinion specialists are instrumental for advertisers when doing this type of work. Targeting has become especially important as media consumption has grown and members of the public are exposed to increasingly diverse content often tailored to their interests. In sum, targeting can help political messaging to cut through the noise and reach its intended audience for maximum impact.[4]

Second, political advertisers can contribute to the development and shaping of the content, format, and tone of political parties' and candidates' ads based on their targets and objectives. The two main categories of political ads are issue-based and image-based. Issue-based advertising generally provides voters with insights into political parties' and candidates' positions, including political and policy matters, legislative priorities, and views on issues of public interest. Image-based advertising is used to introduce, define, and humanize candidates. It highlights personality traits, values, and personal and professional qualifications. It also helps to foster a more personal – and often emotional – connection between voters and candidates.[5] This type of political advertising has gained traction with the increasing personalization of political communication. This phenomenon is characterized by individual politicians – in many cases party leaders – who become the main gateway through which voters are exposed to, make sense of, evaluate, and take part in politics.[6] Political parties and candidates can also turn to the two aforementioned categories of political ads to shape the public's perceptions of their opponents and their ideas, generally in negative ways.

Advertising professionals play key roles in the development of political ads. They can provide guidance on the format of the ad (e.g., textual, visual, audio) and through which media platform it will be shared with the public for effective reach and persuasion. Advertising personnel can also help to set the tone (e.g., positive, negative, mixed, neutral) of a political ad. Tone is especially important. Alongside factors such as political sophistication, tone can stimulate various forms of behaviour among the public, including information seeking and other types of political engagement.

Third, the work of political advertisers can have varied effects on the public. In fact, altering attitudes and behaviours can be viewed as one of political advertising's core functions. Political ads can help to generate, modify, or reinforce specific political attitudes (attitudinal). They can trigger emotional responses leading to shifts in feelings and moods (affective), shape voters' thoughts and decision-making processes (cognitive), as well as foster changes in political behaviour (behavioural).[7] From a broader perspective, political advertisers' ability to generate wide-ranging responses among voters can help to support different facets of their employers' activities, such as mobilizing existing supporters, gaining new supporters, and fundraising. Advertisers' efforts can also lead to a higher share of the vote on election day.

Duties in an Election Campaign

In a context of non-stop campaigning in and out of elections, political advertisers' work begins before the writ is drawn. In the weeks preceding the launch of the campaign – a period defined here as pre-campaign – political advertisers deploy significant efforts to shape the public political narrative and set expectations ahead of the election. Of particular interest is their use of more generic political ads intended for the public at large. Political parties and candidates often rely on issue-based advertising to put forth elements that will be at the core of their messaging during the campaign. Specifically, incumbent parties tend to release ads that have generally positive tones and tout specific political and policy successes. These ads can show how these accomplishments demonstrate their governing effectiveness, have fostered progress and the betterment of society, and can be built on with re-election. Challenger parties adopt a different approach. They frequently turn to issue-based advertising to introduce key elements of their electoral platforms, which can be unknown or not well understood among some groups of voters. They can also lay out and explain their key legislative priorities. As well, they can critique, undermine, and attack the achievements and priorities of the sitting government. In other words, challenger parties can use these types of ads to highlight the weaknesses of members of the government and to portray themselves as viable alternatives.

Political advertisers can turn to image-based ads to establish, strengthen, or sharpen the public images of candidates – typically leaders of political parties – throughout the pre-campaign phase. This is particularly important since politicians' personality traits and personal lives are elements that influence how some voters make up their minds come election day.[8] Specifically, party leaders with less name recognition can use these types of ads to introduce themselves to the public and highlight specific aspects of their identities. This is often done in ways that complement the priorities of their electoral programs and address the preferences, interests, and objectives of target political markets. Candidates with greater name recognition tend to use these ads to fine-tune or sharpen some facets of their public images. In some cases, image-based ads can help them to shore up deficiencies in how they are perceived by the public and position themselves strategically in anticipation of the electoral contest.

Political parties and candidates can also turn to image-based ads to define – or brand – their opponents, often in ways that will be beneficial to them during their campaigns. For example, incumbent parties can release ads raising concerns, doubts, and, in some cases, fears about their challengers' readiness or qualifications to assume the responsibilities of elected office. Conversely, challengers can focus on controversies plaguing an incumbent party to degrade specific aspects of its public image (e.g., honesty, reliability, credibility) and instill doubts in the minds of voters. More broadly, political advertising's main role during the pre-campaign phase is to set the stage for the political marketing efforts that will be rolled out during the campaign.

As the writ is drawn and the electoral campaign gets under way, political advertisers modify their approaches to complement and support political parties' and candidates' voter outreach and engagement operations. The pre-campaign period is dedicated to setting general political impressions among the public. During the campaign, advertisers' activities become surgical. Advertising consultants leverage public opinion data and other forms of political market intelligence to develop and push out messages that consider the wants, needs, and aspirations of specific segments of the voting public. Their tactics need to be constantly rethought and recalibrated to address developments on the campaign trail, shifts in public opinion, and in some cases opponents' policy announcements and communication efforts. Political advertisers' efforts are also informed by the budgets provided by political parties. The budget covers two main types of expenses: the consulting fees of political advertisers and operational costs (e.g., production and circulation of ads, organization of events). The budget can be adjusted during the campaign based on different factors. Among them are the evolution of political parties' and candidates' priorities and objectives, shifts in campaign dynamics, and fundraising yields.

Two key facets of political advertisers' duties during the electoral campaign warrant particular attention. The first aspect is their involvement in selecting which mass media platforms are to be used for sending messages addressing political or policy matters of importance to specific groups of voters. Given that the Canadian political market tends to be more homogeneous than the markets in other countries, particularly the United States, political advertisers use diverse mass media targeting strategies. For example, television – which tends to reach a large and geographically dispersed audience – can be used to broadcast ads with broad political appeal. These ads, which can cut across different political and policy issues and interests, are typically aired during television shows with a large viewership or at peak viewing times. Despite the growing availability of special media channels allowing finer targeting, and the increasing emphasis on social media advertising, political ads intended for larger audiences remain an integral component of the political advertiser's tool box during elections in Canada.

Political advertisers turn to local and regional radio stations to reach out to groups of voters likely to be receptive to messages with a narrower appeal. For instance, radio is used to circulate ads focusing on matters relevant to people sharing specific socio-demographic characteristics (e.g., language, income, ethnicity, education, religion), caring about specific policy matters (e.g., environment, immigration, culture), or located in a particular geographical area (e.g., region, postal code). Regionalism and linguistic and cultural identity remain core elements shaping political life in Canada.[9] Radio-based political ads require less time and technical expertise, and fewer financial resources, to produce and be ready for dissemination than television ads. This is particularly relevant during electoral campaigns. Political parties and candidates are often required to alter their messaging tactics rapidly because of shifts in public opinion or changes in their opponents' policy positions or voter outreach strategies. Radio enables them to roll out new advertising campaigns quickly. Radio-based political ads also offer political parties with less money on hand the ability to engage in low-cost and high-impact forms of political advertising. As noted by some studies, political ads aired on radio during elections can have greater influence on the public's voting decisions than those aired on television.[10]

Finally, social media channels are an integral component of the political media environment in Canada. Political advertisers leverage these digital communication platforms to push out political ads tailored to appeal to slices of the political market with distinct profiles (e.g., mothers, students, young professionals, immigrants). In many cases, these ads are revised versions of existing political ads that are more generic and have been circulated previously through other channels, including newspapers, campaign flyers, and television. They can emphasize specific elements likely to generate a strong response among target audiences. Although this form of hypertargeting can be useful, it is less applicable in Canada than in other national contexts in which the political market might be more heterogeneous.

The second aspect is political advertisers' role in developing the content and setting the tone of political appeals pushed out to voters throughout the electoral race. Of particular interest for this chapter is the notion of change in political ads. Although such ads can touch on a wide range of issues and matters, change is frequently an underlying element driving the overall narrative.

On the one hand, challenger parties devote significant energy and resources to show how change in leadership and in how political and policy issues are dealt with can be beneficial to members of the public. This can be done in many ways. They can release positive ads to offer an uplifting vision of politics. They can also reinforce the concept of change with negative ads that establish clear contrasts between their positions and those of their opponents. On the other hand, as the incumbent party seeks to retain power, it is likely to portray change as potentially detrimental to the public, whether this portrayal is in generic or more targeted political messages. Incumbent parties can promote the status quo by emphasizing their accomplishments and downplaying or attacking challengers' political and policy offerings.

In sum, then, a key aspect of political advertisers' role during elections is to manage how a message of change is presented, perceived, and understood. This can have repercussions on voters' attitudes toward and participation in different facets of the electoral process.

The content and tone of political ads evolve during an electoral campaign. Changes in voters' interests in issues as well as the evolution of journalistic coverage can lead political advertisers to modify the structure and content of political ads. They do so to ensure that the messaging remains relevant and appealing to the public. Adjusting the advertising can strengthen other aspects of the political communications deployed by political parties and candidates. Shifts in public support for political parties and candidates as measured by public opinion polls and fundraising data can cause political advertisers to consider adjustments to messaging and targeting. Parties leading in the polls are likely to release positive ads to protect their positions and to showcase their readiness to occupy elected office. Conversely, candidates trailing in the polls are likely to adopt a more negative approach in order to question and, in some instances, delegitimize their opponents and their electoral platforms. Doing so can help to mobilize their own supporters while also potentially demobilizing members of the public backing their opponents.

Overcoming Obstacles

Quebec is an important electoral battleground visited frequently by party leaders. The Conservatives and their leader, Andrew Scheer, were forced to rethink and retool their advertising approach during the later stages of the 2019 election. Pivoting by the party in response to two developments on the campaign trail reveals the responsive nature of political advertising at work.

Quebec's Bill 21 (An Act Respecting the Laicity of the State) bans newly hired public servants in positions of authority from wearing religious symbols (e.g., kippah, turban, hijab) in the contexts of their duties. Justin Trudeau's announcement of his opposition to the politically divisive issue and his intention to challenge it in the courts if re-elected as prime minister arguably changed the course of the campaign in Quebec. Although a large swath of the provincial electorate supports the legislative measure, many voters oppose it, particularly those outside Quebec. Trudeau leveraged a polarizing issue to establish a clear contrast between his political party and his main opponents. Indeed, the Bloc Québécois and Conservative Party leaders stated throughout the campaign that they were unwilling to intervene in the Bill 21 debate out of respect for Quebec's autonomy. Meanwhile, the position of the New Democratic Party on the issue fluctuated throughout the electoral contest, with leader Jagmeet Singh sending mixed messages to voters. Trudeau's announcement drove a wedge between voters in Quebec as well as affected the Conservative policy positioning and the potency of its messaging.

A further factor was Scheer's performance during the first French-language debate held by Quebec's broadcaster TVA prior to the official debates organized by the Leaders' Debate Commission. During that debate, other party leaders pressed Scheer on several occasions about his personal stance on abortion rights. He refused to address the issue during the debate, and public pressure mounted during the twelve-hour window following the broadcast. After consultations with members of his communication team, Scheer held a press conference the next day at which he affirmed that he is personally pro-life. The Conservative leader reiterated that as prime minister he would oppose any effort from his caucus to restrict reproductive rights. Much like Bill 21, abortion was an issue of importance to many Quebec voters. Scheer's disclosure likely affected negatively Conservative support among them.

These developments contributed to the steady rise of the Bloc Québécois in the polls and the softening of Conservative support among Quebecers. The Bloc capitalized by garnering more public attention, raising money, and releasing ads on local radio stations across Quebec. This situation led to deliberations among members of the Conservative communication team about how to respond to and counter this dynamic. Different options were considered in order to reposition the party and adjust its political appeal in the final stretch of the campaign.

Conservative advertisers ultimately developed and rolled out French-language ads emphasizing a clear narrative: people who voted for the Bloc Québécois on election day in effect would be supporting the Liberals. These ads were crafted strategically as they took into account the two aforementioned dynamics and framed the political appeal of the Conservative Party in ways that complemented its overall messaging. However, because of their release late in the campaign, the ads failed to slow down the momentum of the Bloc, and it made significant gains on election day, whereas the Conservatives lost seats in Quebec.[11] It is believed among Conservative strategists that, even though many Quebecers who voted for the Bloc were unimpressed by the performance of the Liberal government led by Trudeau, political advertising was unable to overcome their concerns about the Conservative Party and its leader's positions on certain policy issues.

As we have shown in this chapter, how political advertisers approach their craft has evolved with the growth of political marketing and digital communication. They place a premium on strategic thinking to match messages, audiences, and media. Much of this is familiar to campaigns past, such as using television to reach mass audiences or using image-based ads to frame how opponents are seen. To date, scholars have taken little notice of social media advertising by Canadian political parties. Although many scholars have shown interest in traditional forms of political advertising in Canada, more research is needed to explore all aspects of strategic advertising in a fragmented media landscape.[12]

Notes

[1] Rose, "Are Negative Ads Positive?"
[2] Dunaway et al., "Political Advertising."
[3] Holtz-Bacha, "Political Advertising."
[4] Schneider, *How to Break Through.*
[5] Tedesco and Dunn, "Political Advertising in the 2016 US Presidential Election."
[6] Balmas and Sheafer, "Personalization of Politics."
[7] Holtz-Bacha, "Political Advertising."
[8] Bittner, "Leaders Always Mattered."
[9] Small, "Canadian Cyberparties."
[10] Overby and Barth, "Radio Advertising in American Political Campaigns."
[11] Compared with the 2015 election, the number of Bloc MPs increased from ten to thirty-two, whereas the Conservatives' Quebec contingent decreased from twelve to ten MPs.
[12] On traditional forms of political advertising, see Daignault, "Cognitive Effects of Televised Political Advertising in Canada"; and Rose, "Are Negative Ads Positive?"

Bibliography

Balmas, Meital, and Tamir Sheafer. "Personalization of Politics." In *The International Encyclopedia of Political Communication*. Hoboken, NJ: John Wiley and Sons, 2015. https://doi.org/10.1002/9781118541555.

Bittner, Amanda. "Leaders Always Mattered: The Persistence of Personality in Canadian Elections." *Electoral Studies* 54 (2018): 297–302.

Daignault, Pénélope. "Cognitive Effects of Televised Political Advertising in Canada." In *Political Communication in Canada: Meet the Press and Tweet the Rest*, edited by Alex Marland, Thierry Giasson, and Tamara A. Small, 39–54. Vancouver: UBC Press, 2014.

Dunaway, Johanna L., Kathleen Searles, Erika F. Fowler, and Travis N. Ridout. "Political Advertising." In *Mediated Communication,* edited by Philip M. Napoli, 431–53. Berlin: De Gruyter Mouton, 2018.

Holtz-Bacha, Christina. "Political Advertising: A Research Overview." *Central European Journal of Communication* 11, 2 (2018): 166–76.

Overby, L. Marvin, and Jay Barth. "Radio Advertising in American Political Campaigns: The Persistence, Importance, and Effects of Narrowcasting." *American Politics Research* 34, 4 (2006): 451–78.

Rose, Jonathan. "Are Negative Ads Positive? Political Advertising and the Permanent Campaign." In *How Canadians Communicate IV: Media and Politics,* edited by David Taras and Christopher Waddell, 149–68. Edmonton: Athabasca University Press, 2012.

Schneider, Mike. *How to Break Through When Political Ads Have Never Been More Competitive. Campaigns and Elections,* 15 July 2019. https://www.campaignsandelections.com/campaign-insider/how-to-break-through-when-political-ads-have-never-been-more-competitive.

Small, Tamara A. "Canadian Cyberparties: Reflections on Internet-Based Campaigning and Party Systems." *Canadian Journal of Political Science* 40, 3 (2007): 639–57.

Tedesco, John C., and Scott W. Dunn. "Political Advertising in the 2016 US Presidential Election: Ad Hominem Ad Nauseam." *American Behavioral Scientist* 63, 7 (2018): 935–47.

13

Third-Party Activism

Thomas Collombat and Magali Picard

Advocacy group leaders play an important role in Canada's democratic system by bringing up issues or constituencies neglected by political parties. During electoral campaigns, Elections Canada groups these activities under regulations for "third parties." The role of their officials is both to define and to carry the electoral strategies of their organizations by reaching out to members and the broader public. Unions form a significant share of registered advocacy groups, and their leaders actively campaign by using their position, connections, and notoriety to advance the interests of their members.

Les dirigeants de groupes d'intérêts jouent un rôle important dans le système démocratique du Canada en attirant l'attention sur des questions ou des segments de l'électorat négligés par les partis politiques. Pendant les campagnes électorales, Élections Canada regroupe ces activités en vertu du règlement sur les « tiers ». Le rôle de leurs représentants est à la fois de définir et d'appliquer la stratégie électorale de leur organisation en rejoignant les membres et le grand public. Les syndicats représentent une part importante des groupes d'intérêts enregistrés, et leurs dirigeants font activement campagne en utilisant leur position, leurs relations et leur notoriété pour défendre les intérêts de leurs membres.

ADVOCACY GROUP leaders play an important role in Canada's democratic system by bringing up issues or constituencies neglected by political parties.[1] Elections Canada regulates their activities during election campaigns under rules for so-called third parties. Over time, legislators and courts have tried to strike a balance between guaranteeing these groups' freedom of speech and ensuring that the groups do not take a disproportionate place in a campaign or circumvent campaign and party financing laws.[2] These regulations guide the conduct of third parties and therefore the kind of work that their officials can and cannot do.

Third-party expenses during campaigns are strictly limited. Historically, the approach in Canada has been to extend both the definition of the activities covered and the time frame during which they apply. Third parties have to report on both partisan activities and advertising, the latter including, during campaigns, issue advertising that does not target a specific party or candidate. Elections Canada has adopted an extensive definition of what qualifies as electoral advertising by including most messages supporting or opposing a position taken by a political party.[3] Third parties have to adjust to this interpretation. Some strategies in past campaigns that were not considered partisan at the time could fall under that category during the next election. The use of social media and other electronic ways of communication also belongs to the list of regulated activities. Digital communications are particularly useful for advocacy groups to improve their political communications.[4] Their relatively weak participation during electoral campaigns is usually explained by the lack of funds and resources as well as by the fear of appearing to be too partisan, which could both jeopardize their charitable status under Revenue Canada's stricter regulations and compromise their relationship with the future government.[5] Each registered third party is allowed to spend up to a certain amount during the pre-election period, usually between three and four months before election day. Each is permitted to spend up to another amount during the official campaign.

Unions form a significant share (about 20 percent) of third parties registered under Elections Canada. In Canada, the labour movement's relationship to electoral politics has been largely dominated by its connection to the New Democratic Party (NDP). The party counted unions among its founders, and its constitution has allowed them to become affiliates and to have formal representation in its governing bodies. Unions were also a major source of income for the NDP until the federal government barred all union and corporate contributions to political parties. Although observers expected this new framework to alter considerably the relationship between the NDP and unions, its impact was not that significant, proving the historical and political strength of the bond between the party and its labour affiliates, despite some policy divergence.[6] Yet not all Canadian unions affiliate with or even support the NDP.[7] This is particularly true of some more conservative craft unions or, for different reasons, most unions in Quebec. Similarly, some unions have decided to promote strategic voting, mostly to avoid a Conservative victory in an election. The decision of then Canadian Auto Workers President Buzz Hargrove to support strategic voting in favour of some Liberal candidates when Paul Martin was the prime minister was considered a sign of defiance toward the NDP. However, other unions have called for strategic voting as well.[8]

The third party that we focus on in this chapter is the Public Service Alliance of Canada (PSAC), the largest union representing federal public employees. Its members are directly affected by the outcome of a federal election given that the political orientations of the government have a significant influence on how it behaves as an employer. Union delegates elect PSAC officials at the convention. Therefore, they are distinct from union staff, often called union representatives, hired by the union. The president, the national executive vice-president, and the regional vice-presidents form the Alliance Executive Committee, the executive body of PSAC.

During electoral campaigns, the national leadership is in charge of applying the orientations adopted by the convention and determining the specific strategies to do so. Often unions have a two-pronged approach to elections: on the one hand, they have to convince their members to vote according to the position of their union; on the other, they try to influence the broader population to support their views and vote accordingly. In this work, union officials also represent the public face of PSAC. They are the ones who address the media in the name of the union and reach out directly to politicians in order to promote their positions. Sometimes they publicly support specific positions or connections, whether they are mandated to do so or not. For instance, in 2011, Nycole Turmel, the former PSAC president, was elected as an NDP MP. She eventually became the interim leader of the party. Her role in the NDP symbolized its labour connections.

Duties in an Election Campaign

Advocacy groups vary greatly depending not only on their sizes but also on the interests that they represent and the internal structures that they adopt. Among those that are member-based (the case with unions), officials are the elected representatives of the members and subject to the accountability mechanisms and governing procedures of the particular organization. Its largest and most representative body usually adopts the political orientation of the group. Executive members participate in those debates, but they do not decide by themselves what the general orientation should be.

Political representation is an important component of PSAC officials' day-to-day work. As the main bargaining agent for federal government employees, these officials act both as labour relations officers and as political representatives of their members. The executive members are at the heart of this dual relationship with the state and with the governing political parties. Their regular contacts with government representatives and political staffers set the groundwork for their duties during the campaign.

The PSAC executive provides training and tools to members for the purpose of political representation. The union leadership updates a lobbying kit monthly. The kit summarizes the positions and priorities of PSAC and how to reach out to politicians in order to promote these goals. When a regular lobbying activity happens during the year of an election, it becomes part of the plan of the union to push forward its agenda. The National Lobbying Day organized by the Canadian Labour Congress – to which PSAC is a major contributor – is one of those events. On that day, rank-and-file members meet with MPs in Ottawa, prioritizing those bearing the portfolio of labour, to promote the positions of their unions. Union officials play a crucial role in preparing union members to communicate with MPs, ensuring that the position put forward by the union is consistent, whether communicated by members or national officers.

For officials of member-based advocacy groups, another crucial element of campaign preparation is knowing where the group's members stand politically. This is all the more important in the case of a large union such as PSAC, whose membership covers a broad range of occupations as well as varying degrees of identification with the union itself and its positions. Information is usually gathered through direct contacts between the executive and the membership as well as through the internal representative structures of the union. Internal polls are also commissioned to inform leaders about the concerns of members, their perceptions of the current government, and their voting intentions for the next election.

Even when they are member-based, advocacy groups often have partial perceptions of their members through the issues that they represent or the services that they provide – hence the necessity to gather more information in order to determine an electoral strategy. For the executive, the goal is not to tailor the organization's position to the dominant one of its membership. Rather, it seeks to adjust the electoral strategy so that it reflects the union's values and ideology, along with the capacity of the union to mobilize its members on this basis.

When an election is scheduled, the PSAC National Convention preceding the election determines the position of the union and adopts a budget specifically dedicated to the campaign. The executive committee is then mandated to put together and bring to life the strategic plan of the union. PSAC usually encourages the election of candidates who support the development of federal public services and are in line with the values of the labour movement. The job of the executive is therefore both to refine the position and to determine the specific tools that will be used by the union to act on that mandate. This task entails writing to party leaders to inform them of the union's priorities and to ask them about their takes on those issues. Because of the historical ties of the NDP to the labour movement, contact with the party is usually easier, though it can vary from union to union and over time. Similar proximities can exist between other advocacy groups and parties, depending on the issues at stake. The parties' answers contribute to pinpointing the union strategy so that the National Board of Directors, the highest governing body of the union between conventions, can adopt a final strategic plan shortly before the official pre-electoral period.

The strategy is twofold: convincing members to vote along the lines of the union's recommendations and reaching out to the broader public to make the organization's positions known. Executive members play a central role in both aspects. As the highest elected officials of the union, they are its voice and have significant influence on its members.

A major part of the electoral strategy is to meet in person with as many members as possible. This is done through a two-month-long nationwide tour of the leaders during which they meet with thousands of PSAC members. Up to six meetings are organized every day, sometimes including weekends. These meetings allow the president and then national executive vice-president to explain the union's positions, encourage members to get involved in the campaign, and exchange ideas. This can be a delicate exercise for the union leadership, and that is when knowing where members stand becomes crucial. Union members, just like members of any advocacy group, do not follow blindly the instructions of their leaders. The meetings are opportunities for union officials to carry their messages and make members aware of the positions of the parties and their potential impacts on the federal public service. This consultation occurs without imposing a view or suggesting which candidate a member should support. The personal qualities of the leaders play a particular role, and they use their legitimacy and access to argue in favour of a position without giving the impression that they are dictating a choice.

For all advocacy group officials, communications with their members are a particularly efficient and privileged way of campaigning because communications are not included in the activities regulated by Elections Canada. Even when member outreach is done during the pre-electoral or the electoral period, these activities are not as restricted as those directed to the broader public. Depending on their resources, advocacy groups may engage in actions focused on key ridings where opinion polls indicate that the race is close and involves a candidate that the organization wishes to support or defeat. The job of the national leadership is to define the criteria to pick those ridings. The PSAC executive usually favours ridings where the NDP candidate has the best chance, though they might support another candidate if that individual has a better chance to beat the representative of the party that the union opposes the most. The capacity of the union to campaign effectively in this riding is also taken into consideration – areas where the union has critical masses of members to help with canvassing are privileged. In addition to picking those ridings, officials might be requested to participate in local campaigns, for example by meeting with candidates.

Media interviews comprise a big part of the leadership's work during the campaign. Whereas all parties and advocacy groups fight for airtime, it is the role of executive officers to use their notoriety and connections to be heard as much as possible. Their main duty is to make sure that the issues most important to the organization are talked about and that candidates are then questioned about them. Beyond the issues themselves, advocacy group representatives sometimes use their media interventions to make the public aware of who their members are and what they do. This is particularly true of PSAC, whose members' work as federal public servants is often less known by the public than the union representing their provincial counterparts. By educating voters about the roles of federal employees, PSAC tries to convince the electorate that it is important to listen to the messages of their representative organizations.

The leadership also supervises the content of the promotional material produced for the campaign. Although advocacy groups can use print materials such as posters, flyers, and newspaper ads during an election, digital communications now form a significant part of the effort and are regulated as such by Elections Canada. A website dedicated to the election is set up and directed to both members and the broader public. Whereas some sections simply present the positions of the organization, others contain information dedicated to members. The PSAC leadership has decided, for instance, to inform members about their rights and restrictions to be politically active as federal public employees. Social media accounts are also used to carry the campaign. When the leader of the organization is particularly well known, that individual's social media profiles might have more followers than those of the organization itself. These profiles can be used to build a prominent platform to spread the message of the campaign.

Finally, it is common for nationwide advocacy groups to be federations themselves, umbrella organizations with which smaller entities are affiliated. This is the case of PSAC, itself a gathering of several unions, each representing workers from specific departments or agencies of the federal government. In this case, the role of the leadership is to make sure that the campaign is unified and that the message carried by the organization is consistent. Even if the affiliates of the organization are represented in the different governing bodies of the union, some might have the capacity and the autonomy to launch their own initiatives for the election. The executive then has to make sure that no unintentional repetitions or contradictory messages are sent to the members and the electorate. This applies to all dimensions of what the organization does, but it becomes particularly crucial during electoral campaigns, when the capacity of an advocacy group to be heard and listened to depends on its ability to articulate a clear and coherent message.

Overcoming Obstacles

One of the main goals of any advocacy group during an electoral campaign is to convince parties and candidates to support its positions. For a union, this involves the values and policy options that it promotes as well as the material conditions of its members, namely their jobs. Unions in general and PSAC in particular usually consider the NDP as a natural ally and tend to support its candidates. Therefore, it came as a surprise when the party decided, a few months before the 2019 general election, to support the idea of a single tax return in Quebec administered by the provincial government. If it were implemented, then it would jeopardize the jobs of hundreds of PSAC members working for the Canada Revenue Agency in Quebec. The national executive vice-president of the union therefore requested a meeting with the leader of the NDP to explain the implications of that position and the impacts that it could have on PSAC's support for the party. Shortly afterward, the party changed its position on the matter.

Another challenge for advocacy groups is to make sure that the issues they care about stay at the forefront of the campaign. For PSAC, the long-lasting issue of the federal government's failing pay system, known as Phoenix, had to be one of the main topics discussed by candidates. Noting that the public discussion was moving away from it in the middle of the campaign, PSAC leaders decided to target the National Capital Region, where the union had the most members affected by this issue and launched a media blitz to put Phoenix at the centre of the campaign again. A few days later both the NDP and the Liberal Party held press conferences to address the issue. It was particularly challenging for PSAC. While blaming the former Conservative government for initiating Phoenix, the union also criticized the Liberal government for not fixing it. This stance presented difficulties in ridings where the best-placed candidate to beat the Conservative one was a Liberal, given that the union's position could then be interpreted as contradictory.

Worth noting in those two cases is how union officials faced those challenges by using not only their connections and notoriety but also the numerical strength of their organization. The historical ties between organized labour and the NDP definitely make it easier for a union to connect with and eventually influence the party. However, the impact on the involvement of the union in the campaign also weighed in the balance, mostly when some Quebec sections of PSAC decided to support another party in the past. The same goes for the media blitz in the National Capital Region, a decision that fit with the strategic plan adopted by the union that favoured ridings and areas where significant numbers of PSAC members live. Ultimately, advocacy group leaders use a broad range of tools to advance their interests in a campaign, whether it is their reputation, their expertise, or their connections. In the case of union members, they do not vote in elections as a bloc with their leaders, but they do tend to support the party favoured by their union in a larger proportion than the rest of the population.[9] The strength of a vast membership remains a significant weapon, even to convince traditional allies.

Notes

1 Grosenick, "Opportunities Missed."
2 Lawlor and Crandall, "Policy versus Practice."
3 Elections Canada, "New Requirements for Third Parties."
4 Laforest, "Going Digital."
5 Pross, "Barriers to Third-Party Advertising in Canadian Elections"; Grosenick, "Opportunities Missed."
6 Janson and Young, "Solidarity Forever?"; Pilon, Ross, and Savage, "Solidarity Revisited."
7 Savage, "Contemporary Party-Union Relations in Canada."
8 Savage, "Organized Labour and the Politics of Strategic Voting."

9 Savage and Ruhloff-Queiruga, "Organized Labour, Campaign Finance."

Bibliography

Elections Canada. "New Requirements for Third Parties: Corporations, Unions, Groups and Individuals." October 2019. https://www.elections. ca/content.aspx?section=pol&dir=thi&document=backgrounder&lang=e.

Grosenick, Georgina C. "Opportunities Missed: Non-Profit Public Communication and Advocacy in Canada." *Political Communication in Canada: Meet the Press and Tweet the Rest,* edited by Alex Marland, Thierry Giasson, and Tamara A. Small, 179–93. Vancouver: UBC Press, 2014.

Janson, Harold J., and Lisa Young. "Solidarity Forever? The NDP, Organized Labour, and the Changing Face of Party Finance in Canada." *Canadian Journal of Political Science* 42, 3 (2009): 657–78.

Laforest, Rachel. "Going Digital: Non-Profit Organizations in a Transformed Media Environment." In *Political Elites in Canada,* edited by Alex Marland, Thierry Giasson, and Andrea Lawlor, 241–58. Vancouver: UBC Press, 2018.

Lawlor, Andrea, and Erin Crandall. "Policy versus Practice: Third Party Behaviours in Canadian Elections." *Canadian Public Administration* 61, 2 (2018): 246–65.

Pilon, Dennis, Stephanie Ross, and Larry Savage. "Solidarity Revisited: Organized Labour and the New Democratic Party." *Canadian Political Science Review* 5, 1 (2011): 20–37.

Pross, A. Paul. "Barriers to Third-Party Advertising in Canadian Elections." *Canadian Public Administration* 56, 3 (2013): 491–505.

Savage, Larry. "Contemporary Party-Union Relations in Canada." *Labor Studies Journal* 35, 1 (2010): 8–26.

–. "Organized Labour and the Politics of Strategic Voting." In *Rethinking the Politics of Labour in Canada,* edited by Stephanie Ross and Larry Savage, 75–87. Halifax: Fernwood, 2012.

Savage, Larry, and Nick Ruhloff-Queiruga. "Organized Labour, Campaign Finance, and the Politics of Strategic Voting in Ontario." *Labour/Le travail* 80 (2017): 247–71.

14

The Independent Candidate

Tamara A. Small and Jane Philpott

Local campaigns are understudied in Canada compared with national politics. In particular, we know relatively little about the unique challenges faced by independents in Canadian elections. An independent candidate is not endorsed by a registered or eligible political party. In 2019, Jane Philpott was one of those independent candidates. A cabinet minister in the Liberal government, Philpott resigned from cabinet in light of the SNC-Lavalin affair. The story of her campaign is the story of the challenges plaguing independent candidates in their attempts to convince citizens to look beyond parties when casting their ballots.

Les campagnes locales sont sous-étudiées au Canada par rapport à la politique nationale. Nous en savons relativement peu sur les défis particuliers que doivent relever les candidats indépendants lors des élections canadiennes. Un candidat indépendant n'est pas appuyé par un parti politique enregistré ou admissible. En 2019, Jane Philpott est devenue une candidate indépendante. Ministre du gouvernement libéral, Philpott a démissionné du cabinet à la suite de l'affaire SNC-Lavalin. L'histoire de la campagne de Philpott est celle des défis que doivent relever les candidats indépendants alors qu'ils tentent de convaincre les citoyens de regarder au-delà du parti lorsqu'ils choisissent de voter.

ACCORDING TO CANADIAN election law, candidates who are not endorsed by a registered or eligible political party are considered independent.[1] Among the reasons that there are few independent candidates in Canada is that electoral success is so elusive for them. In federal elections between 1980 and 2019, only seven independent candidates won a seat in the House of Commons. Generally, successful independent candidates are those running for re-election directly after a severed relationship with a political party. Moreover, party candidates have several benefits that independents do not have during an election campaign.

Although we talk about an election as a singular political phenomenon, in fact a Canadian federal election consists of 338 simultaneous local electoral contests. As such, the local or ground campaign is an important hub of activity during an election. Given the importance of political parties to the functioning of both legislative and electoral politics, most candidates in Canada are party candidates. That is, they are nominated to be the local representatives of a given party. Of the approximately 2,146 candidates who ran in the 2019 federal election, over 94 percent of them were party candidates; the remaining candidates were independents.

Every independent campaign is different and reflects unique local dynamics, in particular the individual candidate. Occasionally, an independent attracts national media attention. Jane Philpott was one such person. In the 2015 federal election, she was elected as an MP with the Liberal Party of Canada in the Ontario riding of Markham–Stouffville. As a member of the Liberal government, she served in numerous cabinet positions, including as minister of health, minister of Indigenous services, president of the Treasury Board, and minister of digital government. In March 2019, she resigned from cabinet, citing a loss of confidence in the government's management of the SNC-Lavalin affair.[2] She was expelled from the Liberal caucus in April 2019. Philpott then served as an independent MP and sought re-election as an independent candidate in the federal election that fall. Another prominent independent candidate was former Attorney General Jody Wilson-Raybould, at the centre of the SNC-Lavalin affair.

To be sure, as a high-profile candidate, Philpott was atypical of most independent candidates in a number of ways.[3] She was an MP seeking re-election. Incumbents have name recognition, direct ties to their local communities, resources associated with their position as office-holders, and potentially greater abilities to raise campaign funds.[4] Moreover, as parliamentarians, incumbents have political experience as well as the ability to claim credit for projects in their ridings.[5] Research shows that incumbency matters in Canadian elections. Incumbent candidates have a 9.4–11.2 percent increased probability of winning compared with non-incumbents.[6] They are also more likely to benefit from a personal vote separate from the party or the leader.[7] As a former cabinet minister, Philpott had considerable name recognition, experience, and political clout. Additionally, the unusual circumstances under which she became an independent candidate brought her national attention. Well-known candidates such as Philpott tend to benefit from additional volunteers and donations compared with their counterparts.[8]

Nevertheless, her bid for re-election was unsuccessful. Her Liberal Party rival (a former provincial minister) won the seat with 38.9 percent of the vote. Wilson-Raybould was the only independent candidate to win a seat, the first to do so in more than a decade.

Duties in an Election Campaign

Local campaigns are understudied in Canada compared with national politics.[9] In particular, we know relatively little about the campaigns of independents and the unique challenges that they face in Canadian elections. The task of any campaign is to mobilize a coalition of people to vote in support of a particular candidate or party.[10] On one level, an independent's task is no different from that of any other candidate: to convince local voters to prioritize the local candidate over other options.

However, independents face challenges that party candidates do not. Simply put, political parties matter in Canada. The importance of local campaigns and candidates pales in comparison to that of the national campaign and party leaders when it comes to voter decisions. Data from the 2000 election reveal that, even though 44 percent of Canadian voters form preferences for local candidates, such preferences are decisive factors for just 6 percent of voters in English Canada.[11] Parties and their leaders provide important information shortcuts or cues to voters about ideology and policy. Moreover, they command media and public attention.

The importance of political parties to Canadian politics shapes the direction of an independent campaign. The biggest challenge can be trying to convince voters that an independent MP will be able to represent them effectively in the House of Commons. Parties dominate the legislative process. The ability to participate regularly in Question Period and to sit on parliamentary committees is related to being a recognized parliamentary party (twelve MPs). Most Canadians vote, at both the federal level and the provincial level, for party candidates. Therefore, an independent campaign needs to communicate consistently to voters that they will still be well served, even without party backing.

Philpott launched her campaign in May 2019 at a press conference timed to coincide with a similar announcement by Wilson-Raybould. While canvassing or door knocking is a central aspect of the ground campaign, Philpott and her team aspired to attempt one-on-one conversations with every household in Markham–Stouffville because they wanted to make this particular appeal directly to voters. Before the writ dropped, the campaign had reached 14,000 doors, and by election day it had made 60,000 door knocks. Moreover, it had made about 15,000 personal phone calls with voters in the riding. These were not robocalls in which a pre-recorded message is delivered via a computerized autodialler but volunteers making live calls. The desire to have one-on-one conversations with voters influenced the decision not to use robocalls. Philpott and her team described this as a "high-touch campaign." Although they made use of digital technologies, including a website and social media, the high-touch campaign was about talking directly with people either in person or on the phone. Canvassing was the central method of communication. The involvement of more than four hundred volunteers was central in communicating a message of independent representation to voters.

Another area where party candidates might be at an advantage over independents is on the issue of policy. Although some local party candidates develop policy planks independent of the party, especially in regard to local issues, for many the decisions on election policies and messages are made in the central campaign. Political parties provide resources to their candidates, including campaign materials such as templates for brochures, websites, lawn signs and logos, and access to voter contact data/management systems. Independent candidates must develop policy positions on the important issues of the campaign on their own.

Electors in Markham–Stouffville expected Philpott to have policies in hand when she spoke to them at the door. To that end, she developed and published policy statements on her blog for a dozen key issues, including climate change and electoral reform. The research on and preparation of policy statements were time-consuming activities not shared by candidates with party backing. Nevertheless, policy research was necessary to convince voters that Philpott would be an equally effective representative in the House of Commons on the key issues facing Canadians. Personal policy development was one of the big differences from her previous campaign as a Liberal candidate. Although it is more work, independents have more control over their communications. They can have conversations with voters that are more authentic. Moreover, party candidates can be hamstrung during an election in cases in which the policy planks or campaign techniques are incompatible with local political priorities.[12]

These experiences are typical of other independents; however, Philpott was an atypical independent. One way of seeing this is to reflect on vote share; together Philpott and Wilson-Raybould obtained 43 percent of all independent votes in the 2019 campaign. Put another way, the remaining eighty-four independent candidates shared the rest of the vote, averaging less than 1 percent of the vote each. There are several aspects of local campaigning in which Philpott likely differed from other independents. As mentioned, her campaign was able to attract a high number of volunteers, thus allowing her to get out her message in the riding. Although this seemed to be consistent with other high-profile candidates, it was significantly more than the typical candidate.[13] Indeed, this was twice the number of volunteers as she had in 2015. Also related to personnel, Philpott had an extensive campaign team to support her candidacy. In addition to a paid campaign manager, other core team members coordinated aspects such as the phone bank, data management, volunteers, and canvassing.

Fundraising is another area of difference. Electoral law favours party candidates; independent candidates cannot provide receipts that are eligible for tax credits for donations received before they become official candidates, whereas registered parties, including constituency associations, can. Some local campaigns, especially in the case of a high-profile candidate or a competitive race, benefit from money flowing down from the national party.[14] This lack of access to funds can be problematic for independents given the importance of money to local election campaigns.[15] However, fundraising was not an impediment for Philpott. According to Elections Canada, the spending limit for Markham–Stouffville was over \$119,000. Because of her national profile, Philpott raised well above that. Fundraising was so effective that her campaign stopped accepting donations. Flush with cash, her campaign was significantly easier to operate than those of other independent candidates. Her campaign paid for the US-based data management system NationBuilder, used for the campaign website, tracking in-person and telephone contacts with voters, and analyzing email contacts. One activity that her campaign engaged in that was atypical for a local campaign was public opinion polling.

Philpott was the subject of intense media attention throughout the campaign. Research consistently shows that the Canadian media focus on the national campaign, especially on party leaders, with little attention given to local campaigns.[16] Yet Philpott was featured in national media across the country, including *La Presse* and the *National Post,* in both the pre-campaign period and during the writ period. Although the campaign was committed to meeting with all local media, the media attention was so great that Philpott had to decline many national media opportunities. Her candidacy was loosely similar to descriptions of political parties' star candidates who attract national media attention but are unable to translate that into local votes.

Despite these opportunities, Philpott was unable to convince the voters of Markham–Stouffville to take a chance on an independent. She came in third place in the riding, behind both the Liberal candidate and the Conservative candidate. Despite the success of Wilson-Raybould, the story of Philpott reminds us of the challenges confronting independent candidates in Canadian elections. Not that it was up for debate, but it reminds us of the importance of political parties in shaping the electoral preferences of Canadians.

Overcoming Obstacles

As mentioned, election laws are stacked against independent candidates especially regarding their campaign finances. The inability of independents to issue receipts eligible for tax credits for donations prior to the official campaign period can mean that independent candidates cannot fundraise on a level playing field with party candidates before the campaign begins.

One of the most fascinating facts of Philpott's campaign was the phenomenal financial support that it received from across the country, almost without asking for it. Despite the disadvantages described, her campaign received substantial donations that allowed

Philpott to rent an office and order materials, including signs, in the pre-campaign period.

As soon as the writs were issued, her campaign manager filed the paperwork regarding her candidacy. The next day they received a note from Elections Canada confirming Philpott as an official candidate. Thus, her campaign could receive donations eligible for tax credits. From that point forward, donations poured in from voters in Markham–Stouffville and across the country. The campaign received donations online from every province and territory, many of them from complete strangers. Supporters in Markham–Stouffville walked into the campaign office every day with cheques. People mailed in cheques accompanied by beautiful handwritten messages for Philpott, such as these samples show:

> Thank you for your courage and strength in adversity and holding to truth and what is right. You are an inspiration to all Canadians. – SM

> So proud of you. Carry on and I will do my best to support you. – CC

> I will be 81 in a couple of weeks and had all but lost hope of seeing any semblance of honour or integrity in government. Canadians now have living proof that honesty and integrity can be upheld, and a new inspiration will grow. – BB

Within two weeks of the official campaign start, Philpott's campaign had received an additional $100,000 in contributions. This amount, in addition to what had already been received, was more than enough. Therefore, the campaign made the unusual decision to stop receiving donations and issued a statement announcing that financial goals had been met.

The story of this financial endorsement was one of the objective measures by which Philpott's team could demonstrate the extraordinary support that they received both locally and nationally. To her team, it was an indication of the appetite among Canadians for seeing politics done differently. The financial backing was matched by the generous practical help of people who volunteered hundreds of hours of their time to do the hard work of local campaigning. Despite an outcome that was not what Philpott and her team had hoped for, it was an entirely positive, optimistic campaign. There are more ways to measure the success of a campaign than the final tally of votes.

Notes

1. The Canada Elections Act allows either unaffiliated or independent designations. We use the term "independent" to cover both in this chapter.
2. For an overview of the SNC-Lavalin controversy, see Dion, *Trudeau II Report.*
3. Sayers, *Parties, Candidates, and Constituency Campaigns.*
4. Carty and Eagles, *Politics Is Local.*
5. Marland, "The Electoral Benefits and Limitations of Incumbency."
6. Kendall and Rekkas, "Incumbency Advantages in the Canadian Parliament."
7. Marland, "The Electoral Benefits and Limitations of Incumbency."
8. Sayers, *Parties, Candidates, and Constituency Campaigns.*
9. Killin and Small, "The National Message, the Local Tour."
10. Flanagan, "Campaign Strategy."
11. Blais et al., "Does the Local Candidate Matter?"
12. Sayers, *Parties, Candidates, and Constituency Campaigns.*
13. Carty and Eagles, *Politics Is Local.*
14. Ibid.
15. Eagles, "The Effectiveness of Local Campaign Spending."
16. Carty and Eagles, *Politics Is Local.*

Bibliography

Blais, André, Elisabeth Gidengil, Agnieszka Dobrzynska, Neil Nevitte, and Richard Adeau. "Does the Local Candidate Matter? Candidate Effects in the Canadian Election of 2000." *Canadian Journal of Political Science* 36, 3 (2003): 657–64.

Carty, R. Kenneth, and Munroe Eagles. *Politics Is Local: National Politics at the Grassroots.* Don Mills, ON: Oxford University Press, 2005.

Dion, Mario. *Trudeau II Report*. Office of the Conflict of Interest and Ethics Commissioner. Parliament of Canada. August 2019.

Eagles, Munroe. "The Effectiveness of Local Campaign Spending in the 1993 and 1997 Federal Elections in Canada." *Canadian Journal of Political Science* 37, 1 (2004): 117–36.

Flanagan, Thomas. "Campaign Strategy: Triage and the Concentration of Resources." In *Election,* edited by Heather MacIvor, 155–72. Toronto: Emond Montgomery, 2010.

Kendall, Chad, and Marie Rekkas. "Incumbency Advantages in the Canadian Parliament." *Canadian Journal of Economics* 45, 4 (2012): 1560–85.

Killin, Julie, and Tamara A. Small. "The National Message, the Local Tour: Candidates' Use of Twitter during the 2015 Canadian Election." In *Political Elites in Canada: Power and Influence in Instantaneous Times,* edited by Alex Marland, Thierry Giasson, and Andrea Lawlor, 223–42. Vancouver: UBC Press, 2018.

Marland, Alex. "The Electoral Benefits and Limitations of Incumbency." *Canadian Parliamentary Review* 21, 4 (1998): 33–36.

Sayers, Anthony M. *Parties, Candidates, and Constituency Campaigns in Canadian Elections.* Vancouver: UBC Press, 1999.

Conclusion

Revealing the Campaign Machine

Anna Lennox Esselment and Thierry Giasson

In this conclusion, we present a summary of the different contributions comprising the book. We reflect on the challenges inherent in descriptive research coauthored by academics and practitioners. We highlight three themes common to professional election practices: caretaking in governance during elections, the essential roles that collaboration and coordination play in campaigns, and the centrality of communication in elections. We also reflect on the hybrid character of postmodern campaigns in which digital and traditional forms of electioneering coexist. Finally, we look toward future Parliaments and elections in Canada.

Ce dernier chapitre présente un résumé des différentes contributions contenues dans le livre. Il porte sur les défis inhérents à la recherche descriptive corédigée par des universitaires et des praticiens. Le chapitre met en lumière trois thèmes communs aux pratiques électorales professionnelles, à savoir la gouvernance au cours des élections, le rôle essentiel que la collaboration et la coordination doivent jouer dans les campagnes, et le caractère central de la communication dans les élections. Il se penche également sur le caractère hybride des campagnes postmodernes où coexistent les formes numériques et traditionnelles des tactiques électorales. Le chapitre se termine en initiant une réflexion sur l'impact de la campagne permanente sur les prochaines législatures et élections canadiennes.

AN ELECTION CAMPAIGN demands the Herculean effort of marshalling diverse roles for the common goal of winning power and influence. In Stephen Clarkson's book *The Big Red Machine: How the Liberal Party Dominates Canadian Politics*, an analogy links a campaign with a Rube Goldberg machine whose complexity greatly overwhelms the task.[1] The straightforward objective of a campaign machine is to win an election. Achieving that task, however, is a complicated and an involved undertaking. Indeed, a campaign operation can have varied goals – from a political party winning the most seats to form the government to a single candidate in an electoral district seeking to become an MP. This volume unveils the parts that make up the machine; in other words, it exposes the roles responsible for the whirring, steaming, whistling, and clanking that go into an election campaign in Canada.

The information presented here is unique. This is the first Canadian book to provide a concise detailing of behind-the-scenes work on campaigns from practitioners of various partisan or professional backgrounds. Their willingness to share their knowledge goes some way toward clarifying the different roles required to prepare for and engage in modern campaigning. We now have a greater awareness of how those positions contribute to the task of winning seats in the House of Commons and how personnel confront challenges that arise during an election. At its core, this book describes groups of talented individuals committed to a process at the root of the democratic experiment. Some of them quietly keep the government going while the parties engage in their public battle for votes. Others manage the news cycle to ensure that Canadians receive stories that will inform them about the parties and their leaders. Alternatively, they guard against the tarnishing of a leader's image.

This book's descriptions of campaign jobs are unorthodox. The willingness of practitioners to offer their time, expertise, and patience in walking us through their roles speaks to their interest in helping Canadians understand their work. As set out in the Introduction, there are challenges with embarking on this kind of project. Securing a practitioner coauthor was sometimes a difficult task. Whereas academic careers involve publishing peer-reviewed research, offering such an enticement to a potential practitioner collaborator can land with a thud. The motivations of those who agreed to take part were much different. The chance to dispel myths, clarify a position, tout a new role, affirm their expertise, and/or advance their interpretations of the world they occupy are some possibilities. There is a keen recognition that the balance of power is heavily in one camp. The practitioners are the doers; they are in the thick of it. As academics, we are the observers, the hangers-on, the ones hoping to be invited in. That a practitioner could withdraw from collaborating was always a possibility that would compromise the venture. What's more, the academic authors had to be sensitive to the contents, observations, and findings with which the practitioners would be comfortable. Academics are trained to provide critical perspectives and embedding observations deep in scholarly literature, but this project was a different sort of undertaking and therefore had to be seen through a novel lens.

Volumes like this one aim to involve viewpoints from all parties and all possible campaign roles, but an ongoing challenge for researchers is to convince decision makers and campaign operatives to open up about their worlds and give us peeks inside them.[2] Efforts to include Liberal Party practitioners were less successful. Governing party status is the likely culprit here. Parties on the opposition benches tend to have more enthusiasm for such projects; had the Conservatives been in power, we expect that their willingness to be involved would have been equally tepid – this is the reality confronting researchers in this field. Our hope is that the contribution of books like this one will encourage more campaign insiders to pull back the curtain and explain to Canadians what they do. The roles are fascinating and affect politics in this country; we simply want to learn more about them.

In the end, the partnerships presented here were fruitful, congenial, honest, and revealing. Inevitably, events in the 2019 federal election campaign are prominent, and the chapters in this book are the first of what will be numerous published analyses of that election. Our purpose here is to draw out broader themes that might augment understandings of professional practices and functions from campaigns in the recent past, the present, and the near future. Ours is a rapid response to recent events. This book should therefore be received as foremost a contribution to knowledge in the emerging subfield of political management and, to a lesser extent, a first draft of the 2019 campaign story.

What We Know about Campaign Work in Canada

Trying to understand what happens behind the scenes in an election campaign is like trying to open the proverbial black box. Campaigns are complicated operations hidden behind layers of secrecy. For decades, social science has been studying voter behaviour, so we know a lot about the statistical aspects of how voters make their decisions – which, in Canada, rely more on socialization, snippets of information about leaders, and deeply ingrained partisanship than we care to admit.[3] We can refer to inventories of descriptive accounts of what happened during almost all of Canada's federal election campaigns.[4] These time capsules transport us back to other eras to document the details of who did what. Occasionally, we are treated to a book authored by a practitioner who spills secrets, or an academic who reveals aspects of campaign operations. We can also draw on a variety of journal articles, book chapters, and news reports that profile campaign jobs.

Research in the previous edited collections in the UBC Press series Communication, Strategy, and Politics is part of the small body of Canadian literature about campaign work. What does it tell us? Primarily that Canadians should eschew American news media and Hollywood portrayals. American-style campaign operations do not exist in Canada. In their examination of the role of political strategists in Canada, two political scientists asserted that "there exists a media myth of hired gun, American-style political consultants who mastermind campaigns, but in reality we have an insular, party-oriented, and small political strategist industry."[5] The election spending limits and infrequent elections in Canada mean that there is not much of an industry of campaign professionals in this country. The researchers observed that Canadian election campaigns are replete with party insiders, many of whom learn on the job and work their way up through the party. Partisans are on the lookout for strategic thinkers fiercely loyal to the party and its leader. There is a demand for campaign staff who have "expertise and experience in polling, branding, advertising, digital campaigning, or political strategy" and a particular need for astute digital strategists.[6] The researchers conclude that the talent pool is rather thin in Canada, a situation made worse by turnover and lack of institutional memory.

Yet at least one American-style import does have a profound effect on Canadian politics. The introduction of fixed-date election legislation has taken much of the guesswork out of when the next election will occur.[7] Previously, the prime minister asked the governor general to dissolve Parliament at a time likely to provide the governing party with optimal electoral advantage. The practice of snap elections at the federal level and governing to the constitutional limit of five years now seem to belong to a bygone era. The main exception, of course, is during a period of minority government when political competitiveness is intense and the prospect of Canadians being plunged into a sudden election is ever present.[8]

A deeply transformed communication environment has further implications for campaign work. Canadian political journalism is undergoing profound changes as digital actors join the ranks while the readership for print media declines.[9] Engaging with social media and digital metrics commands ever more attention from news editors and journalists. During an election campaign, they must contend for public attention with private citizens who have digital acumen and automated bots.[10] Unconventional political actors play the role of disrupter by uncovering embarrassing information about politicians and by engaging in digital agitation.[11] Local candidates in Canada are active users of social media, with incumbents having much greater reach, yet most candidates fail to engage in direct dialogue with electors or to post information about themselves.[12] Likewise, political party leaders use social media foremost for broadcasting information in a one-way direction, ignoring the digital promise of two-way interaction with Canadians.[13] The party hierarchy's interest in social media resides in publicity and rapid response – but especially in garnering supporters' digital data to add to the party database.[14] Where advocacy groups are concerned, the use of digital technologies has muddied accountability because traditional engagements with members are replaced by digital relationships.[15] The smallest Canadian non-profits simply lack the resources to organize communication campaigns.[16]

Another observation stemming from the Communication, Strategy, and Politics series is how the permanent campaign intersects with election campaigning and how interconnected activities climax on election day. Leaders and political parties build their brands incrementally.[17] Often electoral success is the result of work over several federal electoral cycles, and there is interplay with party fortunes at the provincial level. Political strategists import strategies and tactics from other countries, but mostly they learn from observing successes and failures in the Canadian political system. Gradually, what used to be new and innovative becomes a normal practice for all of the mainstream parties.[18] Between elections, the party harnesses the resources available to its parliamentary caucus and staff, blurring parliamentary work and campaign work.[19] Behind the scenes, public servants patiently await the next government. Politics permeates when a new cabinet seeks to implement its agenda and as the Prime Minister's Office begins to place its political imprint on the machinery of government.[20] Within the public service, counterpressures exist as an impartial organization both resists and embraces partisan initiatives.[21] The permanent campaign once again builds from a slow churn to a well-oiled operation in high gear when the writ of election is issued.

What We Have Learned about Campaign Work

The permanent campaign and the official campaign are academic distinctions. The Introduction of this book refers to Canadian political strategist John Duffy's observation that election campaigns are divided into the pre-writ period and the writ period.[22] Indeed, a number of chapters in this book reveal that practitioners organize their thinking according to this calendar-style division of labour. However, there are other ways of differentiating campaign work.

This book distinguishes between visible and invisible campaign activities. There is the election campaign itself, pregnant with the excitement, passion, and adrenalin that drive all of those directly involved in it to throw themselves into the task. They work tirelessly until the last door is knocked on, the final ad is aired, the remaining rally is organized, and all of the votes are tallied on election day.

There is a less obvious side to an election, one that takes place primarily outside the spotlight, in the offices of the government and its agencies, in the boardrooms of polling companies, and in the newsrooms of media organizations. Election preparedness is undoubtedly an ongoing process for both political parties and governments, but several chapters here reveal that interest groups and the media are not exempt from similar states of readiness. Long-term and extensive strategic preparations based on market research, consultations with various publics, and the use of data and analytics are common practices in every corner of the Canadian political environment, not just in partisan life. In short, the professional testimonies collected in this book seem to confirm the pervasiveness of the permanent campaign ethos in Canadian politics, in which election readiness extends far beyond the confines of the official campaign period. We organize its description into the following three broad themes.

Public Administration, Political Staffers, and Electoral Administrators

We learn in the first section of the book that Ottawa's administrative machine moves into election-preparedness mode approximately six months to a year before a federal general campaign begins. The period prior to the drop of the writ propels electoral preparations in every ministry and agency, especially Elections Canada. In Chapter 1, Andrea Lawlor and Marc Mayrand explain how Canada's election administrator deploys its massive workforce across the country to ensure that eligible voters have access to ballots. They also remind readers of the various initiatives that Elections Canada and other government agencies undertake to safeguard the integrity of the election from rogue influences and disinformation tactics.

And what of the remaining political staff left to languish in ministers' offices while a campaign is under way? In Chapter 2, Paul Wilson and Michael McNair explain how the "caretaker convention" affects political staffers in cabinet offices. The vast majority of political staffers working for ministers migrate into their party's campaign workforce during an election, but some of those political operatives must stay behind and fulfill certain duties so that ministers can keep control of the government in the interim. Under the caretaker convention, ministers exercise self-restraint since, with no House of Commons present to grant confidence, opportunities to hold the governing party accountable are reduced. Yet ministers remain ministers during the election campaign, and they need support from their offices to keep their departments running. These political staffers are therefore an integral part of maintaining the political control of the government during an election.

As the campaign gets under way, the work of government administration carries on, and bureaucrats prepare for a smooth transition of power. In Chapter 3, Lori Turnbull and Donald Booth describe how the caretaker mode also guides public administrators in governance. Government business slows down, but high-ranking civil servants working in departments and central agencies supervise teams of bureaucrats charged with preparing files on the policy priorities of the different parties. Doing so is an indication to the future government of their willingness to serve loyally as well as their capacity to provide informed advice rapidly to ministers selected for cabinet.

Election preparedness is a central mission of other federal agencies. In Chapter 4, Brooks DeCillia and Michel Cormier describe how the newly created Leaders' Debate Commission organized its first two national debates. In a few short months following its inception, the commission was able to bring in experts, parties, and media to develop and broadcast two debates: one in English and one in French. Approximately half of the Canadian population tuned in to see the leaders spar with one another as they tried to differentiate themselves, stand out, and persuade voters to their side. The authors recount the difficult process of determining participation in the debates, which ultimately resulted in a stage crowded by six leaders, a record in Canadian electoral history. Following their broadcast, David Johnston, the debates commissioner, ruminated that separating the debates – one with just the main contenders and another with all party leaders who qualify under the commission's criteria – is a suggestion worth considering.[23]

Implementing the Strategy: Tactics and Logistics at Play

Leaders' debates, like many other aspects of the campaign, are meticulously calibrated affairs. Some chapters describe how implementing carefully orchestrated battle plans demands high-level collaboration among those holding various campaign positions. Under the watchful eye of the national campaign director, teams responsible for platform design, fundraising, advertising, communication, the leader's tour, media relations, and voter mobilization must cooperate and find innovative, reactive, and efficient ways to carry out a cohesive, disciplined, yet somewhat flexible campaign plan.

We learn, however, that digital communication technologies put pressure on campaigns and can disrupt this discipline. David

McGrane and Anne McGrath highlight the strategic preoccupation with technology in Chapter 9, on the national campaign director. Even with careful planning, issues occur throughout an election that demand immediate responses, often in the absence of thoughtful preparation. For a national director, time is a rare resource; speedy consultation among the campaign team, along with information gleaned from social media monitoring, guides their public reactions and responses. Strategic decisions are increasingly shaped by interactions with digital technologies. This development will affect future campaigns, for there are few controls and regulations in place in Canada regarding digital communication.

Along a similar vein, in Chapter 11 Mireille Lalancette and Marie Della Mattia delve into the role of senior political adviser and the job of managing the image of the party leader. Team collaboration is especially key here since the leader's image is a crucial part of the overarching campaign strategy. The authors also comment on Jagmeet Singh's efforts and challenges as the first racialized party leader to contend for the office of prime minister. They indicate that who the leader is – and the values embraced and defended by that leader – drive campaign messaging, platform priorities, and voter identification and mobilization. Senior advisers must therefore keep the leader buoyed and energized. Shielding a party leader from the hustle and bustle of the day-to-day campaign has become standard practice, as has reacting to events in real time. Creating a safe environment around the leader is presented as a confidence-building tactic in which information is selectively presented to the leader on a must-know basis. Strategists insist that the leader's role in the campaign should be to meet with voters and explain the party's platform, not to micromanage the logistical minutiae of the tour. Furthermore, the imperative is to keep the leader's morale high; an energetic and positive leader has a trickle-down effect of maintaining engaged and positive troops of partisan volunteers.

Critics will contend that this protective approach can isolate leaders or place them in a somewhat misinformed electoral reality;

they can be left in the dark about how their campaigns are actually performing. However, positivity is key during a campaign. The accounts of strategists who have contributed to this volume imply that staffers, supporters, and reporters surround leaders during the campaigns. Yet a party leader's personal experience can be lonely. Protecting leaders from the usual vagaries of an election that can bounce them up and down in the polls goes some way toward improving the solitary nature of election campaigning.

Political Communication

Along with caretaking and collaboration, a third element of political management stands out: the centrality of communication in campaigns. Electoral campaigns, at their core, are communication campaigns. Sending partisan messages to specific groups of voters through social media platforms and online networks and communities, via both broadcast media and at voters' doors, is a critical undertaking. Chapters on national campaigning and communication indicate that electoral communication strategies are planned, deliberate, and tested. Parties engage in social media monitoring so that they have a grasp of what Canadians are talking about on their digital platforms. Obsessed with voter engagement, they run A/B testing of online ads or emails to uncover which issue, argument, font, or background colour is more likely to lead a voter to click on the distributed content. Yet elections are perilous, with best-laid plans requiring flexibility. Stéphanie Yates and John Chenery aptly point out in Chapter 10 that all of this careful attention to communication details can run up against an electoral system that encourages strategic voting.

In this volume, accounts of communication practices paint the picture of hyper-reactive individuals who face many high-stakes decisions every day of the campaign. They must navigate a hybrid, fast-paced communication environment that requires constant consultation and coordination; the capacity to respond with speed and agility is a job requirement. In an age of concurrent and short-lived news cycles as well as instant access to information at everyone's fingertips, the most effective campaigns are often the most reactive ones.

This is true for political parties that run in elections, and it is equally true for news media, third parties, independent candidates, and polling aggregators. Media organizations want to inform Canadians about the campaign, but they also want to set the political agenda. As Colette Brin and Ryan MacDonald remind us in Chapter 5, the media's appetite for following the official leaders' tour is waning. The staged events are costly adventures that are tightly scripted and controlled, rarely offering added value for audiences, and they primarily serve partisan interests. Canadian news organizations are developing new forms of electoral coverage that focus more on citizens' interests, demands, and needs. Many of them commission public opinion polls that end up being data sources for unaffiliated polling aggregators that attract large followings. Chapter 6, by André Turcotte and Éric Grenier, demonstrates how these online instruments have become staples of political communication, often cited by the press and used by parties, in recent Canadian election cycles.

The final two chapters remind us that, even though campaigns are predominantly partisan affairs, other voices are hoping to command the attention of voters. Thomas Collombat and Magali Picard explain in Chapter 13 how third parties experience the campaign, not just with voters and political parties, but also with their members. Using the case of the Public Service Alliance of Canada – the largest union representing federal public employees – they reveal how it consults with its members through polls and assemblies in order to define its electoral strategy. This channel of communication remains open with members as the campaign unfolds. In Chapter 14, Tamara Small and Jane Philpott recount the latter's run as an independent candidate and the difficulties that she had to overcome in her campaign, including reaching out to voters without the benefit of a party electoral machine. Philpott's political notoriety made her a high-profile candidate and helped her to run a well-financed and professional campaign in her Ontario riding of Markham–Stouffville. She lost her bid for re-election but ran an intensive and personal campaign during which she and her team of volunteers engaged with 75,000 voters. Philpott's journey might not be representative of all independent candidates, yet it does reveal the challenges that even a high-profile independent must confront in a political system that favours party candidates.

These chapters show that voters are the targets of numerous sources of persuasive communication during a campaign. Although parties can position themselves as the loudest voices in the mix, the media and third parties join the chorus of electoral communication.

There are other aspects of campaigns that might not be fully captured here, but they are worthy of future scrutiny. Data, for instance, are vital in campaigns. As chapters in this volume indicate, those directly involved in campaign operations often rely on information that has been collected and stored in party databases. Ensuring a successful rally means primarily packing a room with supporters. Campaigns turn to their databases to identify those partisans and invite them to the boisterous gathering. Jared Wesley and Renze Nauta show in Chapter 8 that party platform builders develop policies by using an array of information. Drawing from the principles of political marketing, platform builders use data to detect which voter groups are likely to support the party as well as which electoral promises can fulfill the needs of those groups.[24] In Chapter 7, Erin Crandall and Michael Roy reveal how fundraising is also a critical aspect of successful campaigning – knowing who has donated in the past, how much, and how to ask for more. Such information is attached to names in a party database.

A digital campaign strategy is an extension of what data contribute to election planning. It also recognizes that many citizens experience politics through digital communication channels. Campaigns have adopted and adapted to digital technologies – reaching out to voters occurs on doorsteps as well as through online communities and networks.[25] Pushing out campaign messages or responding to attacks requires the assistance of social media influencers.[26] In Chapter 12, Vincent Raynauld and Dany Renauld insist that a party's advertising placement strategy requires a good knowledge of online platforms and who is using them. Ground operations benefit from mobile applications that enhance the ability to send information back to campaign headquarters. Canadian campaigns are now hybrid operations, involving both traditional offline and innovative online practices.[27] Online technologies offer parties different opportunities to engage with voters. Large-scale digital strategies that integrate advertising, voter outreach, fundraising, and field organizing have emerged at the epicentre of election planning to create a single user experience with the campaign. How digital strategy is developed and woven into Canadian campaigns is an area ripe for further exploration.

The rise of digital platforms as an integral part of campaigning has also introduced new threats to those who lead parties, who stand as candidates, or who take on roles within the campaign itself.[28] Securitizing campaigns from foreign interference by cyberthreat actors is an added layer of responsibility for the government, national security agencies, and political parties, though the last group are not compelled to do so by any law or regulation, nor do they have the same level of resources to devote to cybersecurity measures. Although there was minimal interference in the 2019 federal election, it is unknown how well prepared the parties were for cybersecurity threats.[29] Such threats can be targeted at systems and devices (e.g., servers, networks, platforms, and email accounts), at the spreading of disinformation, or at candidates themselves through coordinated trolling efforts. Securitizing campaigns has gone far beyond the need to protect the leader physically – notwithstanding Trudeau's need to wear a bulletproof vest at a campaign event in 2019. Today security centres on vulnerabilities exposed with digital technologies.

From Campaigning to Governing like a Campaign

This book has offered students and observers of Canadian politics something new. It is not just the perspective of one insider who tells the tale of a particular campaign. Nor is it focused on just one party or electoral role. Instead, this volume aims to detail aspects of elections in Canada that are common for governments, electoral administrators, and the political parties competing for power. The volume takes readers behind the scenes and attempts to shed light on rather opaque operations. The authors have tried to demystify the roles involved, outline the challenges that face operatives in these positions, and show how obstacles are conquered in the course of a campaign. They have also aimed to encourage more partnerships between academics and practitioners to reveal how things actually work – the whirring, steaming, whistling, and clanking of the campaign machine should not have a stupefying effect; instead, those noises should be seen as invitations to investigate their origins closely.

The book also demonstrates that elections in Canada, for the most part, are carefully managed affairs. Political management is a popular career choice in the United States, but it is downplayed in Canada. Limited election cycles are the primary reason, but there should be little doubt that careful handling of a party's campaign remains a serious undertaking. As noted elsewhere, the skills required to build and maintain a leader's image, galvanize social networks, respond rapidly to attacks, fundraise, and develop messages that resonate with citizens are all transferable to other sectors.[30] After the election, many campaign staffers apply their talents to the private and non-profit sectors, whereas others move into positions on either the government benches or the opposition benches. The point is that political management does not end with a campaign; the same thinking that drives strategic decision making in an election continues in government; political management matters because it is how parties govern today.

We anticipate the profiles and challenges inherent in each role described in this collection to be useful to Canadians as future Parliaments unfold, whether majority or minority, but minority situations heighten the requirement for campaign-like supervision. Fixed election dates are less reliable in a minority situation, and parties will be on a constant election footing. On average, minority governments tend to last two years, and replenishing their war chests is a preoccupation of all parties. Permanent campaigning is in full effect in every party.

Minority Parliaments also tend to increase partisanship inside the House of Commons, particularly between Liberals and Conservatives. Opposition leaders keep prime ministers on notice, and the rancour from the campaign itself spills into the theatre of the Commons. Attacks by one leader against another result in swift responses. In such a tense context, disciplined communication and leader image management are usually front and centre. A fixation on public opinion polls and aggregators is more acute. Any resources at the disposal of the governing party are employed to move its agenda forward so that policy achievements can be touted in the next election. A campaign-like atmosphere descends, like a heavy weight, over the Parliament of Canada.

Minority governments require a good deal of negotiation and cooperation. Collaboration among parties is as inevitable as acrimony. In many instances, partisan differences are set aside to accommodate the policy ideas of opposite members in order to secure the requisite number of votes to move legislation forward. Some effort at collaboration can be beneficial; the regional rifts that mark Canadian politics demand some reflection on how the parties can better bridge these differences. Whether the tactics that parties regularly use in campaigns can do this is an entirely different question but one worthy of posing. As this volume has shown, collaboration between academics and public sector practitioners might hold the promise of answering such questions.

Notes

1 Clarkson, *The Big Red Machine*.
2 Marland and Esselment, "Negotiating with Gatekeepers to Get Interviews with Politicians."
3 Gidengil et al., *Dominance and Decline*.
4 Among them, Marland and Giasson, *Canadian Election Analysis*.
5 Coletto and Gillies, "Political Strategists in Canada," 169.
6 Ibid., 177, 179.
7 Lagassé, "Institutional Change."
8 On political competitiveness, see Esselment, "Market Orientation in a Minority Government."
9 Paré and Delacourt, "The Canadian Parliamentary Press Gallery."
10 Chacon, Lawlor, and Giasson, "Hybridity and Mobility." See also contributions on the media in Marland and Giasson, *Canadian Election Analysis*.
11 McKelvey, Côté, and Raynauld, "Scandals and Screenshots."
12 Killin and Small, "The National Message, the Local Tour." See also their work in Marland and Giasson, *Canadian Election Analysis*.
13 Small, "Are We Friends Yet?"; Small, "The Not-So Social Network."
14 Patten, "Databases, Microtargeting, and the Permanent Campaign." See also his work in Marland and Giasson, *Canadian Election Analysis*.
15 Laforest, "Going Digital."
16 Grosenick, "Opportunities Missed." See also contributions about organized interests in Marland and Giasson, *Canadian Election Analysis*.
17 Wesley and Moyes, "Selling Social Democracy."
18 Marland, "Amateurs versus Professionals."
19 McGrane, "Election Preparation in the Federal NDP."
20 Esselment and Wilson, "Campaigning from the Centre."
21 Craft, "Governing on the Front Foot."
22 Duffy, *Fights of Our Lives*.
23 Wright, "Debates Commissioner David Johnston Suggests Separate Debate."
24 Patten, "Databases, Microtargeting, and the Permanent Campaign."
25 McKenna and Han, *Groundbreakers*.
26 Singer and Brooking, *Like War*.
27 Giasson, Le Bars, and Dubois, "Is Social Media Transforming Canadian Electioneering?"

28 Communications Security Establishment, "Cyberthreats to Canada's Democratic Processes."
29 On the level of interference, see Canadian Press, "So Far, Federal Election Has Had Little Misinformation or Disinformation."
30 Kinsella, *The War Room.*

Bibliography

Canadian Press. "So Far, Federal Election Has Had Little Misinformation or Disinformation: Researchers." *National Post,* 10 October 2019. https://nationalpost.com/news/politics/election-2019/election-has-been-mostly-free-of-mis-and-disinformation-research-shows.

Chacon, Geneviève, Andrea Lawlor, and Thierry Giasson. "Hybridity and Mobility: Media Elite Status on Political Twitter Hashtags." In *Political Elites in Canada: Power and Influence in Instantaneous Times,* edited by Alex Marland, Thierry Giasson, and Andrea Lawlor, 184–203. Vancouver: UBC Press, 2018.

Clarkson, Stephen. *The Big Red Machine: How the Liberal Party Dominates Canadian Politics.* Vancouver: UBC Press, 2005.

Coletto, David, and Jamie Gillies. "Political Strategists in Canada." In *Political Elites in Canada: Power and Influence in Instantaneous Times,* edited by Alex Marland, Thierry Giasson, and Andrea Lawlor, 168–83. Vancouver: UBC Press, 2018.

Communications Security Establishment. "Cyberthreats to Canada's Democratic Processes." 2019. https://cyber.gc.ca/en/guidance/cyber-threats-canadas-democratic-process.

Craft, Jonathan. "Governing on the Front Foot: Politicians, Civil Servants, and the Permanent Campaign in Canada." In *Permanent Campaigning in Canada,* edited by Alex Marland, Thierry Giasson, and Anna Lennox Esselment, 28–46. Vancouver: UBC Press, 2017.

Duffy, John. *Fights of Our Lives: Elections, Leadership, and the Making of Canada.* Toronto: HarperCollins, 2002.

Esselment, Anna. "Market Orientation in a Minority Government: The Challenges of Product Delivery." In *Political Marketing in Canada,* edited by Alex Marland, Thierry Giasson, and Jennifer Lees-Marshment, 123–38. Vancouver: UBC Press, 2012.

Esselment, Anna Lennox, and Paul Wilson. "Campaigning from the Centre." In *Permanent Campaigning in Canada,* edited by Alex Marland, Thierry Giasson, and Anna Lennox Esselment, 222–40. Vancouver: UBC Press, 2017.

Giasson, Thierry, Gildas Le Bars, and Philippe Dubois. "Is Social Media Transforming Canadian Electioneering? Hybridity and Online Partisan Strategies in the 2012 Quebec Election." *Canadian Journal of Political Science* 52, 2 (2019): 323–41.

Gidengil, Elisabeth, Neil Nevitte, André Blais, Joanna Everitt, and Patrick Fournier. *Dominance and Decline: Making Sense of Recent Canadian Elections.* Toronto: University of Toronto Press, 2012.

Grosenick, Gina C. "Opportunities Missed: Non-Profit Public Communication and Advocacy in Canada." In *Political Communication in Canada: Meet the Press and Tweet the Rest,* edited by Alex Marland, Thierry Giasson, and Tamara A. Small, 179–93. Vancouver: UBC Press, 2014.

Killin, Julie, and Tamara A. Small. "The National Message, the Local Tour: Candidates' Use of Twitter during the 2015 Canadian Election." In *Political Elites in Canada: Power and Influence in Instantaneous Times,* edited by Alex Marland, Thierry Giasson, and Andrea Lawlor, 223–42. Vancouver: UBC Press, 2018.

Kinsella, Warren. *The War Room: Political Strategies for Business, NGOs, and Anyone Who Wants to Win.* Toronto: Dundurn Press, 2007.

Laforest, Rachel. "Going Digital: Non-Profit Organizations in a Transformed Media Environment." In *Political Elites in Canada: Power and Influence in Instantaneous Times,* edited by Alex Marland, Thierry Giasson, and Andrea Lawlor, 243–60. Vancouver: UBC Press, 2018.

Lagassé, Philippe. "Institutional Change, Permanent Campaigning, and Canada's Fixed Election Date Law." In *Permanent Campaigning in Canada,* edited by Alex Marland, Thierry Giasson, and Anna Lennox Esselment, 167–83. Vancouver: UBC Press, 2017.

Marland, Alex. "Amateurs versus Professionals: The 1993 and 2006 Canadian Federal Elections." In *Political Marketing in Canada,* edited by Alex Marland, Thierry Giasson, and Jennifer Lees-Marshment, 59–75. Vancouver: UBC Press, 2012.

Marland, Alex, and Anna Lennox Esselment. "Negotiating with Gatekeepers to Get Interviews with Politicians: Qualitative Research Recruitment in a Digital Media Environment." *Qualitative Research* 19, 6 (2018): 685–702.

Marland, Alex, and Thierry Giasson, eds. *Canadian Election Analysis: Communication, Strategy, and Democracy.* Vancouver: UBC Press, 2015. https://www.ubcpress.ca/canadianelectionanalysis2015.

McGrane, David. "Election Preparation in the Federal NDP: The Next Campaign Starts the Day after the Last One Ends." In *Permanent*

Campaigning in Canada, edited by Alex Marland, Thierry Giasson, and Anna Lennox Esselment, 145–64. Vancouver: UBC Press, 2017.

McKelvey, Fenwick, Marianne Côté, and Vincent Raynauld. "Scandals and Screenshots: Social Media Elites in Canadian Politics." In *Political Elites in Canada: Power and Influence in Instantaneous Times,* edited by Alex Marland, Thierry Giasson, and Andrea Lawlor, 204–22. Vancouver: UBC Press, 2018.

McKenna, Elizabeth, and Hahrie Han. *Groundbreakers: How Obama's 2.2 Million Volunteers Transformed Campaigning in America.* New York: Oxford University Press, 2014.

Paré, Daniel J., and Susan Delacourt. "The Canadian Parliamentary Press Gallery: Still Relevant or Relic of Another Time?" In *Political Communication in Canada: Meet the Press and Tweet the Rest,* edited by Alex Marland, Thierry Giasson, and Tamara A. Small, 111–26.Vancouver: UBC Press, 2014.

Patten, Steven. "Databases, Microtargeting, and the Permanent Campaign: A Threat to Democracy?" In *Permanent Campaigning in Canada,* edited by Alex Marland, Thierry Giasson, and Anna Lennox Esselment, 47–64. Vancouver: UBC Press, 2017.

Singer, P.W., and Emerson T. Brooking. *Like War: The Weaponization of Social Media.* Boston: Houghton Mifflin Harcourt, 2018.

Small, Tamara A. "Are We Friends Yet? Online Relationship Marketing by Political Parties." In *Political Marketing in Canada,* edited by Alex Marland, Thierry Giasson, and Jennifer Lees-Marshment, 193–208. Vancouver: UBC Press, 2012.

–. "The Not-So Social Network: The Use of Twitter by Canada's Party Leaders." In *Political Communication in Canada: Meet the Press and Tweet the Rest,* edited by Alex Marland, Thierry Giasson, and Tamara A. Small, 92–108. Vancouver: UBC Press, 2014.

Wesley, Jared, and Mike Moyes. "Selling Social Democracy: Branding the Political Left in Canada." In *Political Communication in Canada: Meet the Press and Tweet the Rest,* edited by Alex Marland, Thierry Giasson, and Tamara A. Small, 74–91. Vancouver: UBC Press, 2014.

Wright, Teresa. "Debates Commissioner David Johnston Suggests Separate Debate for Main Contenders." CBC News, 12 November 2019. https://www.cbc.ca/news/politics/debates-for-top-leaders-johnston-1.5356825.

List of Contributors

DONALD BOOTH is the director of policy at the Machinery of Government Secretariat at the Privy Council Office, where he provides advice and guidance on the structure of the government and the cabinet decision-making system. He also serves as the Canadian secretary to the queen. Don is a lifelong rugby fan and an avid bagpiper.

COLETTE BRIN is a professor of journalism at Université Laval and the director of the Centre d'études sur les médias. She coordinates the Canadian edition of the *Digital News Report* and coedited *Journalism in Crisis* (University of Toronto Press, 2016).

JOHN CHENERY is the director of communications with the Green Party of Canada. He began his career in journalism in his native Australia, New York, and the United Kingdom and then held senior communication positions with the Earth Council in Costa Rica, the Biodiversity Institute of Ontario, and the Canadian Lung Association.

THOMAS COLLOMBAT is an associate professor of political science at l'Université du Québec en Outaouais. He publishes on the socio-political dimensions of the labour movement in Canada and Latin America, and he is the president of the Canadian Association for Work and Labour Studies.

MICHEL CORMIER is the executive director of the Canadian Leaders' Debate Commission. He is the former executive director of news and current affairs at Société Radio-Canada. In thirty years of public broadcasting, he was the parliamentary correspondent in Ottawa, the bureau chief in Quebec City, and a foreign correspondent posted to Moscow, Paris, and Beijing.

ERIN CRANDALL is an associate professor of politics at Acadia University. She publishes on Canadian judicial politics and election law. Her work has appeared in the *Canadian Journal of Political Science/Revue canadienne de science politique* and *Public Policy and Administration,* among other publications.

BROOKS DeCILLIA spent twenty years reporting and producing news at CBC. He splits his time now between studying public opinion at the University of Calgary and teaching communication and journalism at Mount Royal University.

SUSAN DELACOURT is a political journalist and author who has covered Parliament Hill since the 1980s. During the 2019 election campaign, she was Ottawa bureau chief and national columnist for the *Toronto Star.*

ANNA LENNOX ESSELMENT is an associate professor in the Department of Political Science at the University of Waterloo. Her research interests include elections and campaigns, political marketing, and political parties. She is a coeditor of *Permanent Campaigning in Canada* (UBC Press, 2017).

THIERRY GIASSON is a professor and the chair of the Department of Political Science at Université Laval. He is the director of the Groupe de recherche en communication politique. His research focuses on political journalism, online technologies, and political marketing. He is the coeditor, with Alex Marland, of the series Communication, Strategy, and Politics at UBC Press.

ÉRIC GRENIER is a senior writer and CBC's polls analyst. He was the founder of ThreeHundredEight.com and has written for the *Globe and Mail, Huffington Post Canada, Hill Times, Le Devoir,* and *L'Actualité.*

MIREILLE LALANCETTE is a professor of political communication at l'Université du Québec à Trois-Rivières. She publishes on leadership, image management and social media, and politics. She is the editor (with Vincent Raynauld and Erin Crandall) of *What's Trending in Canadian Politics? Understanding Transformations in Power, Media, and the Public Sphere* (UBC Press, 2019).

ANDREA LAWLOR is an associate professor of political science at King's University College at Western University. Her research looks at election administration, public policy change, and the role of the media in the policy process. Her work can be found in the *Journal of Social Policy, Canadian Journal of Political Science,* and *Journal of Ethnic and Migration Studies,* among others.

RYAN MacDONALD is the head of programming at the *Globe and Mail,* where he has held editorial positions since 2007. Previously, he was the national editor at the *Ottawa Citizen.* He was appointed the overseeing editor for the *Globe and Mail's* coverage of the 2019 election campaign.

ALEX MARLAND is a professor of political science at Memorial University of Newfoundland. He is the author of *Whipped: Party Discipline in Canada* (UBC Press, 2020), which examines how party discipline has evolved into message discipline in Canadian parliamentary politics.

MARIE DELLA MATTIA is a political strategist with over thirty years of experience. She has helped to elect seven NDP premiers in five provinces. She was the lead political adviser on John Horgan's 2017 tour in British Columbia, Andrea Horwath's 2018 tour in

Ontario, and Jagmeet Singh's 2019 campaign in the Canadian general election.

MARC MAYRAND is the former chief electoral officer of Canada (2007–16). During his time as the CEO, he oversaw improvements to the accessibility of Canadian elections and encouraged Parliament to adapt the laws to respond to innovations in digital media and technologies.

DAVID McGRANE is an associate professor of political studies at St. Thomas More College and the University of Saskatchewan. He is a specialist in Canadian social democracy and the author of *The New NDP: Moderation, Modernization, and Political Marketing* (UBC Press, 2019).

ANNE McGRATH has worked for the NDP, unions, and progressive organizations in Canada for the past thirty years. Among other positions, she was the chief of staff to Jack Layton and more recently to Premier Rachel Notley. She is currently the national director of the federal NDP.

MICHAEL McNAIR holds master's degrees from the London School of Economics and Political Science and from Columbia University's School of International and Public Affairs. He was policy director for Prime Minister Justin Trudeau from 2012 to 2019.

RENZE NAUTA served as the platform director for the 2019 Conservative campaign. He has held several positions in federal politics, including in the Prime Minister's Office under Stephen Harper.

JANE PHILPOTT was MP for Markham–Stouffville from 2015 to 2019. She served in multiple cabinet posts before running as an independent candidate in the 2019 federal election.

MAGALI PICARD is the national executive vice-president of the Public Service Alliance of Canada. She is highly involved in the political orientation and strategies of Canada's largest federal public workers' union. She was the regional executive vice-president for Quebec from 2012 to 2018.

VINCENT RAYNAULD is an assistant professor in the Department of Communication Studies at Emerson College and an affiliate professor in the Département de lettres et communication sociale at l'Université du Québec à Trois-Rivières.

DANY RENAULD is a partner in a public relations and public affairs company. Over the past twenty years, he has participated in many election campaigns as a communication strategist.

MICHAEL ROY is one of Canada's top political digital directors and online fundraisers. As the digital director for the NDP, he set the record for the largest number of donors to any Canadian political party in a single calendar year, a record that still stands as of the date of publication of this volume.

TAMARA A. SMALL is an associate professor of political science at the University of Guelph. She publishes about digital politics in Canada and is the coauthor of *Fighting for Votes: Parties, the Media, and Voters in an Ontario Election* (UBC Press, 2015).

ANDRÉ TURCOTTE is an associate professor in the School of Journalism and Communication at Carleton University. He writes about public opinion research, political marketing, and elections.

LORI TURNBULL is the director of the School of Public Administration at Dalhousie University. Her research and teaching focus on parliamentary governance, elections and voting, and public and political ethics. She is a freelance writer with the *Globe and Mail* and a contributing writer to *Policy* magazine.

JARED WESLEY is an associate professor of political science at the University of Alberta. He researches the links between elections and community values. He is the author of *Code Politics: Campaigns and Cultures on the Canadian Prairies* (UBC Press, 2011).

PAUL WILSON is an associate professor in the Clayton H. Riddell Graduate Program in Political Management at Carleton University. Formerly the director of policy at the PMO under Prime Minister Stephen Harper, he focuses his research on ministerial and parliamentary political staffers.

STÉPHANIE YATES is a professor of communication at l'Université du Québec à Montréal. She works on lobbying, public participation, and social acceptability, and she is the editor of *Introduction aux relations publiques: Fondements, enjeux et pratiques* (Presses de l'Université du Québec, 2018).

Index

abortion: as a political issue, 16, 94, 182

activism. *See* third-party activism

advertising: digital, 14, 35; evolution of, 37; parties as marketing machines, 5, party discipline in, 6, 175; and third-party spending, 39–40 (*see also* third-party activism). *See also* political advertisers

amplification, 11, 92, 154, 164, 174

Bernier, Maxime, 15–16, 34, 79, 81–82. *See also* People's Party of Canada

Bill 21 (Quebec), 166, 181–82

Blanchet, Yves-François, 16, 79. *See also* Bloc Québécois

Bloc Québécois, 15–17, 79, 90–91, 181–82

brands, 6, 160, 163; and election platforms, 125–26; and party leaders, 162; and party messaging, 6, 8, 148, 153; and positioning, 114, 177, 212

brownface/blackface scandal, 16, 93–94. *See also* Trudeau, Justin

Byrne, Jenni, 137

Caddell, Pat, 101

campaign directors: and crisis management, 142–44; literature on, 135; media profile of, 136; powers of, 137; role of, 138–41, 145

campaign machines, 208, 221

Campbell, Kim, 47, 153

Canada Elections Act, 32–34, 35; Section 91, 40–41. *See also* election administrators; Elections Canada

Canadian Broadcasting Corporation (CBC), 72, 89, 106

Canadian *Charter of Rights and Freedoms*, 40

Canadian Debate Production Partnership (CDPP), 76–77

Canadian Election Study (CES), 74, 80

Canadian Labour Congress, 189

Canadian Security Intelligence Service (CSIS), 38

Canadian Television Network (CTV), 89

and finance, 34, 39, 114, 202, 204; and incident preparedness, 36, 37; and inter-election period, 33; and third parties, 15, 34, 39, 186–87. *See also* election administrators

Elections Modernization Act, 14, 33

e-mail: and cybersecurity, 220; and fundraising, 113, 115, 119; and party databases, 118, 202, 217; and political staff, 49, 141

employment insurance (EI) 131–32

Facebook, 13, 77, 78, 91, 149; *New Mom, Who Dis?*, 14

Fair Elections Act, 2014

Federal Accountability Act, 2006, 33

fixed election dates, 53, 89, 126, 211, 222

Flanagan, Tom, 8, 136

fundraising, 110–20; cash for access, 113; director of fundraising, 115; and evolution of party fundraising, 112; and federal party finance regulations, 113; and fundraising tools, 113; obstacles faced by, 117–20; role of modern, 114. *See also* party fundraisers

Gallup, George, 100–1

get out the vote (GOTV), 14, 18, 115

Global Affairs, Department of, 38, 48

Globe and Mail, 16, 87, 89, 90–94

Google, 91, 149

governor general, 47

Green Party of Canada, 15, 17, 72, 154–55

Gregg, Allan, 101

Grey, Deborah, 75

Hargrove, Buzz, 187

Harper, Stephen: and accountable government, 67; and caretaker convention, 53; and Jenni Byrne, 137; and leaders' debates, 73

Hart, Peter, 101

House of Commons (Canada): appointment of CEO, 32; at dissolution, 54, 62; evolution of representation in, 72; independent members in, 198, 200–1; Liberal/Conservative Party rivalry in, 131; and political staffers, 46–47

Howard, Jennifer, 137

identification (ID): voter, 13, 33, 36, 216

Income Tax Act, 132

independent candidates, 198, 218–19; challenges faced, 200, 203; definition of, 198, 205n1; and election fortunes, 16, 17, 198, 199, 202, 203; and fundraising, 199, 202, 203; as incumbents, 199; objectives of, 199; and policy, 201; and volunteers, 199, 201. *See also* Philpott, Jane; Wilson-Raybould, Jody

Indigenous peoples, 35, 76, 119

Instagram, 77

Institute for Research on Public Policy, 73

National Lobbying Day, 189
National Post, 89, 203
NationBuilder, 202
New Democratic Party of Canada
    (NDP), 142–43; and candidate
    recruitment, 15; and fundrais-
    ing, 113, 116, 118–19, 120; and
    labour movement, 187–88; and
    PSAC, 191, 193; and Quebec,
    166–67. *See also* Singh, Jagmeet
news editors: and changing media
    environment, 86–87; obstacles
    faced by, 93–96; role of, 86–92
newsrooms: independence of,
    86; local, 89; preparation for
    an election by, 87, 89; public
    opinion polls and, 90; resources
    and, 87, 95

Obama, Barack, 17, 105
opposition research (oppo), 151,
    154

Parliamentary Budget Office
    (PBO), 128
party discipline, 6, 12, 175
party fundraisers: and grassroots
    fundraising, 113; history of, 112–
    13; and messaging, 116; skills
    of, 114, 118. *See also* fundraising
party platform builders. *See* elec-
    tion platforms
People's Party of Canada, 15, 34,
    80
permanent campaign, 3–7
Perrault, Stéphane, 36
Philpott, Jane, 218–19; cabinet
    positions held, 198; campaign
    launch, 200, 204; and cam-
    paign team, 202, 205; and

fundraising, 202–4; as a high-
    profile candidate, 199, 201–3;
    and policy development, 201;
    and SNC-Lavalin affair, 16,
    198; and voter interactions,
    200–1, 204. *See also* independ-
    ent candidates
photo ops, 9
political advertisers: contribution
    to campaign, 175; description
    of, 174; impact of, 176; role of,
    180; strategies of, 176–79; third-
    party, 39. *See also* advertising
political management, 17–18
political marketing, 6, 12; as a
    discipline, 102; and election
    platforms, 124, 219; tactics,
    163, 177
political staff, 45–47; Leaders'
    Debate Commission staff, 75,
    80, 82; PMO staff, 48–49; and
    public engagement, 62; role of,
    50–55, 145, 214; and Westmin-
    ster system, 68
pollsters, 7, 17, 100–7, 126, 174,
    178
prime minister: and caretaker con-
    vention, 55; media coverage of,
    16, 78; and PMO, 48–49, 64;
    powers of, 6, 35, 65–66, 211;
    relationship with deputy min-
    isters, 61; relationship with
    opposition leaders, 222
Prime Minister's Office (PMO), 66,
    212; role of, 6; staffers in, 46,
    48–49, 51–55, 131
Privy Council Office (PCO): clerk
    of, 52; and interactions with
    PMO, 51–55; and Machinery
    of Government Secretariat,

TikTok, 168
Time, 93
Toronto Star, 78, 89
transparency, 53, 68, 81. *See also*
    secrecy
Trudeau, Justin, 14–15, 53, 66,
    86, 181, 183; and brownface/
    blackface scandal, 16, 93, 143–
    44. *See also* Liberal Party of
    Canada
Tupper, Sir Charles, 47
Turmel, Nycole, 188
Twitter, 13, 39, 77, 78

unions, 23, 113, 187, 188–89, 193.
    See also Public Service Alliance
    of Canada (PSAC)
United States, 73, 178; comparison
    with Canada, 68, 211, 221

wagon master, 10
Wakeman, Frederic, 100
war room, 8–9, 47, 153–54

websites: and Leaders' Debate
    Commission, 77; of media, 78,
    86; and Philpott campaign, 201–
    2; of political parties, 13, 114,
    130, 201; and Public Service
    Alliance of Canada, 192
Westminster parliamentary system,
    47, 60, 65, 68
Whirtlin, Richard, 101
Wilson-Raybould, Jody, 16–17, 199,
    201, 203. *See also* independent
    candidates
writ drop: and campaign strategy,
    139, 141, 163; and caretaker con-
    vention, 61; history of, 5; and
    impact on campaign staffers,
    46–49; and Jane Philpott cam-
    paign, 200, 204; and media
    coverage, 89; and platform
    release, 130; political strategy
    behind, 35; and polling, 102–3

YouTube, 78